CANADA

W9-BMU-689

MINNESOTA

St.Paul ★

WISCONSIN

Mississippi

MICH.
Lansing ★

Madison ★

IOWA

Des Moines ★

ILLINOIS

Springfield ★

MISSOURI

Jefferson
City ★

IND.
Indianapolis ★

OHIO
Columbus ★

Ohio

Frankfort ★

KENTUCKY

PENN.
Harrisburg ★

Charleston
W.
VA

NEW YORK

Hartford

Albany ★

MAINE
Augusta ★

Montpelier
VT NH
Concord ★
★
Boston
Providence

MA

RI
CT

Trenton ★
NJ
Dover ★
Annapolis ★
DE

MD

Richmond ★

VIRGINIA

N.
CAROLINA

Raleigh ★

Nashville ★

TENNESSEE

ARKANSAS

Little ★
Rock

Oklahoma

S.
CAROLINA
Columbia ★

Atlanta ★

ATLANTIC
OCEAN

MISS.

Jackson ★

ALABAMA

Montgomery ★

GEORGIA

LOUISIANA

Baton
Rouge

Tallahassee ★

FLORIDA

Gulf of Mexico

0   100   200   300   400
Miles

The United States: A Brief Narrative History

THIRD EDITION

Link Hullar
Lone Star College — Kingwood

Scott Nelson
Texas Community College Teachers Association

A John Wiley & Sons, Ltd., Publication

Harlan Davidson, Inc. was acquired by John Wiley & Sons in May 2012.

Registered Office
John Wiley & Sons, Ltd, The Atrium, Southern Gate, Chichester, West Sussex,
PO19 8SQ, UK

Editorial Offices
350 Main Street, Malden, MA 02148-5020, USA
9600 Garsington Road, Oxford, OX4 2DQ, UK
The Atrium, Southern Gate, Chichester, West Sussex, PO19 8SQ, UK

For details of our global editorial offices, for customer services, and for
information about how to apply for permission to reuse the copyright material
in this book please see our website at www.wiley.com/wiley-blackwell.

Library of Congress Cataloging in-Publication Data

Hullar, Link.
The United States: a brief narrative history / Link Hullar, Scott Nelson. — 3rd ed.
  p. cm.
Includes bibliographic references and index.
ISBN 978-0-88295-278-9 (alk. paper)
1. United States—History—Textbooks. I. Nelson, Scott A. 1950- II. Title.

E178.1.H92 2011
973.dc22   2010038885

Cover design: Linda Gaio, Harlan Davidson, Inc.
Cover photograph: Teton Barn. © Mike Norton | Dreamstime.com

Manufactured in the United States of America
14 13 2 3 4 VP

TABLE OF CONTENTS

MAPS:

PREFACE

In presenting this third edition of *The United States: A Brief Narrative History*, our intent remains to provide a basic, readable, affordable core text for the introductory survey of United States history. Most assuredly, the book is not designed as the only resource for students in such courses. Its length, approach, and price give an instructor the freedom to complement it with an abundance of supplemental books, research projects, and primary documents (many of which are now available on the Internet). With more than fifty years of combined teaching experience, from middle school through graduate seminars in history, we know there is a real and growing need for a book such as this. Increasingly we find that the average student is intimidated, overwhelmed, and drained financially by the massive texts that dominate the genre. Even so-called brief editions often weigh in at a thousand pages or more, leaving the reader lost in a maze of confusing—and expensive—information.

Needless to say, in order for this book to fulfill its mission, we had to leave a great deal out. In deciding what to include, we worked toward a cultural-literacy approach. Names, terms, and concepts with which an educated American should be familiar are highlighted. By no means, however, is this book a quasi-dictionary or almanac. Big ideas, major themes, important events, and basic facts are arranged in a chronological narrative that tells a lively story without talking down to the reader. As generalists, we have studiously avoided most controversies within the various specialties, ideologies, and schools of academic historians. Students who read this book can obtain the big picture of United States history, while each instructor may provide added depth and perspective by using supplemental material to emphasize particular interests or areas of expertise. As historians, we would be the first ones to object to the idea that our book tells the whole story, but as teachers, we think such an approach works best for introductory students.

It's staggering to contemplate how much has been added to the American story since the last edition of this book appeared in 2006. In addition to taking the narrative right up to the present, we have made corrections and changes in response to feedback from student readers and other instructors. We have also added new maps and, in an ongoing effort to make ours the most accessible U.S. survey available, re-edited the entire work with an eye toward simple—but by no means simplistic—and engaging language.

We have benefited greatly from the careful reading of Andrew J. Davidson, who shares our vision of an intelligent, readable, student-friendly text, and is an accomplished editor. We also appreciate the thousands of students who have passed through our classrooms over the years and sincerely hope this book will help many more in the future.

Link Hullar
Scott Nelson

America's First Nations

The First Americans

Scientific and linguistic analysis suggests that the first people came to America some 15,000 to 25,000 years ago, during the last Ice Age. There was never a large or continuous migration of these early settlers to North America, the ancestors of the American Indians. Rather, they came to this continent in small hunting groups over a period of thousands of years. Archaeologists who have studied the early Indians' material culture (pots, tools, weapons, and the like) estimate that the migrations ended less than five millennia ago. According to a recent calculation, the last migration, composed of Eskimo or Inuit groups, took place about 2500 B.C.

The Ice Age began long before the first human beings came to America. Scientists estimate that it started some 3 million years ago and ended about 10,000 years ago. During this period temperatures were so cold that the seas and oceans froze, the water turning into mile-thick glaciers. As the water froze and massive glaciers covered vast areas of the North American continent, global water levels dropped, sometimes by as much as hun-

---

* Philip Weeks is Professor Emeritus of History at Kent State University, where, as a Distinguished Teaching Award recipient, he taught American Indian and United States history for many years. He is the author or co-author of several books, including his acclaimed *Farewell, My Nation: The American Indians and the United States in the Nineteenth Century* and *They Made Us Many Promises: The American Indian Experience, 1524 to the Present* (both published by Harlan Davidson, Inc.).

dreds of feet. The Bering Strait, which today separates northeastern Asia from northwestern North America, became a stretch of dry, wind-swept land hundreds of miles wide. Over this frigid Bering land bridge, also called **Beringia**, the first people evidently migrated from Asia to America.

The newcomers, after settling in present-day Alaska for a long time, slowly began to follow the game herds southward through the ice-free corridors along the slopes of the Rocky Mountains. They eventually passed below the southern edge of the glaciers into the present-day continental United States. Doggedly pressing forward toward the east, the west, and the south, humans eventually reached the southernmost part of the Western Hemisphere, present southern Chile and Argentina, by 8000 B.C.

The early Indians who migrated to the present-day United States encountered a comparatively uniform climate warmer than that of Alaska. Temperatures were mild and rainfall abundant. The land was covered by dense forests, tall grasses, numerous lakes and swamps, and lush plant life. The first Americans were hunters who used simple weapons and tools made of stone or wood to bring down prey like mammoths and mastodons, the giant animals of the Ice Age. They also hunted smaller game such as wolves, deer, elk, and rabbits. Between 25,000 B.C. and 8000 B.C., the early Indians, as they explored and settled the American continents, improved their technology by carving stones into sharp-pointed darts, which look similar to arrowheads. They attached some of these sharpened stones to the tips of wooden spears and used them as weapons for protection and hunting. Other stone tools served as knives to skin animals.

The Archaic Age

The Ice Age came to an end about 8000 B.C. As it did, the weather became warmer, the massive glaciers steadily melted, and North America's climate changed as the weather patterns that we know today began to emerge. The eastern portion of what is today the continental United States remained humid and rainy. In the Southwest, however, dry plains and deserts began to appear. The great Ice Age animals, apparently incapable of adapting to the newer climate and environment, soon became extinct. The Indians of the **Archaic Age**, which lasted from about 8000 B.C. to 1200 B.C., had to alter their way of life to survive in this changing environment. Compelled during this time of dramatic changes to look for new sources of food and to develop better technology, Archaic Indians met these challenges with remarkable ability.

Western Archaic Indians lived in a region that had become dry and barren, where animal and plant resources were in short supply. Life for them was hard and demanding as they had to move continuously to find enough food. Eastern Archaic Indians, on the other hand, had a far easier existence because they lived and developed cultures in a region full of forests and lakes. Fish, animals, and plants were plentiful, with the result that the population in the East grew much larger than that of the West.

Archaic Indians lived in small, mobile, extended-family groups. They began to use a variety of materials to make tools, weapons, and utensils. In addition to stone and wood, they now also crafted items from bone, horns, shells, hide, and copper. Archaic Indians became more than just hunters: they fished when possible; gathered edible items such as seeds, nuts, berries, and roots; and ascertained how to catch animals with nets, traps, and pits dug in the ground. To assist them with hunting and to help guard their camps, they began to train wolf pups, beginning the process of the domestication of dogs. They also learned how to use fire for cooking and for warmth.

The most important and far-reaching advancement Archaic Indians made, however, was farming, as they discovered how to adapt wild plants, such as corn, to home cultivation. Farming changed their way of life dramatically. Those people who learned how to grow crops no longer had to wander in search of food. For them, farming provided a more dependable source of food than had hunting and gathering alone. A more sedentary way of life became feasible.

Early Indians of the West

The spread of agriculture across the Southwest gave rise to three great early Indian cultures—Mogollon, Hohokam, and Anasazi.

Mogollon society developed first, sometime around 300 B.C. It was centered in the mountain region of southwestern New Mexico and eastern Arizona. The Mogollon were skilled craftspeople who made beautiful pottery and fine bows and arrows. They relied on hunting and gathering to supplement the fruits of their new agricultural skills. Mogollon farmers raised corn, beans, and squash.

Hohokam society, located in present-day southern Arizona, relied principally upon crops for sustenance, but the predicament these people faced was that their land received little rainfall. Sustaining an agrarian way of life was enormously challenging due to the dry soil. To solve this problem, Hohokam farmers developed a system of irrigation for their land. Large work crews built and maintained a network of canals that directed floodwater and water from rivers like the Gila, Salt, and Santa Cruz to crops in their fields. The canals were almost six feet deep, thirty feet wide, and often ten miles long.

For recreation, the Hohokam people played a game similar to basketball on outdoor ball courts. Some courts were almost as large as modern football fields. Sometimes the game was played for more than recreation, also being used as a tool of diplomacy—a way to settle arguments between villages.

The last great early western culture was the **Anasazi**, or the "old ones." The Anasazi lived in the four-corners region where the borders of the present states of Utah, Colorado, Arizona, and New Mexico meet. They were the ancestors of the modern Pueblo, Hopi, Zuni, and Tewa Indians. The Anasazi had the most advanced culture in the West during this period.

Anasazi settlements, peopled with skilled farmers and basketmakers as well as excellent designers and builders, were constructed high above river valleys along canyon walls. There, safely protected from their enemies, the Anasazi lived in tall, apartment-like buildings. Some of the buildings were five-stories high and contained up to 800 rooms. Ground-level dwellings were built without doors. The upper levels were reached by ladders that could be pulled up in case of an enemy attack. Within each building were a number of rooms in which family members lived, worked, and slept.

The Anasazi practiced the domestication of animals. They used dogs to guard their households, and they found that turkeys were easy to tame and breed as a food source. The Anasazi were a deeply religious people who believed in supernatural beings or spirits. In or near each settlement was a *kiva*, a circular underground building or room used for religious purposes. The Anasazi believed that spirits from within the earth could appear to them in the kiva. Only men were allowed to enter this sacred area.

The great Anasazi buildings were in use from about A.D. 900 to about A.D. 1300. We are not sure why they were abandoned. Perhaps the Anasazi came under assault from more aggressive Indians in the region and decided to relocate their settlements to a safer setting, such as on top of a mesa. It is clear that in some cases the Anasazi vacated their buildings quickly, because they left behind rooms filled with food, tools, and various personal articles.

Early Indians of the East

Three advanced cultures also emerged in the East during the same period. These eastern cultures were centered near the Mississippi, Missouri, and Ohio rivers. The Adena culture arose first, followed by the Hopewell and then the Mississippian cultures. Although these three cultures developed during different time periods between 800 B.C. and A.D. 1250, they shared many similar characteristics.

All three culture groups lived in large, permanent villages typically protected by earthen walls. All were skilled at making pottery, which they used to store food and other objects of value. They were able craftspeople who fashioned beautiful ornaments for both personal and ceremonial use. All three groups traded goods with other Indians who lived in distant places to the east and west. The Adena people secured their food principally through hunting. In contrast, the Hopewell and the Mississippian peoples relied more heavily on farming. Their chief crops were corn, beans, pumpkins, squash, and sunflowers.

What the Adena, Hopewell, and Mississippian peoples are best remembered for are their great ceremonial mounds. For this reason, the three societies are often referred to by a single name: the **Mound Builders**. Like many ancient peoples, the Mound Builders were sun worshippers, their religious beliefs and ceremonies focusing on death and an afterlife. Anthropologists and archaeologists believe that they built the huge mounds for religious purposes. Some mounds were hollow, serving as burial places. Valuable objects were often placed beside the bodies in the tombs. Other mounds were solid, earthen structures built high into the air. Sometimes temples were built on these solid mounds and used by priests for religious ceremonies.

Cahokia in western Illinois, the most sophisticated prehistoric site north of Mexico, had such an assortment of mounds. The city covered nearly six square miles and contained houses arranged in rows, around open plazas, for its population of tens of thousands. Wooden stockade walls surrounded Cahokia, offering protection from attackers. Just west of that ancient city is a site now referred to as "Woodhenge." Long ago tall vertical posts, arranged in a huge oval, lined up with the sun at certain times of the year and served Cahokians as a calendar for their civil and religious festivals, the agricultural cycle, or solar alignments like the solstices and the equinoxes.

Other groups of Mound Builders constructed earthen mounds in the shapes of animals, called **effigy mounds**. The Great Serpent Mound in Adams County, southwestern Ohio, for example, zigzags for 1,348 feet from tail to open jaws. It is the largest known serpent effigy in the United States.

The Mound Builder cultures prospered for well over a millennium. They began to vanish around 1250, or about 250 years before the coming of European explorers. Scholars are not sure why this happened. They do know that other, less-developed but more warlike Indian groups lived in the same region. The Mound Builders feared these hostile groups, taking great care to strengthen their villages against attack. It is possible that, in the end, the Mound Builders were unable to defend themselves and thus were destroyed. Other theories suggest that depletion of local resources, climate changes affecting crop production, or bitter arguments and infighting tore their societies apart, ultimately causing their downfall.

Variety and Indian Societies

It is a common belief that the Americas were thinly populated at the time the Europeans first explored and settled there. Actually, the opposite is true. In about 1500, at the time of Christopher Columbus's voyages, the indigenous population numbered approximately 60 to 70 million people. This was larger than the population of the continent of Europe at that time. Comparatively, the nation of England, in the colonial era, had about 4 million inhabitants. About 7 to 12 million Indians lived north of the Rio Grande in what is today the United States and Canada. Another 25 million natives lived in Mexico and Central America. The rest, some 30–40 million people, lived on islands in the Caribbean Sea and in South America. Within a hundred years of colonial settlement, the Indian population declined drastically (perhaps 30 to 50 percent) due to the introduction of European diseases, especially smallpox. This undoubtedly contributed to the common European perception that North America was sparsely populated by native peoples. One historian suggests that while many colonizers were confident that they were settling in a virgin land, they were in fact taking up residence in a **widowed land**.

The diffusion of native peoples across the American continents brought the parallel diffusion of native languages. Estimates of the number of Indian languages vary, but it is probable that as many as 300 different languages were spoken north of Mexico. These languages belong to at least a half-dozen different American Indian linguistic stocks, that is, stocks without a common origin. It is hypothesized that as many as 2,000 separate languages were spoken among the tribes of North and South America. These are languages, not dialects, nor are they variations of a single, universal Indian tongue. The Sioux, for example, spoke a language completely different from that of the Cheyenne of the same Great Plains region. Indian languages were as different from each other as were the English, French, and Spanish languages spoken by European explorers and settlers.

Indian political organization also took a wide variety of forms. The Plains Indians, for example, organized themselves into small tribal groups. Others, like the Indians of the Southeast, often organized into confederacies, or unions of independent groups or societies. Some, like the five tribes of the League of the Iroquois of New York State, were democratic in some of their governmental activities. The Natchez of Louisiana, on the other hand, lived in a theocracy ruled by religious leaders.

American Indian societies varied greatly not only in language and methods of government, but in culture and way of life. Many were farmers who grew a wide variety of crops. Others engaged in fishing or hunting. Still others combined hunting, gathering, and farming. The Indian societies living in what is now the United States can be divided into at least **seven cultural areas**, according to the geographic locales they occupied.

1. Eastern Woodland Indians lived in the great forests of the present-day northeastern United States, mainly east of the Mississippi River and north of Tennessee and North Carolina. They lived in permanent villages, their lifestyle based primarily on farming, but supplemented by hunting. Plenty of forests, fertile farmlands, lakes and rivers, and game allowed these people to develop stable, sedentary communities.

2. The Southeastern Indians lived south of the Eastern Woodland tribes, likewise developing stable, sedentary communities based on an agricultural

economy. Many tribes of this thickly populated region were organized into political confederacies.

3. The homeland of the Plains Indians was the central portion of the country, roughly between the Missouri River and the Rocky Mountains. Although some tribes were sedentary, the majority were roving bison hunters.

4. The Great Basin and Plateau Indians lived in the arid and semiarid lands between the Rocky Mountains on the east and the Sierra Nevada on the west. Because of the harsh environment, the region had only a small population. The Shoshone who lived there fished, hunted, and gathered. Plant and animal life were sparse, however, making life very difficult for these Indians.

5. The Indians of the Southwest made their homes in the desert areas of what is today Arizona, New Mexico, western Texas, and parts of Utah, Colorado, and northern Mexico. Many Southwest Indians lived in villages, some on top of high mesas, and their homes were made of *adobe*, or sun-dried bricks. Most who lived in the pueblos were farmers. Other groups were hunters and gatherers.

6. The lands along the Pacific coast were home for people called the California Indians. They enjoyed a temperate climate and plenty of food—acorns, game, fish, fowl, and various wild plants. California Indians prospered in a land of plenty.

7. Finally, the Northwest Coast Indians lived along the Pacific coast in the area of northern California, Oregon, and western Washington. They relied primarily on salmon and halibut fishing, as well as seal hunting for their food supply. Northwest Coast Indians were skilled at working with wood. They crafted beautifully carved totem poles. They also fashioned wooden boats—used for fishing and warfare—that were as long as 60 feet.

Indian societies living in what became the United States varied dramatically. By looking at three groups—Eastern Woodland, Great Plains, and Southwestern Indians—one can see this extensive variety more clearly.

Eastern Woodland Indians

The northeastern section of the country was covered by dense forests, its rolling hills and valleys well-supplied by lakes, rivers, and streams. The region was crossed by a network of natural waterways connecting the Atlantic to the Great Lakes and the Ohio River Valley. Except in the northernmost regions, the rich soil and temperate climate made it suitable for intensive agriculture. Wild animals, such as bison, bear, and deer, roamed freely, providing sustenance for the inhabitants. Birds and wild plants were also in abundance, and the waterways teemed with several species of fish.

On the whole Eastern Woodland Indians were farmers and hunters. Some also fished and conducted intertribal trade. Two linguistic groups dominated the region: the **Algonquian** and the **Iroquois**. Although most tribes spoke Algonquian languages (like the Shawnee, Delaware, and Miami), many Iroquois-speaking people penetrated Algonquian territory and lived in its central region. These Iroquois settled in Upper New York State, in Pennsylvania, and along the shores of the eastern Great Lakes.

The Algonquians of the Eastern Woodlands depended only partly on farming for survival. While they established villages and farm fields on rich land along rivers, they occupied these villages only during the growing season. After the harvest, the Algonquians left their summer villages and separated into smaller winter hunting bands. For summer travel, the Algonquians used birch bark canoes, which were light and efficient. In winter, they used snowshoes to travel or pursue animals. Algonquians lived in wigwams, bark-covered lodges with rounded roofs and wooden frames.

The Iroquois of present Upper New York State were aggressive warriors who raided westward against their political (native) enemies and fur-trading rivals, usually Algonquians but also other Iroquois-speaking peoples like the Erie. The New York Iroquois claimed dominion over many tribes and established a virtual monopoly of the beaver trade in lands that are now Ohio and Indiana. Their strength also came from uniting to form a political confederation: five separate Upper New York Iroquois tribes (the Mohawk, Oneida, Onondaga, Cayuga, and Seneca) united in the 1500s to form the Haudenosaunee, or **League of the Iroquois**. This powerful alliance, its leaders skillfully employing the might that political, military, and diplomatic unity provided, dominated much of the present northeastern United States until the American Revolution.

The League of the Iroquois was ruled by a council of fifty *sachems*, or leaders, from among the five tribes. The council ruled only on affairs that affected the five member tribes collectively, and it had no say over the internal affairs of each member tribe. Women had political influence, and their views were respected in the Iroquois League. Sachems were always male, but women within each member tribe always selected the successor of a sachem who had died.

The name *Iroquois* means "the People of the Longhouse." As their name suggests, they lived in long, wooden, rectangular lodges with rounded edges. Longhouses were community dwellings housing up to twenty families and located in large towns, frequently protected by stockade walls. In many cases, hundreds of acres of cultivated farm land surrounded a town. Although the fields were cleared of trees and brush by the men, women did the farming.

Indians of the Great Plains

The Great Plains straddle the center of the nation. This is a vast region of grasslands stretching north to south from mid-North Dakota down to Texas and east to west from the Mississippi River to the foothills of the Rocky Mountains. The plains are treeless except for the river valleys. Enormous herds of bison and antelope once grazed there, and other game—deer, elk, rabbits, grizzly bears—were plentiful as well.

Two different Indian groups lived on the Great Plains. Sedentary farming peoples, like the Mandan, Hidatsa, and Arikara, occupied the timbered Missouri River valley and some of its major tributaries on the eastern plains. The plains farmers lived in large, permanent villages with circular houses built of poles and heavy timber covered with a thick layer of dirt. The dirt covering served as excellent insulation during the winter months. The earthen lodges were large, measuring thirty to fifty feet in diameter, and housed as many as forty people.

Some two dozen nomadic bison-hunting societies, collectively referred to as the **Plains Indians**, dominated the remainder of the region. The *Dakota*, or Sioux, controlled the northeastern portion of the plains. The powerful Cheyenne and Arapahoe, long each others' comrades and allies, ranged widely over the central plains. Across the Arkansas River to the south lived their traditional enemies: the Kiowa and the Comanche. The Comanche, the dominant tribe on the southern plains, was also the most populous, with seven thousand members. The Plains Indians were expert hunters, daring warriors, and, after Europeans introduced horses to America, superb riders. Their highly specialized way of life centered on two animals: bison, which were native to the plains, and domesticated horses, which were not.

The enormous herds of bison found throughout the region became the dietary staple of the mounted Plains Indians. The animals also supplied most of their material needs. Clothing, robes, moccasins, saddles, teepee walls, bedding, water vessels, and boats were made of bison hide. The hooves were made into glue, horns carved into cups and spoons, and tendons made into bowstrings, cord, and trail ropes for the horses. Their dried manure, called "buffalo chips," was used for fuel, and their stomachs were fashioned into water bottles. The bison-hunting tribes had little need for permanent homes, using the *tepee*, a portable cone-shaped tent, for shelter. The Indians built a fire in the center of the tepee and placed their beds on the ground around it. Tepees were always made, erected, and maintained by the women of a tribe.

The use of the horse transformed Indian life on the Great Plains, especially with regard to food gathering. Before the introduction of the horse by Spanish explorers, Indians lived a meager life, always near the brink of want. They traveled and hunted on foot, which was slow, tedious, and difficult. The horse changed these conditions forever, allowing Indians to move rapidly over the immense reaches of the Great Plains, traveling and hunting in rhythm with the movement of the great bison herds. The horse also turned the Plains Indians into formidable, highly-mobile fighters—the best light cavalry in the world, as one American soldier put it. Becoming skilled and respected warriors was important to the males of Plains Indian tribes, and it was necessary for warriors to establish a record of battle feats to earn the respect of tribal members and merit positions of leadership. Tribes gave warriors recognition for taking the scalp of or killing an enemy. Those warriors exposing themselves to the greatest danger in such endeavors received the greatest honors. For example, a warrior received great honor if he touched a live enemy in battle without receiving any wounds himself.

Indians of the Southwest

The Southwest has a desert climate, with little rainfall. Most Indians there lived harsh lives, relying on gathering wild vegetation—berries, nuts, fruits, roots, seeds—but hunting when game was available. One group of Southwestern Indians, however, used agriculture successfully.

The Pueblo Indians lived in villages with stone and adobe apartment-like dwellings. Today thirty such dwellings remain in Arizona and New Mexico.

Acoma Pueblo, known as Sky City, was built on top of a 357-foot sandstone mesa in New Mexico, making it easily defensible. Modern Acomans claim that their seventy-acre village is the oldest continuously inhabited city in the United States. The Pueblos grew corn, squash, beans, tobacco, and cotton. Eastern Pueblos, located in north central New Mexico, planted their crops on lands near the Rio Grande and Chama River, using river water in irrigation systems. Western Pueblos living in the deserts of the Southwest had no such options. Consequently they planted drought-resistant crops, like certain hearty types of corn. Pueblo men did most of the farming, but they were assisted by women at planting and harvesting time. In addition to being excellent farmers, the Pueblos were skilled craftspeople and traders. The women excelled in making fine pottery, baskets, cotton cloth, and blankets, which Western Pueblos traded, along with surplus crops, with other groups of Indians.

The Pueblo Indians believed that the object of life was to live in harmony with one another. Thus, they encouraged cooperation and succeeded in creating an orderly and relatively peaceful society. The Pueblos believed that if they achieved harmony, the spirits of the dead would permit the rain to fall, the harvest to be good, and the people to be healthy.

There was yet another major group of Southwestern Indians. These were nomadic hunters and gatherers who arrived in the Southwest between 900 and 1500 A.D. In time, they separated into two groups: the **Apaches** and **Navajos**, both of whom were known as good hunters, brave fighters, and aggressive raiders. The Apaches and the Navajos attacked the Pueblo Indians, raiding their villages, crops, and animal herds. In fact, the two tribes received their present names because of such activity: the Pueblos called them *Apache de Navaju*, "raiders and burners of our crops." The Apaches and Navajos, though, called themselves *Diné* or "the People." The Pueblos took measures to protect themselves from these attacks, walling up the first-floor windows and doorways of their homes. Some northern Pueblos apparently abandoned their villages in the face of the raids, seeking refuge in other villages that grew larger as a result of accepting them.

The Apaches' and Navajos' way of life changed after their arrival in the Southwest. At first both were nomadic peoples who relied on hunting, gathering, and raiding, but as time went on, the Navajos dropped their nomadic way of life and became expert sheep herders and weavers. The

Apaches, on the other hand, stayed largely on the move and continued as before. In contrast to other American Indian groups across the United States, many present-day Southwest Indians still live in the same places as did their ancestors.

Changes Coming

The way of life of American Indians in each of the seven cultural areas declined during the next period of history, which witnessed the exploration and settlement of the Americas by Europeans. The coming of Europeans changed the lives of Indians forever, as great numbers of Indians died in battles fought against the newcomers, and even more died from European diseases. In fact, whole tribes were wiped out by disease, some even before the Indians ever set eyes on a white person. The Indians' reaction to the newcomers is summed up well by Chief Hiamovi of the Cheyenne: "Then came strangers from across the Great Water. No land had they; we gave them our land. No food had they; we gave them of our corn. The strangers [have] become many and they fill our country. . . . In a little while, the old Indians will no longer be."

✤ Chapter Review

Identify

Beringia	Plains Indians
Archaic Age	Acoma Pueblo
Hohokam	Apaches
Anasazi	Navajos
Kiva	
Mound Builders	
Cahokia	
effigy mounds	
widowed land	
seven cultural areas	
Algonquian	
Iroquois	
League of the Iroquois	

Short Paragraph

1. How do many scientists think people were first able to migrate to North America?

2. How did the development of farming change early Indian societies?

3. In what ways did American Indian groups in the Eastern Woodlands, Great Plains, and Southwest differ in lifestyle and culture?

1

Discovery, Exploration, and Colonization

❖

Background to "Discovery"

As early as about A.D. 1000, Europeans had visited the continents known today as North and South America. The Norse (or Viking) explorer **Leif Ericson** was among the first Europeans to travel to these newly discovered lands, but the Western Europe of Leif Ericson's day was not prepared to take advantage of them. During this historical era the European nation-states were organizing into the now-familiar political units of England, France, Spain, Portugal, and others. By 1100, these nations were involved in the **Crusades**, a series of Holy Wars waged to capture the Holy Land (Palestine) from the Muslims and drive them out of Western Europe.

During the course of the Crusades over the next two centuries, the people of Western Europe were introduced to the many luxuries of the advanced civilizations already in place in the Mid and Far East. From these experiences a regular overland trade developed between the East (Asia) and the various countries of Western Europe. In time this trade provided the motivation for Europeans to undertake the early voyages of maritime exploration. In an effort to discover a viable sea route to Asia—knowledge of which would make trade with the Far East both quicker and more profitable—daring seafarers ventured out into vast, unknown waters.

Portugal and Spain

Under the guidance of the monarch known as Prince Henry the Navigator in the 1440s, Portugal began its efforts to reach Asia by sailing south, down the coast of Africa. In 1448 **Bartholomew Diaz** had managed to round the Cape of Good Hope (the southern tip of Africa), and in 1498 **Vasco da Gama** repeated the feat, then sailed east, and on to India.

Meanwhile, in 1492, an Italian sailor named **Christopher Columbus** led a small expedition of three ships under the flag of Spain to find a new and, hopefully, more-direct trade route with Asia by sailing west from Europe. After more than a month at sea, Columbus was convinced he had succeeded when he made landfall in the present-day Bahamas. Although he would make a total of four voyages to the Caribbean, Columbus died in Spain in 1505 still believing that he had reached the East Indies. Others, however, were convinced that what Columbus and successive explorers had encountered across the Atlantic Ocean wasn't the Orient at all but a rich New World of boundless opportunity. One such person was the Italian **Amerigo Vespucci**, who led Portuguese and Spanish expeditions along the coast of South America. In his honor, the term *America* was adopted by European cartographers to label the continents of the great New World.

The New World

The Europeans soon found the New World to be a place rich in natural resources, the most obvious of which was the land itself. The cultures of Western Civilization had always valued land ownership, with wealth and social position directly linked to one's ownership or control of land. Without a doubt, the tremendous quantity of seemingly unsettled land was a major attraction for most Europeans. In addition to land, the forests (for timber products), fish, furs, and, of course, gold and silver held out by the New World proved to be strong temptations for Europeans brave enough to heed the call.

The early explorers and the settlers who followed gave little consideration to the people who already inhabited this so-called New World. Columbus had simply called these people *Indians* because he had believed himself to be in the Indies, and the label stuck. At the time of the arrival of the Europeans, there may have been as many as 70 million people living in North and

South America, with up to 12 million of this population scattered across what is now the United States. In all, the Americas comprised hundreds of different culture groups who used hundreds of distinct languages and dialects. It is likely that the first inhabitants of North and South America had arrived from Siberia during the last Ice Age while in search of big game. Over thousands of years, their descendants had spread south and across both continents, developing a wide variety of cultures, from the hunting-and-gathering societies of the eastern North American woodlands to the more advanced civilizations of the Aztec in the central valley of Mexico and the Inca in Peru.

The Conquistadors

Because the voyages of Columbus had provided them a foothold, the Spanish got off to an early lead in the exploration and conquest of the Western Hemisphere. Small bands of private soldiers or adventurers known as **conquistadors** pushed the Spanish claim for land and riches in Central America, South America, and the North American Southwest. Notable among these conquistadors and explorers were such men as **Hernando Cortes**, who conquered the Aztec empire of Mexico in 1519; **Francisco Pizarro**, who brought down the Inca empire of Peru (1531–35); **Juan Ponce de Leon**, who explored the Florida Peninsula in 1513; **Hernando de Soto**, the Spaniard who traveled throughout the southeastern region of North America in 1539–42; and **Francisco Vasquez de Coronado** explorer of the North American Southwest (1540–42). These conquistadors killed and enslaved the native populations they encountered, taking control of the land and extracting gold and silver from the New World to enrich themselves, Spain, and the Roman Catholic Church.

The French

French exploration of the New World began in 1524 with the voyages of yet another Italian sailor, **Giovanni da Verrazano**. Like many others, Verrazano searched for a Northwest Passage through North America in order to reach Asia. **Jacques Cartier** sailed under the French flag in 1535–36, exploring the Gulf of St. Lawrence and the St. Lawrence River. The Father of New France (French possessions in North America) was **Samuel de Champlain**, who founded Quebec in 1608. While the Spanish had aggressively pursued riches and conquest, the French were more interested in establishing trade with the Indians and fishing along the continent's Grand Banks. French fur traders, in pursuit of highly prized beaver, mink, and other pelts, traveled and lived among the Indian peoples of North America and explored much of the interior of the continent. Both the Great Lakes and the river system of the mid-continent provided these frontier explorers with good transportation routes, with Roman Catholic priests following close behind to spread their faith throughout the native populations of the inland forest.

England: Exploration and Settlement

Francis Drake engaged in exploration of the New World as a result of his voyages in pursuit of Spanish treasure. Drake was an English privateer, or Sea Dog, who, with the blessings of Queen Elizabeth of England, raided Spanish ships and New World settlements, relieving them of their stores of gold and silver. In 1580 Drake returned from one such voyage that had taken him around the world. Upon his return to England he was knighted by the queen in recognition of his exploits. In 1587 the British attempted to plant an American colony of their own on an island off the coast of present-day North Carolina. The **Roanoke Island** settlement was established with 117 people under the leadership of Governor **John White**. White's granddaughter, **Virginia Dare**, was the first English child born in North America. At one point it became necessary for White to return to England. When he arrived back at the settlement, he found it deserted, and Roanoke came to be known as the "lost colony." In spite of this and other faltering early efforts at settlement, England would not lose interest in establishing colonies upon the eastern coast of the North American continent.

Jamestown, Virginia, and the Southern Colonies

The first permanent English settlement in North America was **Jamestown**, established by the Virginia Company in the colony of Virginia in 1607. There, a small group of colonists struggled to plant their colony in the New World. While many died in this effort, Captain **John Smith**, a seasoned soldier and adventurer, emerged as a leader who managed to bring order and discipline to a body of people giving way to hunger, chaos, and fear. The early colonists of Virginia searched for a passageway through the continent (in an effort to reach the Pacific Ocean and on to Asia), tried in vain to find large deposits of gold, silver, or other precious metals (as the Spanish had done in Mexico and South America), and negotiated with the local Indians with the idea that a profitable trade might be established (as the French had managed to do in the interior). None of these activities proved profitable. Ultimately, it was tobacco that would save Virginia.

John Rolfe, an early settler, developed a variety of tobacco that would grow in the tidewater soils of Virginia yet provide the smooth, sweet smoke that the British had become accustomed to over the years. As demand for it grew after 1616, tobacco became the staple, or principal cash crop, of all the southern colonies, its cultivation laying the basis of the southern colonial economy. In turn, the plantation system, which growing and curing tobacco fostered, laid the foundation for southern life and culture for many generations to come. Out of the plantation system of agriculture developed the southern dependence upon slave labor, a distinctive lack of large towns and cities (which hampered the development of an adequate educational system), and a social structure dominated by a relatively small elite of wealthy planters. Besides tobacco, other staples in the southern colonies came to include rice and indigo.

In addition to Virginia, the southern colonies comprised the following. **Maryland** was founded in 1634 by the Calvert family of England as a refuge for British Catholics. **Carolina** was chartered in 1663 to create a buffer zone between hostile Indians and the more settled populations of Virginia. **South Carolina** became a separate colony in 1719, as the two regions, north and south, had been settled by different populations—North Carolina by immigrants from Virginia, and South Carolina by planters from Barbados. Founded by James Oglethorpe in 1733, **Georgia** became the last of the original thirteen British colonies in the North American mainland and the final southern colony. Georgia was originally intended as a grand social experiment, a refuge for debtors and petty criminals who might make good if given a second chance with a clean slate, but the experiment largely failed. By 1752 Georgia's trustees had turned their colony back over to the king.

Their economies firmly grounded in plantation agriculture and slave labor, the southern colonies ended up fitting quite nicely within the model of the growing British Empire. By providing raw materials (tobacco, rice, and indigo) to the mother country (England) and, in turn, using the proceeds from those sales to purchase manufactured goods from British merchants, the southern colonies functioned comfortably within the empire's notion of **mercantilism** (the idea that colonies should complement and supplement, but not compete with, the economy of the mother country).

Plymouth, Massachusetts, and the New England Colonies

In 1620 a group of religious dissenters left England for the New World, where they established the colony of Plymouth. Believing the Church of England to be corrupt, these settlers intended to separate themselves from that church. Hence they were called **Separatists**. Since they had traveled on a long, religious journey (a pilgrimage) they became more widely known as the Pilgrims. The Pilgrims crossed the Atlantic Ocean in the tiny ship *Mayflower*, on which they agreed to abide by laws made by their own elected officials once they reached America. This agreement was the **Mayflower Compact**. Led by William Bradford, these settlers established their colony with the assistance of an English-speaking Indian named Squanto. In the fall of 1621, the surviving Pilgrims celebrated their good fortune with a harvest feast, including the local Indians in their celebration. This gathering is recognized as the first American Thanksgiving.

A little farther south along that same eastern seaboard another colony was soon planted that would eventually absorb the small settlement at Plymouth. This was the **Massachusetts Bay Colony**. There, **John Winthrop** stands out as an important early leader. From planning to governing, he was an active force in the new settlement. Like most of the other early settlers of Massachusetts, Winthrop was a Puritan. Like the Separatists, **Puritans** believed the Church of England to be corrupt, but instead of separating from that church they intended to purify it. Winthrop and his Puritan settlers came to Massachusetts to set an example of a godly society for all the world to see. With this in mind, Massachusetts was founded in 1629. Settlement in Massachusetts and throughout New England, for the most part, followed an orderly pattern that centered around the town. The New England town also became the focal point of social life in this region as well, for church, school, and local government all found a home in the town meeting house.

Unlike the southern colonies, the New England colonies never found a suitable staple, so agricultural production in the area was largely a matter of small family farms engaged in subsistence agriculture (growing food for one's own family with a small surplus for trade or sale). Therefore, as the New England colonies developed, their economic base would not be agriculture but shipping and commerce. With Boston, Massachusetts, as the leading port, New England merchants were engaged in trade throughout the world. In fact, the **triangular trade** patterns developed by New Englanders proved to be a point of contention between those colonists and "Mother England." Triangular trade referred to trade routes by which the New Englanders sold rum to traders (both European and African) on the west coast of Africa, with which they bartered for slaves who were then traded and sold in the West Indies. From there the colonists purchased molasses, which they brought back to New England in order to make more rum. While there were many variations on this cyclical pattern, the important point is that New England merchants often found themselves at odds with the prevailing theory of mercantilism. In other words, the New England colonies did not necessarily complement and supplement the economy of the mother country; often they competed with the English economy.

In addition to Massachusetts, the other New England colonies were as follows. **Rhode Island** was founded by **Roger Williams** and **Anne Hutchinson**, both of whom were religious dissenters from the Puritan theocracy in Massachusetts. Williams had been banished from the Puritan colony in 1635, Hutchinson in 1638. Williams received the Rhode Island charter in 1644. Settlers led by Thomas Hooker, another religious dissenter, left Massachusetts in 1633 to establish the colony of **Connecticut** (chartered in 1637). Both **New Hampshire** and **Maine** were primarily settled by immigrants from the Massachusetts Bay Colony, with both colonies involved in controversy with Massachusetts over boundaries and their own independent existence. New Hampshire finally won a separate charter in 1679, but by 1691 Maine had been absorbed back into Massachusetts.

In general, colonial New Englanders were rugged, independent farmers committed to a grass-roots democracy that had grown up as a result of their local town meetings. Economically, the region was dominated by shipping and commerce, with key merchants operating from bustling port cities, the most important of which was Boston.

Pennsylvania and the Middle Colonies

William Penn, a member of the Society of Friends, or Quakers, founded the colony of **Pennsylvania** in 1681 as a refuge for Quakers, who were persecuted and discriminated against in England. The Friends believed in equality among all peoples, were committed to peace, and embraced the right of the individual to interpret scripture and communicate with God. William Penn promoted his colony as a place of religious tolerance and rich farmland, a combination that brought prosperity and rapid growth to Pennsylvania. Indeed, Philadelphia, Pennsylvania, grew to become one of the largest cities in the British Empire before the American Revolution. In contrast to both the southern and New England colonies, the middle colonies developed large family farms engaged in profitable commercial agriculture. Often called the bread basket, this region was soon exporting many grain products, along with beef and pork. Not only would commercial agriculture play a large role in the prosperity of the middle colonies, but the city of Philadelphia would become a major port city. Like their counterparts in Boston, the merchants of Philadelphia participated in shipping and trade with interests throughout the world. Also like the merchants of Boston, Philadelphia's international business leaders would soon find themselves an irritant to the royal government for operating outside the colonial norm known as mercantilism. Along with the middle colonies' economic diversity came a cultural diversity; the religious tolerance of this region attracted settlers from many European nations, peoples with a variety of cultural and religious backgrounds.

The other middle colonies were as follows. **New York** had originally been settled by the Dutch as New Netherland in 1624, with the settlement at New Amsterdam begun in 1626 by Governor **Peter Minuit**. In 1664, the Dutch colony was surrendered to the British and New Amsterdam became New York City and New Netherland became the colony of New York, so named after the duke of York, the brother of the king of England. Also in 1664, the duke of York granted lands to other British nobles, who created the colonies of East and West Jersey, united in 1702 to form **New Jersey**. **Delaware** was originally settled by Swedish immigrants as New Sweden. Once a private tract of land given to William Penn by the duke of York in 1682, the area separated from Pennsylvania in 1701 to function as its own colony. Culturally and economically diverse, the middle colonies constituted a prosperous, rapidly growing region.

Great Britain and the Colonies

Throughout the colonial period England had, for the most part, let the American Colonies pursue their own interests. This included the development in each colony of an assembly that acted, in practice, as the government, or at least as the legislature. While British laws, in theory, applied to colonial America (especially a set of laws governing the conduct of trade and commerce in the empire known as the **Navigation Acts**) they were largely ignored. And the British government, preoccupied at home with a drawn-out war with France, did not bother to enforce its mandates in its American colonies. This tendency for the British government to overlook violations of the law in its far-flung colonies is known as **salutary neglect**. In other words, despite the concept that the British **Parliament** (the legislative branch of government) and monarchy were supreme, the reality of colonial life was such that the assembly in each colony functioned as the effective government of the people. As long as England continued to ignore or neglect its colonies along the eastern seaboard, relations between the thirteen colonies on the North American mainland and the mother country remained reasonably stable. By 1763, however, events began to unfold that would forever alter this relationship.

✤ Chapter Review

Identify

Leif Ericson	Jacques Cartier
Crusades	Samuel de Champlain
Bartholomew Diaz	Francis Drake
Vasco da Gama	Roanoke Island
Christopher Columbus	John White
Amerigo Vespucci	Virginia Dare
conquistadors	Jamestown
Hernando Cortes	John Smith
Francisco Pizarro	John Rolfe
Juan Ponce de Leon	Maryland
Hernando de Soto	Carolina
Francisco Vasquez de Coronado	South Carolina
Giovanni da Verrazano	Georgia

mercantilism	New Hampshire
Separatists	Maine
Mayflower	William Penn
Mayflower Compact	Pennsylvania
Massachusetts Bay Colony	New York
John Winthrop	Peter Minuit
Puritans	New Jersey
triangular trade	Delaware
Rhode Island	Navigation Acts
Roger Williams	salutary neglect
Anne Hutchinson	Parliament
Connecticut	

Short Paragraph

1. Describe the three basic regions (the Southern, Middle, and New England colonies) of Colonial America.

2. Describe the relationship between Great Britain and the colonies.

3. Describe the concepts of mercantilism and salutary neglect; how are these concepts related to the British colonies in North America?

2

Revolution and Independence

The French and Indian War

England and France were often at war during the years of American colonization and throughout the years of the early American republic. One war
in this long series of conflicts would have a major impact on the movement
of the colonies toward revolution and independence. While it had repercus-
sions throughout Europe, the Great War for Empire began in the American
colonies and involved the climactic struggle between France and Great Britain over the control of North America.

Early in the 1750s, the French crossed Lake Erie and began to push their
claim to territory into the Ohio River Valley, building a line of forts along the
western Pennsylvania border to serve as a blockade to British and American
expansion. This greatly displeased the British as well as the Virginia and
Pennsylvania colonists, who also laid claim to the area. In 1753 a young
officer in the Virginia militia, **George Washington**, was dispatched by the
Governor of Virginia on a mission to order the French to evacuate this territory. They refused. Quickly this stalemate turned into an armed conflict,
known in America as the **French and Indian War**, since most of the Indians
in the Ohio country participated on the side of the French. Washington
would engage the French in the first battle of this war in 1754. With the
conflict still raging, in 1760 **King George III** came to power in England determined to seek peace in this most recent dispute with France. By 1763 the

British and colonial forces secured victory. The French and Indian War officially came to an end with the signing of the **Treaty of Paris**, under terms of which France gave up all territory east of the Mississippi River (except New Orleans) and Spain (an ally of the French in the war) lost Spanish Florida. To appease their loyal ally, the French gave New Orleans and claims to territory west of the Mississippi River to Spain.

With the French and their Indian allies defeated, the barrier to the expansion of the British colonies in North America had been removed. There was no longer a hostile power on the western borders of the English colonies. The frontier was open to settlement. However, with this victory in 1763, Great Britain and its American colonies would embark upon new directions that would result in the formation of a new nation.

Social and Intellectual Movements

While 1763 is a pivotal date in the history of colonial America, there were, throughout the colonies and Western Europe, powerful social and intellectual movements afoot that served to move many loyal colonists in the direction of revolution. The great intellectual movement of the late eighteenth century known as the **Enlightenment** represented the triumph of reason in Western culture. As early as the 1660s, advances in science and philosophy brought a new attitude toward both religion and politics. The idea that the universe was governed by natural laws discernable by all people of reason was a notion that deprived those in authority of some of the mystery of their office. For if ordinary people were capable through reason of understanding the principles that govern the universe, then the authority and power of monarchs and church officials were undermined to the extent that, in theory, all people were at least capable of equality. The English philosopher **John Locke** was an important figure of the Enlightenment. His ideas regarding the role of reason and **natural law** (laws that are higher or more important than man-made laws) played an important role in the thinking of American colonial leaders. In British colonies along America's eastern seaboard, the man who best represented the Enlightenment was the inventor and scientist **Benjamin Franklin** of Philadelphia. Indeed, by the 1750s Franklin's reputation had spread throughout the colonies and Western Europe. From his status as a scientist, thinker, and inventor of international renown, he would increasingly find himself in a position of colonial leadership in the years after 1763.

Another force in the shaping of the American mind was a religious revival known as the **Great Awakening**. In the 1730s a dramatic camp-style movement swept through the colonies. This great awakening emphasized individual accountability and the nurturing of the individual's personal relationship with God. This new empowerment of the individual in religious matters carried over into the social and political arenas as well. People touched by this revival movement were far less likely to engage in simple-minded or blind deference to church or government officials. Among the leaders of the Great Awakening were Massachusetts minister and theologian **Jonathan Edwards** and the English minister and evangelist **George Whitefield**, who toured the colonies preaching to thousands.

The Road to Revolution

Although Great Britain had routed France, its hated adversary, from its colonial possessions in mainland North America, the Treaty of Paris left the British government with a variety of problems. Among the difficulties now facing King George III and Parliament was the extensive debt brought on by the recent war with France and the question of just how to effectively govern the growing number of British subjects in the newly expanded territories in North America. In an effort to pay off the government debts and reorganize the administration of the American colonies, Parliament set out to tighten its control over trade and commerce within the empire and arrange for the American colonists to pay some share of the British tax burden.

The colonists, having grown used to governing themselves through their own colonial assemblies and largely indifferent to British laws and regulations, naturally resisted efforts on the part of the king and Parliament to assert more influence in their affairs. One of the earliest points of contention between the British government and the American colonies focused upon the **Proclamation of 1763**. The measure was designed to bring peace to the frontier by, at least temporarily, stopping the flow of American settlers into Indian lands, and thereby calling a halt to the westward movement of American colonists beyond the Appalachian Mountains. Americans, however, regarded expansion into these western territories as one of the hard-won victories of the French and Indian War. This attempt to prohibit their migration angered them.

Adding to these tensions was the Parliament's passage of the **Sugar Act** of 1764. In an effort to raise more money (revenue) from its colonies and to regulate trade within the empire, Parliament levied new duties (taxes) upon such regularly imported items as wine, coffee, and sugar. As irritating as these measures were to the colonists, they provoked only moderate responses of displeasure when compared to the outpouring of resentment that followed the passage of the **Stamp Act** in 1765. This new regulation required the placing of revenue stamps on a variety of common items, including legal documents and newspapers. The stamps, which had to be purchased from British agents, were ostensible evidence that the taxes had been paid. These so-called stamp taxes cut across colonial society to impact large numbers of people. In response, protests erupted throughout the colonies, often led by members of a militant society known as the **Sons of Liberty**. Now delegates from nine of the colonies met in New York and convened a meeting known as the **Stamp Act Congress**. Meanwhile a movement to protest British taxes through **nonimportation** (a boycott of British goods) spread throughout the colonies. Eventually the Parliament relented by repealing the Stamp Act, but its desire to increase revenue from the colonies remained.

In 1767 the British government decreed the **Townshend Acts**, which once again attempted to place duties on a variety of items that the colonists regularly imported from Great Britain, such as glass, paint, and tea. This move proved every bit as unpopular as had the Stamp Act, with a boycott of British goods once again serving as protest against the new legislation. Again, Parliament responded to the pressure by repealing the offensive legislation, removing duties on all of the items except tea. In response, the colonists lifted their boycott of all British imports—except tea.

From Agitation to Revolution

From the Proclamation of 1763 through the controversy surrounding the Townshend Acts, a tension had developed that slowly began to erode the good will between England and its American colonies. Soon the stressful atmosphere turned decidedly more hostile. On March 5, 1770, a group of nervous British soldiers fired into an angry mob that was protesting outside the Boston customhouse, with eleven casualties (five killed) resulting. This violent event, known as the **Boston Massacre**, fueled the anti-British fires and gave credence to the colonists' suspicions that the British soldiers had been dispatched to Boston in the first place in order to repress potential rebellion. A tense and uneasy quiet marked relations between Great Britain and the colonies for many months to come, but this was simply the calm before the storm.

In an attempt to assist the struggling British East India Company, in 1773 the Parliament passed the **Tea Act**, which removed a number of duties and allowed the company to sell its tea at a reduced price; nevertheless, the Townshend duty, to which the colonists had strongly objected, remained in place, and the colonists still refused to buy British tea, in many places even refusing to allow tea to be unloaded from East India Company ships. In Boston, this dispute resulted in the infamous **Boston Tea Party**. On the night of December 16, 1773, a group of men under the leadership of the Sons of Liberty boarded British ships docked in Boston Harbor and proceeded to "unload" them by dumping crates of tea into the water. This dramatic destruction of private property was met with an angry response by Parliament. Passing the **Coercive Acts** in 1774, the British government suspended representative government in Massachusetts and took a variety of additional punitive measures. The colonists denounced this last bit of legislation as the **Intolerable Acts**. Clearly, the conflict between England and the colonies was intensifying.

Responding to the Intolerable Acts, delegates from each of the thirteen colonies met in Philadelphia in 1774 to convene the **First Continental Congress**. This group agreed, yet again, to resort to nonimportation, and proceeded to engage in lengthy deliberations over their problems with the British Parliament. Quickly, however, events moved beyond any real hope of reconciliation. In April of 1775, fighting broke out between militia members in Massachusetts and British soldiers. Intending to seize a cache of weapons and arrest certain leaders of the Sons of Liberty, the British had marched out of Boston en route to Concord, an outlying town some twenty miles to the west. Even as the British began their march, the warning went out that the "British are coming!" With mounted patriots such as **Paul Revere** riding through the countryside spreading the word, local militia units known as the **Minute Men** (for their self-proclaimed ability to be ready to fight in a minute) prepared for action. Early morning of April 19 found the British soldiers approaching the town of **Lexington**, about halfway to Concord, where the local militiamen had assembled on the town's commons to meet them. The tension soon erupted into a bloody fight, with ten American patriots wounded and another eight killed. After the skirmish the soldiers continued on to Concord, where they found little to justify their long and violent march. On their way back to Boston, the British army suffered terrible losses as armed patriot Minute Men sniped at them from behind trees and walls. The American Revolution had begun!

Independence and Revolution

The **Second Continental Congress** met in Philadelphia in May of 1775. This time there was much to decide. Already a war had begun, with the Massachusetts militia surrounding the British forces in the city of Boston. After naming George Washington of Virginia as commander of the Continental Army, the Congress scrambled to deliberate the best course of action to take with England. Back in Boston, meanwhile, another bloody battle had been fought. The **Battle of Bunker Hill** (actually fought on nearby Breed's Hill) saw a British victory, but at the cost of more than 1,000 British casualties. Furthermore, anti-British sentiment among the colonists was on the rise. Early the next year, in January 1776, Thomas Paine's widely distributed and highly persuasive pamphlet **Common Sense** stirred American feelings against the monarchy and urged rebellion. The official break with England finally came with the **Declaration of Independence**, which the delegates in Philadelphia adopted on July 4, 1776. The declaration, drafted by the Virginian **Thomas Jefferson**, outlined the justifications for the rebellion and declared the colonies "free and independent states." There would be no turning back.

The American Revolution

The factors that influenced the outcome of the American War for Independence are numerous, and at the Revolution's onset it seemed that the colonists had the deck stacked against them. First and foremost, at this time the British army and navy were among the finest in the world, while the Americans would have to create an army and navy virtually from scratch, even as they tried to conduct a war with a superpower. In addition British forces were backed by a long-standing and powerful government, one with considerable financial resources; the Americans, of course, had neither a standing federal government nor a treasury and would have to attempt to forge some semblance of both in the midst of war. To make matters even worse, approximately one-third of the American population were **Loyalists** (called **Tories** by the Patriots) who actively supported the British, both in spirit and in practice.

In spite of all the negatives, other key factors kept the Americans' battle for independence alive. Perhaps most important, the great distance separating the colonies from England worked against the British military (making the transportation of troops and supplies costly and slow), as did the large territory of the colonial eastern seaboard (making it quite difficult for the British army and navy to be in the right place at the right time). Another key consideration is that the American patriots had a definite sense of fighting for a cause and, in addition, were fighting in defense of home and family, while British soldiers were far from home fighting a war that held little purpose from their point of view. Also, the Continental Congress had chosen their military commander well, for George Washington proved to be a decisive factor in the war by keeping his army in the field and, more or less, intact. Finally, the entry of France and Spain into the war against England forced the British to divert military and financial resources to fighting their old enemies on the European continent. Thus hamstrung, they paid far less attention than they otherwise would have to the upstart colonies in North America.

The drama unfolded from the Battle of Lexington in 1775 to the Battle of Yorktown in 1781. In the course of the fighting, Washington achieved a stunning victory over the British by leading his forces across the icy Delaware River under the cover of darkness on Christmas evening 1776 and striking the enemy at **Trenton**, New Jersey. Surprise victories of this nature would, however, be few and far between for the struggling Continental Army. Indeed, strategic retreat might best describe Washington's strategy, but he continually succeeded in keeping his army from being captured or destroyed. After withdrawing from New Jersey and suffering defeats in campaigns around Philadelphia, General Washington and his remaining men endured a harsh winter at **Valley Forge**, Pennsylvania, in 1777. Nonetheless, American forces proved victorious on other fronts. At **Saratoga**, New York, the British General John Burgoyne surrendered his troops to American General Horatio Gates on October 17, 1777. Demonstrating to the world that American armies would continue to fight and, indeed, win battles against the British forces, this victory proved an important factor in the decision of France (and then Spain) to enter the war against England early in 1778. With Washington and his forces engaged along the eastern seaboard, American and British armies clashed in campaigns that stretched from the western frontier to the deep south. Final victory for General Washington and the Continental Army came at **Yorktown**,

Virginia, in 1781. There, with the assistance of French ground troops under the Comte de Rochambeau and the support of the French navy under Admiral de Grasse, Washington forced the surrender of the British army under the command of Lord Cornwallis on October 17, 1781. The American Revolution had come to an end.

The Treaty of Paris

Americans negotiated the official terms of the peace with Great Britain in 1782. In addition to peace, the resulting **Treaty of Paris**, signed in 1783, recognized American independence and gave to "these united states" the lands east of the Mississippi River. With the issue of their independence from Great Britain settled, the former colonists now turned to the considerable task of attempting to restore order and stability after the devastation and chaos of revolution.

✦ Chapter Review

Identify

George Washington	Townshend Acts
French and Indian War	Boston Massacre
King George III	Tea Act
Treaty of Paris (1763)	Boston Tea Party
Enlightenment	Coercive Acts
John Locke	Intolerable Acts
natural law	First Continental Congress
Benjamin Franklin	Paul Revere
Great Awakening	Minute Men
Jonathan Edwards	Lexington
George Whitefield	Second Continental Congress
Proclamation of 1763	Battle of Bunker Hill
Sugar Act	*Common Sense*
Stamp Act	Declaration of Independence
Sons of Liberty	Thomas Jefferson
Stamp Act Congress	Loyalists
nonimportation	Tories

Trenton   Yorktown

Valley Forge   Treaty of Paris (1783)

Saratoga

Short Paragraph

1. Describe the events that brought the American colonies to revolution and independence from Great Britain.

2. What factors most influenced the outcome of the American Revolution?

3. Describe the Treaties of Paris 1763 and 1783; what wars did each conclude, and what were the major provisions of each treaty?

The First Thirteen States, 1779

3

The Young Republic

Even as Americans fought for their independence from Britain, they struggled to create their own system of government. Most crucial was the formation of **state constitutions**, which replaced assorted colonial charters and oaths of allegiance to the British crown. In many ways these creative exercises in self-governance are as important to the founding of the United States as the better-known documents that tourists stand in line to see today. The inhabitants of the first thirteen states varied widely in culture and habits of daily life, but they all shared a belief in **republicanism**, the concept that political power should derive only from the people and their legitimate representatives.

The Articles of Confederation

Early Americans instinctively distrusted all central authority, feeling more loyalty to and more closely identifying with their respective states and communities. It is hardly surprising, then, that the first actual constitution of the United States, entitled the **Articles of Confederation**, effected a loosely knit federal government. Under the Articles, approved by the Congress in 1781 from an early committee proposal in 1776, the legislative branch was the sole institution of national authority. It was charged with the power to wage war, conduct foreign relations, and borrow and issue money. In this new congress, each state had a single vote regardless of the size of its population, and the consent of all thirteen state legislatures was required to amend the Articles.

Discussions of the United States under the Articles of Confederation traditionally focus on the national government's weaknesses, and there were plenty of them. No power existed to regulate trade or interstate commerce, draft troops, or tax the people. To raise the funds necessary to operate, Congress had to make formal requests to the state legislatures, which had full authority to refuse such entreaties. Since there was little enforcement of national law, people tended to disregard it. A variety of different currencies were in circulation, complicating business transactions, with the U.S. dollar often at the bottom in value. Moreover, states routinely charged tariffs on goods passing through their territory, raising prices significantly and, in turn, making American goods less competitive in world markets. During this fragile period the prestige and stature of the young nation were at stake, as well as its very survival. Ominously, British troops remained in the Great Lakes region long after the peace had been negotiated.

But to label the Articles of Confederation a complete failure would be a distortion. Under the Articles, the United States conducted the first successful colonial war for independence in history, driving out a world power and establishing a republic nearly as large as Europe. Furthermore, the average American seemed to approve of a loose union, one that, for example, allowed Virginians to concentrate on agriculture and New Yorkers to focus on trade and commerce.

Whatever the opinions of average folk, American political leaders began to criticize the lack of central authority. Most alarming was the inability of the United States to pay its debts to lenders, both at home and abroad. Complete bankruptcy of the nation was a real possibility. To make matters worse, an economic depression that lasted from 1784 to 1787 drastically reduced the nation's money supply. Hit especially hard were farmers in New England, where riots became commonplace. The most significant of these disturbances was **Shays's Rebellion**, which took place in western Massachusetts during 1786–87. Daniel Shays, a highly decorated military officer in the Revolution, led an armed revolt composed mostly of farmers who were furious over state taxes, mortgage foreclosures, and the common practice of the courts to mete out jail sentences for debtors. At the peak of this unrest, Shays and his men marched on a government arsenal in Springfield. Eventually the state militia managed to put down the revolt (some, including Shays, were sentenced to death and later pardoned), but the national government appeared pitiful and helpless throughout the entire episode. In retrospect, the timing of Shays's Rebellion, which began in 1786, was crucial. Earlier that same year American leaders had gathered to consider the need for a stronger central authority.

The Constitutional Convention

One early advocate of a stronger national government was Alexander Hamilton of New York, who helped organize the Annapolis Convention to discuss problems with the Articles of Confederation. Although only five states sent delegates to this meeting, those convened urged Congress to call a special assembly for the purpose of drafting a new constitution. At Annapolis, Hamilton found a strong ally in Virginian **James Madison**, who would later be called the "father of the U.S. Constitution." During debate, opinion was divided sharply on the need for strengthening the central government. On the subject of Shays's Rebellion, for instance, Thomas Jefferson (at the time serving as ambassador to France) noted that "a little rebellion, now and then, is a good thing . . . ," while George Washington from his home in Virginia exclaimed, "Good God!" and immediately made plans to travel to Philadelphia, where the constitutional convention was scheduled to be held after the turn of the year. Washington, as the most beloved and respected American, proved crucial to the convention's success, and was chosen as convention chairman.

As the Constitutional Convention commenced work in the spring of 1787, a total of fifty-five delegates representing all states but Rhode Island eventually participated. Those who framed the U.S. Constitution are often collectively called the nation's founding fathers, but such a label obscures the fact that many important leaders of the day were not present (including Jefferson and fellow collaborator on the Declaration of Independence, John Adams of Massachusetts). Furthermore, quite a few notable and patriotic Americans who were in attendance, such as Virginia firebrand Patrick Henry, ultimately opposed the proposed document. At any rate, the delegates of 1787 were hardly typical American citizens of the day: only two were farmers; many of them were college educated; lawyers were plentiful in their ranks; and fourteen among the group owned slaves. Nevertheless, the assembly was a remarkable and timely collection of talented and highly regarded political figures. In order to promote frank discussion, the convention voted to conduct meetings in secret—a fact critics would seize upon for generations. Cosmopolitan Philadelphia proved an ideal host city for the attendees, who were entertained by local celebrity and fellow delegate Benjamin Franklin. Throughout the long, hot summer, James Madison kept a private journal, one of the few sources on the details of the meeting.

Madison and his fellow Virginians had come to Philadelphia well prepared; immediately this group put forward the so-called **Virginia Plan** to fashion a stronger central government composed of three branches of national authority: one legislative, one executive, and one judicial. Controversy quickly surfaced, however, regarding the determination of each state's amount of representation in the crucial legislative branch of government, as fierce debate between the representatives of the large and small states threatened to abort the entire convention. The Virginians (from a state with ten times as many people as Delaware) naturally wanted population to determine each state's number of representatives in the national legislature. In response, William Paterson, champion of the small states, put forth an alternative, the **New Jersey Plan**, which would give each state an equal number of votes. Bickering continued for weeks, with old Ben Franklin offering wise and calm counsel, including a moment of prayer (which was perhaps a sign of desperation since Franklin was hardly religious). In what became known as the **Great Compromise**, the delegates finally agreed upon a bicameral (or two-chambered) legislature, with each state given two representatives in the Senate, or upper chamber, and the population determining the number of representatives in the lower chamber, the House of Representatives. Naturally, the delegates from the southern states wanted to count slaves for purposes of representation, but they only succeeded in having each slave count as three-fifths of a person. Indeed, slavery was an embarrassment to many of the delegates (the Constitution never specifically mentions the words *slave* or *slavery*, referring to human property as "other persons"), and slavery remained one of the unresolved issues of 1784. With regard to slavery and all the other subjects left out of the Constitution entirely (such as precisely who qualifies to vote), such matters remained the province of the state governments, which, for the time being, were free to operate as they wished.

The Constitution of the United States embodies several key concepts. The **separation of powers** (into the Legislative, Executive, and Judicial branches of the federal government) and a system of **checks and balances** (such as the presidential veto) were intended to help prevent tyranny from arising, and to force deliberation and compromise. The system of government the Constitution effected, known as **Federalism** (with powers shared between the national and state governments), was a natural conclusion, for in those days each of the states claimed sovereignty, a notion that would have been unthinkable to abandon. Interestingly, the practice of judicial review (the power of courts to void government actions because of unconstitutionality) was not provided for by the Constitution, but within a few years the Supreme Court began to assume such a role in practice. On September 17, 1787, the thirty-nine delegates still in attendance signed the Constitution and, fearing stiff opposition to the new document's acceptance, announced that the approval of only nine of the states was necessary to ratify their work in state conventions.

During the two years in which Americans deliberated the adoption of the Constitution, known as the **ratification period**, supporters of the proposed stronger central government cleverly dubbed themselves *Federalists*, a term which then implied a large role for the states in a system of shared powers. This left their opponents with the undesirable tag of *Antifederalists*. Although it is impossible to measure what average Americans thought on the subject, it is clear that the Federalists were better organized and equipped in the war of words. Most notable was the publication of the so-called *Federalist Papers*, a series of essays penned by James Madison, Alexander Hamilton, and John Jay that ran in New York newspapers under the pseudonym "Publius." These essays were widely circulated and to this day remain the most concise explanation of the *intent* behind the U.S. Constitution. Although the Antifederalists ultimately failed to block the acceptance of the Constitution, they were successful in persuading the leadership to add to it the **Bill of Rights** (in the form of the first ten amendments) as a guarantee of personal liberties under the new and much stronger federal government.

The true motives of those who drafted and supported the ratification of the new U.S. Constitution have been debated for more than two hundred years. Often these founding fathers have been portrayed as godlike figures who created democracy as we know it for the good of all Americans—a version of history found most prominently in the patriotic education of American children. But in the early twentieth century another view emerged, this from historian **Charles A. Beard** in *An Economic Interpretation of the Con-*

stitution, published in 1913. Beard argued that the founders were a group of economic elitists primarily interested in protecting and advancing their own interests. The system of checks and balances, for instance, was not an attempt to block tyranny in the new government but a plot to prevent majority rule. Today most historians dispute this view, but the Beard thesis remains influential. At any rate, and whatever their inner motives, the Federalists won the day, as the Constitution was ratified by all thirteen states by 1790.

One of the most significant laws passed by the newly formed U.S. Congress was the **Judiciary Act of 1789**. Among other provisions, it created a national system of circuit and district courts and gave the U.S. Supreme Court the power of Judicial Review over the decisions reached by state courts in matters of constitutionality. As noted earlier, the Constitution did not specify which branch or level of government would be expected to exercise review over national laws. Over the many generations to follow, this omission was to provide ample fuel for the fires of controversy.

The Genesis of Political Parties

Not surprisingly, George Washington was chosen unanimously by the **Electoral College** as the first President of the United States. The Electoral College consisted of men chosen by the states, with each state awarded the same number of votes as it had representatives in the House and Senate. Today the Electoral College essentially approves the decision of the public vote, but in the early days of the Republic it was expected to choose the best candidate. A reluctant politician who hated controversy, Washington felt that the President should remain above politics. Significantly, the Constitution does not mention parties, for most of the founders felt that political factions were undesirable. Perceptive leaders such as James Madison, however, realized that factionalism was part of human nature and could not be extinguished without harm to liberty. Soon the stage was set for the emergence of a two-party system in American government, which began as an informal political split among strong personalities.

The **Federalist Party** originated within the Washington Administration under the leadership of Treasury Secretary **Alexander Hamilton**. Hamilton was unabashedly aristocratic, and he believed that stable and effective government can only exist under the leadership of an elite (and presumably better-educated) ruling class. A savvy and clever politician, he realized the need for a national banking system that could enable people of wealth and property to invest in the country's future. He also insisted that the nation's development and expansion rested on its ability to borrow money. Above all else, Federalists such as Hamilton believed in a strong central government—one to which the state governments need be subservient. They further believed that if the United States was to be taken seriously in the world arena, its trade and commerce must flourish. Therefore, it is hardly surprising that most Federalists hailed from the booming cities of America rather than the farms and villages. And, finally, despite constant tensions with Great Britain, Hamilton, an admirer of Parliament, whenever possible moved the government toward a pro-British stance. A striking and important event that divided Americans deeply during this period was the **French Revolution**, which began in 1789. Conservative and aristocratic Americans such as Hamilton were horrified at the violent radicalism overturning France, a phenomenon which, in their eyes, made stoic England a much more civilized model for American nationhood.

The **Republican Party** (no relation to today's Republican Party) arose in opposition to Federalist objectives. **Thomas Jefferson** became the principal leader of the Republicans, aided by fellow Virginian James Madison. Republicans felt that the Federalists were engaged in a conspiracy to nullify the freedoms gained in 1776 and to impose a tyrannical aristocracy upon the common people. Jefferson and his followers began to set up committees, newspapers, and centers of party organization. Republicans favored states' rights, in the belief that liberty flourished more purely through decentralization (an ironical view since states' rights would later be used to impose limits on liberty through slavery and segregation). Jefferson believed that agriculture was preferable to the corruption of business and commerce, and he envisioned a nation of yeoman (self-sufficient) farmers raising crops for world markets. Deeply averse to the idea of a national debt, the Republicans maintained that a balanced budget was crucial to progress, and would prevent the banking and manufacturing interests from gaining too much power. (It is interesting to note that Hamilton's nationalistic, probusiness, urban vision of America was much more prophetic than Jefferson's agrarian ideal, yet it is Jefferson who is held in higher esteem today by most Americans.) As for the French Revolution, as horrifying as the mass executions were, Republicans felt that liberty was ultimately being advanced by it. In the Republican mind, almost any state of affairs was better than traditional aristocracy and monarchy.

The rhetoric of the Federalists and Republicans grew increasingly intense during the eight years of the Washington Administration, as the leaders of each party reached out for allies in Congress and the states. Many worried that the competition would lead the young republic to ruin, but the two-party system proved to be remarkably durable.

The Washington and Adams Administrations

Historian James Thomas Flexner has called George Washington the "Indispensable Man." This is no exaggeration. It is indeed unlikely that any other mortal was capable of serving as president during this critical period in American development. Almost every decision Washington made (or avoided) in the course of his presidency became tradition. The Constitution is worded vaguely in terms of presidential power and authority, and some aristocratically minded Americans probably would have been perfectly happy with a president for life. But the wealthy and dignified Washington would have no part in such talk, and he yearned for the day when he could return to his tobacco plantation at Mount Vernon.

By no means, however, was Washington simply a caretaker president. Although reluctant to take sides in the partisan debates, he supported Hamilton on most key issues. Under Washington, the U.S. government funded the national debt, assumed the debts of the states, and backed the establishment of a nationally chartered bank. And it was George Washington who was instrumental in explaining to the American people that a strong national government was necessary if the country was to prosper and defend itself. As a Virginian, Washington helped lessen the frequent charge that New Yorker Hamilton's policies favored the interests of northern manufacturers over those of southern agriculturalists. In making presidential appointments, Washington tried at first to obtain the advice and consent of the Senate, as the Constitution stipulates. He discovered, however, that getting such advice was an invitation for seemingly endless bickering and began instead to simply send the names of his chosen nominees for Senate confirmation—a practice that continues today. Most significant, as the disputes between the Federalists and Republicans grew increasingly bitter, the president used his considerable prestige to hold the nation together.

In 1792 Washington won unanimous reelection, at which point in his tenure foreign policy took center stage. England and France were once again at war with each other, and the administration had great difficulty fashioning a policy of neutrality that would allow the United States to continue to trade with both nations. Certainly war with England was possible during these years. Many Americans still harbored resentment toward Parliament and the king, and British troops were still poised to the North. Most disturbing, the rules of war (between England and France) allowed American ships to be stopped on the high seas and searched. American sailors were often impressed into service of the British Navy. Neutral Americans felt such rules of war did not apply to them. Federalists worried that a failure to appease England would result in another war with that nation, a condition that would stop all imports, crippling Hamilton's financial plans since most revenues came from tariffs. To complicate matters, Washington's State Department was headed by the admitted Francophile Thomas Jefferson. In an attempt to find a favorable solution to the predicament, Chief Justice of the Supreme Court John Jay (an ardent Federalist) was dispatched by Washington to England. The resulting agreement was **Jay's Treaty**, which achieved many if not all of Washington's goals—including British acceptance of U.S. sovereignty over the Northwest Territory—but remained a sore point between the two countries for years. The **Northwest Territory** (also known as the Old Northwest) included a vast section of land that would eventually become the states of Ohio, Indiana, Illinois, Michigan, Wisconsin, and part of Minnesota. Both the United States and England had claimed the region since American independence was won in 1781. Other provisions of the treaty, however, were quite favorable to Britain. The British navy could continue to search American vessels for contraband and apprehend sailors believed to be British subjects. No compensation for previously seized ships was required by the treaty, and American slaveholders would not be paid (as they demanded) for slaves carried off by the British army after the Revolution. Republicans were outraged. In angry protests, Jay was burned in effigy, as many felt the treaty gave too much to the British.

Washington managed to get the treaty ratified in the Senate by raising the unthinkable notion that a movement to impeach him was afoot. Public support swelled for the president. Another important development in foreign policy was **Pinckney's Treaty**, signed by U.S. minister Thomas Pinckney with Spain in 1795 and giving the United States the right to navigate freely up and down the Mississippi River, all the way to the river's mouth at New

Orleans. This was key to the development of the nation's interior, as western farmers finally had use of the mighty Mississippi to transport their goods to world markets.

George Washington refused to run for president again in the **Election of 1796**, setting a tradition of two terms that lasted until 1940. In his **farewell address**, the beloved father of his country spoke forcefully against the nation getting too involved in Europe's problems, articulating a view that would later (and perhaps incorrectly) be construed as a recommendation of isolationism in U.S. foreign policy. In the contest, Washington's vice president, **John Adams**, was elected over Republican Thomas Jefferson, winning by only three votes in the Electoral College. The days of unanimity were over. As constitutionally required then, Jefferson, who had tallied the second highest number of votes, became vice president. Whatever unity George Washington had managed to pull together in his own administration was clearly gone as Adams took the oath of office. His vast service to his country ended, the frail chief executive retired deservedly to his beloved Mount Vernon.

President Adams soon had his hands full. In response to French seizure of American ships, which violated the laws of neutrality, Adams sent a delegation to France to negotiate. But before the negotiations could even begin, three French officials blatantly demanded the promise of a U.S. loan and the immediate payment of bribes. The **XYZ Affair** (named after the anonymous labels given the three French officials) demonstrated the difficulty of conducting foreign affairs in a neutral fashion. Bribes were common in one form or another during this period. (President Washington, for instance, had once paid ransom to Algerian pirates to secure the release of captive American sailors.) In this case, however, the American commissioners were infuriated that a price be paid merely for negotiations to begin. When the news broke in Congress and in the Federalist newspapers, self-righteous Americans rallied around the slogan, "Millions for defense, but not one cent for tribute." A wave of anti-French sentiment ensued. An undeclared naval war erupted from 1798 to 1800, but President Adams was reluctant to propose a formal declaration of war to Congress. This was precisely the kind of entanglement in Europe's affairs that George Washington had urged the United States to avoid.

The conflict with France allowed the (pro-British) Federalists to increase their majorities in Congress in 1798, and they were determined to silence (pro-French) Republican opposition, which the Federalists regarded as treasonous. The result was the implementation of perhaps the most controversial legislation in U.S. history, the **Alien and Sedition Acts**. These laws gave the president extraordinary powers in dealing with foreigners—stifling immigration and persuading some noncitizens to leave the country. Most alarmingly, the Sedition Act allowed the government to suspend constitutional guarantees of individual civil rights to prosecute its opponents and those it merely suspected of treasonous activity. Ten men were arrested under the law, most of whom were Republican newspaper editors whose only real offense was political criticism. A climate of crisis prevailed, as Republicans charged that freedoms gained by the Revolution were suddenly and ruthlessly being snatched away by would-be monarchists.

Republican stalwart Thomas Jefferson responded with the (anonymous) authorship of resolutions adopted by the Kentucky legislature, interpreting the U.S. Constitution to allow states to nullify certain acts of Congress (should the states deem them unacceptable) inside their boundaries. (The U.S. Supreme Court had not yet assumed its role of deciding issues of Constitutionality.) A similar proposal was drafted by James Madison and approved in Virginia. Together, the so-called **Virginia and Kentucky Resolutions** provided ammunition against the Federalists, expressing a view that would take a civil war in the next century to clarify. But even as the nineteenth century dawned, the fate of the young republic seemed up for grabs between two hostile and sharply contrasting visions.

✤ Chapter Review

Identify

state constitutions	checks and balances
republicanism	Federalism
Articles of Confederation	ratification period
Shays's Rebellion	Federalists
James Madison	Antifederalists
Virginia Plan	*Federalist Papers*
New Jersey Plan	Bill of Rights
Great Compromise	Charles A. Beard
separation of powers	Judiciary Act of 1789

Electoral College	Pinckney's Treaty
Federalist Party	Election of 1796
Alexander Hamilton	Washington's farewell address
French Revolution	John Adams
Republican Party	XYZ Affair
Thomas Jefferson	Alien and Sedition Acts
Jay's Treaty	Virginia and Kentucky Resolutions
Northwest Territory	

Short Paragraph

1. Describe the founding fathers of the U.S. Constitution. Why did they feel the need to replace the Articles of Confederation?

2. How did the two-party system get its start in the United States?

3. Describe the presidency of George Washington.

4

Jefferson and the Democratic Republic

The Revolution of 1800

In 1800 **Thomas Jefferson** was elected president of the United States. Author of the Declaration of Independence, Jefferson had already served the nation as a diplomat, secretary of state, and vice president. His bitter disputes with Federalists such as Alexander Hamilton and John Adams had served to create about him the Republican Party, members of which came to be known as **Democratic-Republicans**, and later simply as Democrats. While a member of the elite of the old southern aristocracy, Jefferson was a son of the Enlightenment who professed a deep confidence in the basic abilities of the average person to govern himself. At **Monticello**, the elaborate home in northern Virginia that he had designed himself, Jefferson explored science, philosophy, literature, and the arts. This multifaceted individual reached the apex of his political life when he displaced John Adams as president after the Federalist had served only one term.

Jefferson and his followers hailed the event as the "revolution of 1800." In the eyes of Democratic-Republicans, Jefferson's election was the triumph of democracy over autocracy, a vindication of the values of the American Revolution. On March 4, 1801, the author of the Declaration of Independence was administered the oath of office by Chief Justice John Marshall. A new era of American politics had dawned.

The Louisiana Purchase

As the population west of the Appalachian Mountains (but east of the Mississippi River) continued to grow, the ability to transport sufficient amounts of crops to market became an increasing concern of western farmers. With the key port city of New Orleans in foreign hands, the mighty Mississippi River was not always a dependable route. Always supportive of agriculturalists, Jefferson sent a representative to France to negotiate for the purchase of New Orleans. Instead, due to a variety of circumstances and, in hindsight, excellent timing, **Napoleon Bonaparte**, ruler of France, was willing to sell to the United States not only New Orleans but the entire Louisiana Territory. In 1803 Jefferson's liaison James Monroe successfully arranged the **Louisiana Purchase** from France for the sum of $15 million. This territorial acquisition approximately doubled the size of the young republic and gave western farmers unfettered use of the Mississippi River as well as the thriving port city of New Orleans. Stretching from New Orleans in the south to the Canadian border in the north and the Rocky Mountains in the west, this remarkable acquisition added over 800,000 square miles to the United States of America.

Lewis and Clark

Even before the purchase of Louisiana, President Jefferson had begun to make plans for an expedition into the rugged frontier west of the Missouri River country. **Meriwether Lewis**, then Jefferson's private secretary, and an old army companion of Lewis's, **William Clark**, led a small group of regular servicemen and volunteers that composed the **Corps of Discovery** on an exploratory journey that took them from St. Louis (1803), across the vast Great Plains, through the Rocky Mountains, to the Pacific Ocean, and back again (1806). A young Indian woman named **Sacajawea** served as both a guide and interpreter for the group as they entered heretofore-unexplored territory. Accompanied by her husband, a French trader, Sacajawea met all the hardships of the two-and-one-half-year journey, first while pregnant and then carrying her infant son.

By any estimate, the Lewis and Clark expedition was a major success. The Corps of Discovery returned with tremendous knowledge of the newly purchased territory, with Lewis and Clark having kept copious notes on exciting scientific discoveries regarding plant and animal life and the various native cultures with which they had come into contact. On their way back from the Dakotas down the Missouri River to St. Louis, Lewis and Clark and their men were amazed to meet other Americans heading upstream. The push westward across the Mississippi had begun.

Barbary Pirates

As had Washington and Adams, President Jefferson would struggle to remain neutral in the war that raged on between England and France. He would, however, find himself caught up in a minor conflict across the ocean with the Barbary Pirates. For many years the nations along the Barbary Coast of North Africa had engaged in both piracy and extortion of shipping on the Mediterranean Sea. In order to protect American shipping interests in the area, Jefferson engaged in naval actions against these **Barbary Pirates**, which began in 1801 and did not conclude until a settlement was reached that satisfied all parties concerned in 1805. While the whole episode constitutes one of America's minor wars, it did produce a new hero for the times. Naval officer **Stephen Decatur** led a daring raid into the harbor at Tripoli in 1804 in order to free Americans held prisoner by the pirates, thus sailing into the ranks of American naval heroes. Furthermore, this and other military engagements brought some measure of respect for the young nation in the eyes of Western Europe.

Burr, Hamilton, and Conspiracy

Jefferson's vice president, **Aaron Burr**, had long been a thorn in the President's side. Not only had Burr schemed to deprive Jefferson of the election in 1800, but while serving as vice president Burr had conspired with the extreme Federalists to unite New York with New England in a plan to secede the whole area from the United States. As part of this plot, Burr had hoped to be elected as governor of New York, but the opposition of the more moderate Federalist Alexander Hamilton cost Burr the office. Soon thereafter, Burr challenged Hamilton to a duel in which he shot the former treasury secretary to death in 1804.

When Jefferson ran for reelection in 1804, he replaced Burr with George Clinton. Nevertheless, Jefferson's troubles with the intriguing Aaron Burr were far from over. Soon thereafter Burr engaged in yet another conspiracy, this time to separate portions of the western United States from the nation and establish an empire with himself as ruler. In 1807 his scheme was uncovered and Jefferson ordered Burr arrested. Brought to trial under Chief Justice John Marshall (a political opponent of Thomas Jefferson), Aaron Burr was found not guilty of treason, largely due to Marshall's very strict and narrow definition of the crime. Soon after his trial Burr fled to France but soon returned to the United States to practice law in New York, where he lived a long, active life.

John Marshall and the Supreme Court

As Chief Justice of the United States Supreme Court, **John Marshall** revolutionized the role of that institution in American government. Marshall, a Virginian, originally had been appointed to the court in 1801 by Federalist President John Adams. Marshall used his role as chief justice to expand the powers of the Supreme Court and to support traditional Federalist political views. In the case of **_Marbury v. Madison_** (1803), Marshall and the Court ruled a particular federal law was invalid or unconstitutional, thus establishing the principle of **judicial review** (the right of the Supreme Court to rule on the constitutionality of federal laws). Marshall established the Supreme Court as a powerful branch of the federal government and worked to clarify the supremacy of the federal government and the United States Constitution over state governments and state laws. This made John Marshall one of the most influential figures in the history of the Supreme Court.

Jefferson and Foreign Affairs

During Jefferson's presidency the ongoing conflict between France and Great Britain intensified. France, under Napoleon Bonaparte, had established dominance on the European continent, while the British navy clearly remained supreme on the seas. Both powers, however, increasingly violated the rights of Americans at sea, stopping and boarding vessels engaged in trade with one or the other belligerent nation. With France and England locked in a terrible war, and the United States remaining neutral, Americans stood to make great profits by trading with the belligerent powers. That said, the risks for American shippers were equally great, as both belligerents were determined to prevent trade with the enemy. Eventually, both England and France were repeatedly guilty of violating the neutral rights of American shippers. By stopping and searching American ships and confiscating cargo from them, both old powers were showing little respect for the young United States. Great Britain further aggravated the tense situation by seizing American sailors onboard American ships and forcing them into the service of the British navy, a practice called **impressment**.

Because the British had a larger and more powerful navy than did France, the British violations of American neutrality were the more frequent, and more obnoxious to the American people. After an incident during which the British ship *Leopard* fired on the American ship *Chesapeake* as it cruised just outside of U.S. territorial waters near Virginia, there was a widespread outcry for war. President Jefferson, however, was not prepared to take such a drastic step. Instead, he resorted to an old weapon from the days of the colonial disputes with Great Britain. In 1807, at the President's request, Congress passed the **Embargo Act**. The idea of the embargo was to cease trade with European nations and thus punish France and Great Britain for their offenses while, at the same time, taking American ships out of harm's way. But the embargo was unsuccessful from the beginning, as American ships continued to sneak out of harbors bound for Europe. There was simply far too much money to be made in the trade with Europe, and American merchants could not resist the temptation. So in spite of Jefferson's best efforts, the international clashes on the high seas continued apace, and the United States began to drift closer toward its second war with England.

James Madison

Jefferson's dear friend, his secretary of state and fellow Virginian James Madison, was elected to the presidency in 1808. Taking office in 1809, Madison was already well acquainted with the foreign policy issues he faced. The new President continued to push for America's rights as a neutral power and observance of the rule of international law guaranteeing the freedom of the seas, but, like Jefferson before him, Madison struggled to gain some measure of respect for the United States from the powerful nations of Europe. By June of 1812, the United States of America would once again be at war with Great Britain.

Causes of the War of 1812

Of course, one of the primary causes of the **War of 1812** was the violation of the neutral rights of America's shipping interests. Other causes of this conflict include: clashes with Indians on the western frontier (hostilities often attributed to the British influence on the Indian population in that region); and the agitation of young congressmen—a group known as the **War Hawks**—who supported a war with powerful Britain in the hope of commanding international respect for their new nation and ending the impressment of American sailors on the high seas. Therefore, in spite of evidence that America's embargo, and later the Non-Intercourse Act, was having an effect on British policy, the United States chose to go to war.

The War against England

For Americans the War of 1812 produced indecisive military results. With the exception of a handful of naval and land victories, American offensive efforts were dismal at best. The nation's defensive efforts for the most part proved equally dull. War raged on land and water, including attempts to conquer Canada (a British possession), naval battles on the Great Lakes, land battles in the Northwest Territory, and skirmishes with Indians throughout the frontier. While much of America's military proved ineffective, on September 10, 1813, Commodore **Oliver H. Perry** of the United States Navy managed a stunning victory over the British that resulted in the surrender of their naval squadron on Lake Erie. Soon after this, General **William Henry Harrison** scored an important victory over the British on October 5 at the Battle of Thames in Canada. Despite these flashy victories, in August of 1814 the British navy pushed up Chesapeake Bay to land forces near Washington, D.C. With the British fast approaching (having met only minor resistance), government officials, including the President and First Lady, were forced to evacuate the city. Once in possession of the capital, British soldiers proceeded to burn public buildings, including the White House and the Capitol. This humiliating defeat would not, however, be the concluding note of the war. The final battle took place on January 8, 1815, several weeks after representatives of Great Britain and the United States had met in Ghent, Belgium, to conclude terms of peace. In the **Battle of New Orleans** the British, under General Edward Pakenham, suffered more than 2,000 casualties, while the American forces, under General **Andrew Jackson** of Tennessee, saw only about 20 such losses. The arrogant Pakenham had thrown his army against Jackson's fortified position, with the resulting defeat a staggering one that cost Pakenham his life.

The Indian War

One part of the War of 1812 was played out on America's western frontier, in the form of a war against the Indians. While there long had been a relationship between the British and Indians hostile to Americans in the western territories, the War of 1812 provided a convenient excuse for western settlers to eliminate their so-called Indian problem. **Tecumseh**, a Shawnee leader, had been traveling throughout the western frontier promoting a doctrine of Indian intertribal unity. He maintained that only by putting aside old differences and uniting against the advance of the Americans could the disparate Indian peoples hope to hold on to their lands and retain their native cultures. As early as 1811, William Henry Harrison, Governor of Ohio, had inflicted a smashing but costly defeat upon Tecumseh and his confederation of warriors at the **Battle of Tippecanoe** in Indiana territory. Tecumseh would later be killed while fighting alongside his British allies against the Americans in Canada, at the Battle of Thames in 1813, but his message had already spread among Indian tribes across the frontier. In Alabama, the result was the **Creek War**. A militant band of the Creek Indians, known by the Americans as the Red Sticks, had attacked **Fort Mims**, an outpost in southern Alabama, in August of 1813. More than 200 settlers were killed in this siege, prompting the call for the raising of a volunteer militia. General Andrew Jackson led a force of over 2,000 such volunteers from Tennessee into Alabama to crush the Red Stick faction of the Creek nation. After a number of indecisive engagements, Jackson and his forces (at this point made up of state militia, friendly Creek, Cherokee, and regulars in the U.S. army) met the hostile Creek Indians in a climactic confrontation, the **Battle of Horseshoe Bend**, on March 27, 1814. The Red Sticks had built a fortification (and a village) at the Horseshoe Bend of the Tallapoosa River. Jackson, in retaliation for earlier losses, smashed the warriors and massacred many families gathered at the site, killing more than 800 Creek warriors in the day's fighting. Several months later, Jackson would oversee the signing of the **Treaty of Fort Jackson** (at the site of the old French Fort Toulouse), wherein the Creek would cede over two-thirds of their lands to the United States of America. From here, Jackson would go on to his victory over the British at New Orleans.

Treaty of Ghent

The **Treaty of Ghent**, which ended the War of 1812, was signed on Christmas Eve of 1814 (about two weeks before the Battle of New Orleans). At this point the British were simply too engrossed in their war with France to pay much attention to settling their differences with the fledgling United States. As a result, the Treaty of Ghent simply ended the war, settling nothing else of much consequence. Indeed, none of the causes of the War of 1812 were addressed by the peace agreement, which effectively only called for a cease-fire. While in many respects Americans had fared badly in this war with England, they had come through it without having been defeated by one of the most powerful nations in the world. In addition, they had made significant gains against the Indians in their western territories.

Results of the War of 1812

Regardless of the rather tepid terms of the Treaty of Ghent, there were at least two major consequences of the War of 1812. First, the military victories against both the British and the Indians spurred a surge of nationalism in the young nation. The victories along with the war's conclusion helped fuel a growing pride among the American people. This sentiment, combined with a movement away from simple regional or state allegiances, produced a broader, national perspective. Second, one can not minimize the importance of the War of 1812 in bringing Andrew Jackson to national prominence. As a result of that conflict, he went on to become a truly national hero. Celebrated in books, plays, and songs, Andrew Jackson, champion of the common man, would ride this wave of popularity all the way to the White House.

James Monroe

In the presidential election of 1816, James Madison supported his secretary of state (and fellow Virginian) **James Monroe** to follow him as the chief executive. With Madison's endorsement, Monroe was elected as president.

Monroe's eight years in office are often referred to as the **Era of Good Feelings**, for during this time only one political party was functioning. The old Federalist Party had been torn apart by members' protests against the War of 1812. Furthermore, to many Americans, the plotting and intriguing of the Federalists over the previous ten years had bordered on treason and, at the very least, evidenced an unpatriotic attitude toward the newly proud young nation. In the years following the Treaty of Ghent, the Federalist Party dissolved. With little or no opposition, Monroe served a relatively peaceful two terms in office.

Though things were generally quiet at home, the years of Monroe's administration witnessed growing turbulence in Latin America. Revolutions in Central and South America expelled the Portuguese and the Spanish from their old colonial holdings. In the spirit of liberty, the American people supported their Latin American neighbors in their respective moves toward independence from their Old World agents. In 1823 President James Monroe included the so-called **Monroe Doctrine** in his annual message to Congress. With considerable influence from Secretary of State **John Quincy Adams**, the Monroe Doctrine put forth the notion that the Old and New Worlds were separate and distinctly different places, and that the nations of the Old World should no longer interfere in the affairs of the nations of the New World, and vice versa. Overall, the American people were in agreement with this basic principle, but the Monroe Doctrine had little impact on the world at the time. The importance of this bold proclamation lay not in any practical results but in the growing pride and sense of nationalism it declared. The United States of America, it appeared, was ready to seek its place in world affairs.

✤ Chapter Review

Identify

Thomas Jefferson	War of 1812
Democratic-Republicans	War Hawks
Monticello	Oliver H. Perry
Napoleon Bonaparte	William Henry Harrison
Louisiana Purchase	Battle of New Orleans
Meriwether Lewis	Andrew Jackson
William Clark	Tecumseh
Corps of Discovery	Battle of Tippecanoe
Sacajawea	Creek War
Barbary Pirates	Fort Mims
Stephen Decatur	Battle of Horseshoe Bend
Aaron Burr	Treaty of Fort Jackson
John Marshall	Treaty of Ghent
Marbury v. *Madison*	James Monroe
judicial review	Era of Good Feelings
impressment	Monroe Doctrine
Embargo Act	John Quincy Adams

Short Paragraph

1. Describe Thomas Jefferson and the "revolution of 1800."

2. Describe the causes and outcomes of the war of 1812.

3. How would you characterize the presidency of James Monroe?

5

The Age of Jackson

Jacksonian America

Historian John William Ward has called Andrew Jackson the "symbol for an age." Indeed, Jackson's rise to power from humble frontier origins speaks to the spirit of the nation in the early decades of the nineteenth century. The Age of Jackson, then, was the era of the common man, one marked by robust growth, energy, and change. Andrew Jackson stands both as symbol of the young nation's development and a leader of national prominence who charted its direction. His presidency and his public status as a popular culture icon stamp this Jacksonian age.

Sectional Developments

The first third of the nineteenth century saw the development of three distinctive regions, or sections, within the United States of America. Each section had a particular economic base that predisposed its economic and cultural ties to other areas. The **Northeast** became increasingly urban and industrial during this time. While most residents of this region continued to earn their livelihood through agriculture, the driving trend in the Northeast was toward business, industry, commerce, and trade, all of which thrived in growing urban centers such as Boston, New York City, and Philadelphia.

The **West**, still pretty much confined to the boundaries of the Old Northwest (west of the Appalachian Mountains and east of the Mississippi River), became increasingly settled during this time. As this section evolved from frontier to farmland, a solid, middle-class, and largely agricultural lifestyle became the norm there. Before long, as commercial farming came to constitute the economic base of the West, ties connecting this section with the urban and industrial Northeast grew and strengthened. As the century progressed, both sections found a reliable marketplace in the other: the West purchased manufactured goods from the Northeast, which, in turn, purchased farm produce from the West. These economic ties would help to hold these sections of the nation together during the sectional crisis that steadily intensified over the next several decades.

The **South**, meanwhile, continued as a region dependent on large-scale plantation agriculture. In colonial times, tobacco had fueled the southern economy (with rice and indigo as supporting crops). But in the nineteenth century, **cotton**, a highly labor-intensive crop, became the staple of the southern plantation system, reinforcing slavery as the planters' preferred form of labor. While most white southerners did not own slaves, the planter (slave-owning) portion of the southern population nonetheless dominated the economy and culture of the region. Because factories in the Northeast could purchase only a fraction of the annual southern cotton crop, the South maintained its traditional economic ties to Europe (primarily England and France)—yet one more contributory factor in the sectional conflicts that eventually would lead the nation to civil war.

Henry Clay and the American System

Henry Clay (a congressman and later senator from Kentucky who served various terms between 1806 and 1852) put forth a plan that both reflected and served to develop the growing spirit of nationalism that came to pervade the United States in the early nineteenth century. Ironically, at the same time the nation moved toward disunion over sectional issues, the American people increasingly came to identify with and take pride in their country. Clay's plan was known as the **American System**. Throughout his terms in the House and Senate, Clay would use his power and skills to put his ideas into action through legislation. Clay's American System included three basic components. First, it called for an ambitious series of internal improvements, such as road and canal building. Improvements in transportation, it was argued, would strengthen ties between sections and greatly enhance the distribution of goods throughout the nation. Second, the American System called for a protective tariff. The **tariff** (a tax on foreign goods imported into this country) was designed to protect American-made and American-grown products from competition with foreign imports by raising the price (through taxation) of the imported items. Finally, Clay called for the creation of a new Bank of the United States. Alexander Hamilton had created the first Bank of the United States, but Clay now wanted a new, stronger bank to bring order and stability to the nation's economy, since the first bank's charter had expired.

While the American System was certainly designed to promote greater and stronger nationalism, much of what the plan effected would, in the long run, serve to further alienate the South from the other two sections of the country. For example, most of the roads and canals the plan called for were built in the North and the West, with the money to construct them often coming from revenue generated by the import tariff which, in fact, most heavily taxed the southerners, who continued to do an active business with England and France. For years, the southern planters harbored a smoldering resentment over the tariff. Eventually this resentment would burst forth into the flames of rebellion.

John Quincy Adams and the Election of 1824

As the presidency of James Monroe came to a conclusion, his secretary of state, John Quincy Adams, the son of the former president, made ready to run for the White House. John Quincy Adams had served his country for many years as a skillful and loyal diplomat, but the opposition to his presidential candidacy was almost overwhelming. The election of 1824 saw Adams running against William Crawford of Georgia, Henry Clay of Kentucky, and Andrew Jackson of Tennessee. While Jackson won a plurality of the popular vote, no candidate won a majority in the Electoral College, so the election had to be decided in the House of Representatives. At this point Crawford became ill and dropped out of the running, while Clay, who had come in fourth place, was also no longer a candidate. The race was now down to Adams and Jackson. As

Speaker of the House, Henry Clay was still in a prime position to influence the outcome of the election. In the past, Adams and Clay had seen their share of personal differences, but more often than not they were in agreement on matters of public policy. Clay gave his considerable support to John Quincy Adams, who won the election. **John C. Calhoun**, a powerful congressman from South Carolina, had won the race for vice president. Once president, Adams appointed Henry Clay as his secretary of state. Outraged, Jackson's many supporters accused Adams of having struck a **corrupt bargain**. Since by this time the position of secretary of state had come to be seen as a stepping stone to the presidency, the Jackson faction believed that not only had their candidate—the choice of the people—been deprived of the presidency, but that Clay and Adams had engaged in a corrupt bargain to pave the way for Clay's election in the years to follow. Furious with this development, Jackson's followers plotted to make a shambles of the Adams presidency, and they largely succeeded. For his own part, and in spite of the best intentions, the new president consistently appeared arrogant and aristocratic to those in and out of the government. Four years later, the election of 1828 swept Andrew Jackson into the land's highest office as the people's choice. The era of the common man had arrived.

Andrew Jackson

Andrew Jackson was born on the Carolina frontier. Orphaned at an early age, he worked his way up from the depths of poverty to the White House. Along the way he had worked as a lawyer, a judge, a planter, and a politician, but he was best known as the soldier hero of the Creek War and the War of 1812. It was Jackson who had led American troops to victory over the Red Stick Creek at Horseshoe Bend and again in a smashing blow against the British at New Orleans. As a tough, stubborn commander he had gained the nickname "Old Hickory." While he could be petty and prone to vengeance with his enemies, he was loyal and generous to a fault when dealing with friends. Jackson was a strong believer in the federal union and saw the presidency as the office meant to represent the nation's people, not merely sectional or regional interest groups. He would prove to be a strong, capable chief executive.

The Jackson Presidency (1829–1837)

Jackson faced many issues during his presidency. This was an age of dynamic growth and expansion, both geographically and economically. As President, Jackson left his mark on history by his stand on these explosive issues. With regard to internal improvements and sectional issues, Jackson made his position clear with his **Maysville Road Veto** (1830). Supporters of internal improvements (especially those in the West) promoted a bill that would provide federal funds to construct a road connecting Maysville, Kentucky (on the Ohio River), with Lexington, Kentucky. Jackson vetoed the bill in order to make a strong statement against the use of federal funds for a project intended to benefit a particular state, proving that he would not be a party to regional (or sectional) politics.

Another major issue of the Jackson presidency was **land policy**. An important controversy of the early republic centered around the manner in which the federal government would use lands owned by the United States. While the question of public lands was not settled during the Jackson Administration, the President clearly favored cheaper and more open access to public lands for American settlers. **Indian Removal** was Jackson's position on what to do with the Indian population that remained east of the Mississippi River. Even though these Indian peoples had made every effort to live in peaceful cooperation with their white neighbors, population pressures were forcing them from the lands they legally owned. As violence erupted between the Indian and American cultures, Jackson felt he had little choice but to follow the will of the Americans. Jackson aggressively pursued a policy of removal, sending the eastern Indians to live west of the Mississippi River in the newly created Indian Territory, present-day Oklahoma and Arkansas. Among the Indian nations pushed out of their rightful homes and westward to these new lands were the Cherokee, who referred to the long, bitter, and forced journey as the **Trail of Tears**.

One of the major controversies of the Jackson Administration involved the Bank of the United States (B.U.S.). The B.U.S. (actually the Second Bank of the United States) had been implemented as a part of Clay's American System. Jackson, calling it the "monster," opposed the B.U.S., believing it to be a tool of the eastern financial interests, but he would have been content to leave the issue alone if not provoked by Henry Clay and Bank President

Nicholas Biddle. Requesting an early renewal of the Bank's charter, Clay and Biddle decided to make the B.U.S. an issue in the presidential election of 1832. Jackson not only vetoed the rechartering of the B.U.S., but he also moved to withdraw federal funds from the bank, which crippled the effectiveness of the national economic institution. Now the president directed the placement of federal funds into state banks owned by faithful supporters. Jackson's critics hailed these banks as Jackson's **pet banks**. This **Bank War** between Jackson and Biddle would ultimately lead to a national recession, but by then a new president would be in office.

At about the same time as Jackson engaged Clay and Biddle in the Bank War, he became embroiled in a conflict over the tariff with South Carolina's John C. Calhoun. Vice President Calhoun, like most southerners, supported a lower tariff. Southerners still believed that they were being taxed to pay for internal improvements made in the North and West. They did not think it fair to protect northern business interests at the expense of southern planters, who continued to trade heavily with Europe, the principal market for their cotton. In opposition to the federal tariff, Calhoun went so far as to develop a political theory he called **nullification**. His idea was that each state could exercise its sovereign authority by rejecting or nullifying federal laws that the people of the state found obnoxious. Of course, the implied threat in this stance was that a state might nullify the tariff and then refuse to collect these taxes. The tariff controversy reached a climax following the new tariff bill of 1832. This new tariff was not acceptable to the southern states, and South Carolina attempted to implement Calhoun's theory of nullification. At this point, Jackson considered Calhoun's behavior as treason and believed the people of South Carolina to be in a state of rebellion against the federal government. At the height of this showdown, Calhoun resigned from his position as vice president and took a recently vacated seat in the Senate to fight the battle in that arena. Ultimately, the potentially dangerous conflict between states' rights and federal authority was resolved in the Congress by Henry Clay, who proposed the compromise tariff of 1833 that lowered the tariff by 1 percent each year for the next ten years. The stage had been set, however, for a growing sectional conflict along these same lines.

Another point of interest regarding Jackson's presidency is his open acceptance of what critics have called the **spoils system**. Jackson believed that having long-term or career civil servants (government employees) sowed fertile ground for corruption and therefore argued for a regular turnover in government offices. In this process, however, Jackson ended up appointing his own loyal supporters to the newly vacant offices, a practice of patronage that came to be called the spoils system. Despite his faults, for eight years Andrew Jackson served as a dynamic, forceful President. The Age of Jackson saw an expansion of democracy and the rise of the common man in American life and politics.

Martin Van Buren

Martin Van Buren of New York had followed Calhoun as Jackson's vice president. When Jackson decided to follow the tradition of serving only two terms in office, he gave his support to Van Buren in the presidential election of 1836. With the support of Andrew Jackson, Martin Van Buren won the presidency. Unfortunately for Van Buren, the Democrats, and the nation, the consequences of the bank war struck home in 1837. The **Panic of 1837** was an economic crisis that gripped the nation in the year that Van Buren took office. This panic, or depression, hit virtually all aspects of the national economy and marked Van Buren's term in office with failure, even though his leadership had little to do with the current difficulties.

The Election of 1840, Harrison and Tyler

During Jackson's presidency the **Whig Party** had formed in opposition to the powerful administration and the reign of common-man democracy. Within this new party were remnants of the old Federalist Party along with other factions opposed to Jackson's anti-aristocratic style. With blame for the Panic of 1837 resting on President Van Buren and the Democrats, the Whigs saw their opportunity to gain the presidency. While the Democrats nominated Van Buren, the Whigs selected a war hero from Ohio, William Henry Harrison. Harrison was credited with victories at the Battle of Tippecanoe and the Battle of the Thames, so, like Jackson, he had a national reputation independent of politics. Also like Jackson, Harrison would be portrayed by the Whigs as a simple man of the people (in spite of the fact that Old Tippecanoe was, in fact, a frontier aristocrat). With **John Tyler** of Virginia as his running mate, "Tippecanoe and Tyler Too" were swept into office in 1841. But with victory still fresh in the minds of the Whigs, Harrison died after only a month in office. For the first time in American history, a vice president became president on the death of the chief executive. The Whigs, who had expected to move their agenda forward with the cooperation of Harrison, Clay, and Webster (all part of the Whig Party), were now faced with the Virginia aristocrat John Tyler as their standard bearer. Tyler had left the Democrats due to the controversy and conflict between Jackson and Calhoun, but the new president had little sympathy with the agenda put forward by Clay and Webster. In fact, through use of the presidential veto, Tyler would make a shambles of the Whig victory.

Society and Culture in Jacksonian America

The Age of Jackson saw a flowering of American literature and philosophy as well as a surge in reform activity. Of particular importance in the arts and philosophy are two movements known as **romanticism** (the idea that reason alone cannot explain the world) and **transcendentalism** (the concept that we must rise above or transcend pure reason in order to understand life and the universe). Early leaders of the American transcendentalist movement were **Ralph Waldo Emerson** and his friend **Henry David Thoreau**. Great American literary figures to emerge from this era included such notables as **Nathaniel Hawthorne** (*The Scarlet Letter,* 1850), **James Fenimore Cooper** (*The Pioneers,* 1823), **Washington Irving** (*The Sketch Book,* 1820), **Edgar Allan Poe** ("A Tell-Tale Heart" and "The Pit and the Pendulum"), **Herman Melville** (*Moby-Dick,* 1851), the poet **Walt Whitman** (*Leaves of Grass,* 1855), and others.

In addition to philosophy and literature, religion and reform experienced renewed energy in Jacksonian America. A revival movement swept through the frontier that came to be known as the **Second Great Awakening** or the **Great Revival in the West**. Much like the first Great Awakening of colonial times, this movement emphasized an individual's accountability to God and the individual's personal relationship with the Deity. This would reinforce the renewed social and political emphasis upon the common man that was the focus of the Age of Jackson. This revival movement was characterized by the camp meeting, where people gathered (and camped out) for days at a time to socialize and attend preaching services.

Along with the religious fervor of the times, an increasing number of people became interested in **reform** (improving the world in which they lived). Many women across America took active leadership roles in these reform efforts, but they often found that without political power (the right to vote), it was difficult to influence major issues. Among the reformers and reform movements of the era were **Dorothea Dix** and her efforts to improve conditions in American prisons and asylums for the insane, and the women's rights movement, with leadership from such notables as Dix, **Lucretia Mott**, **Elizabeth Cady Stanton**, and **Susan B. Anthony**. From the frustrations and leadership of these early struggles would emerge the growing voice for women's suffrage (the right to vote). Other reformers included the founders of utopian communities such as **John Humphrey Noyes** and his Oneida Community in upstate New York. These utopian settlements (often communal in nature) attempted to bring about a perfect society in the midst of an imperfect world.

In American society, the arts, philosophy, and politics, the Age of Jackson was a period of growth, change, and exciting opportunity.

✣ Chapter Review

Identify

Northeast	romanticism
West	Whig Party
South	John Tyler
cotton	transcendentalism
Henry Clay	Ralph Waldo Emerson
American System	Henry David Thoreau
tariff	James Fenimore Cooper
John C. Calhoun	Washington Irving
corrupt bargain	Edgar Allan Poe
Marysville Road Veto	Herman Melville
land policy	Walt Whitman
Indian Removal	Second Great Awakening
Trail of Tears	Great Revival in the West
pet banks	reform
Bank War	Dorothea Dix
nullification	Lucretia Mott
spoils system	Elizabeth Cady Stanton
Martin Van Buren	Susan B. Anthony
Panic of 1837	John Humphrey Noyes

Short Paragraph

1. Describe the regional, or sectional, developments of the early nineteenth century.

2. How would you characterize Andrew Jackson and his presidency?

3. Describe the social and cultural developments of Jacksonian America.

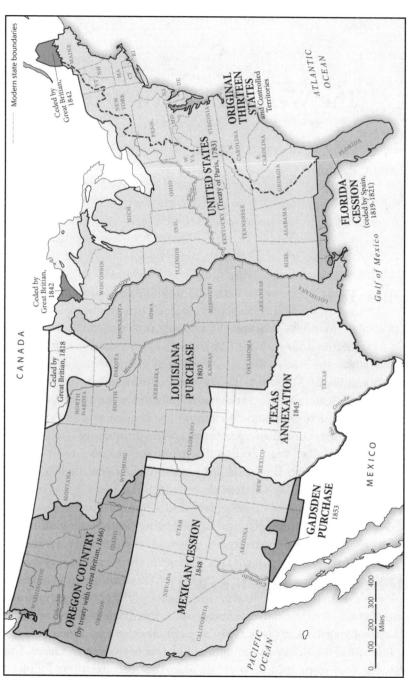

Growth of the U.S. to 1853

CHAPTER

6

The West (Pre–Civil War)

Manifest Destiny

The concept of **Manifest Destiny**, the popular notion that the American people were destined, or ordained by God, to spread the blessings of the Christian faith and American democracy across the continent, helped inspire thousands of Americans to say goodbye to familiar surroundings and head west. Certainly there were many motivations for people to do so throughout the course of the nineteenth century. The desire for land of their own, the search for economic opportunity, and the promise of starting over in a new region ranked high among the many and complex reasons that people decided to endure the hardships of the long and potentially dangerous journey west of the Mississippi River into a vast and rugged terrain. Nonetheless, underlying the practical reasons to undertake such a move remained the foundation belief that it was the destiny of the American people to settle the lands beyond the big river.

Early Explorations and the Fur Trade

Among the earliest of the expeditions to explore the trans-Mississippi West was that led by **Lewis and Clark**. The Corps of Discovery had traversed the Great Plains and the Rocky Mountains, all the way to the Pacific Ocean and back to St. Louis from 1804 to 1806. In 1806–07, other explorers followed on their heels. **Zebulon Pike** explored westward to the area of Colorado, traveling partway up the Rocky Mountain peak that still bears his name. Another of these early western adventurers was **John Charles Frémont**, known as "the Pathfinder" for his work in exploring and mapping the way west in the 1830s and 1840s.

During the 1820s and 1830s, the fur trade in the Rocky Mountains attracted a small number of trappers and traders who came to be known as **mountain men**. Primarily hunting beavers, which then abounded in the cold mountain streams of the Rockies, the mountain men spent most of their days trapping the flat tails, coming together once each summer for a few weeks of trading and celebrating known as a *rendezvous*. By the 1840s, the fur trade had collapsed (due to the dramatic decline in demand for hats made from beaver pelts), but by then the mountain men had blazed many trails and pointed the way to the key mountain passes through which many covered-wagon trains would soon travel en route to California and Oregon.

Oregon and California

In 1818 Great Britain and the United States had agreed to joint occupation of the Oregon Country, essentially the area that is now Oregon and Washington. There was, however, little American presence in this territory until the 1830s, as word of Oregon's rich, fertile soil and moderate climate began to drift east. By the 1840s, a steady stream of settlers were moving west on the **Oregon Trail**. Most of these emigrants rode in covered wagons pulled by oxen or horses. These pioneers endured months of difficult and dangerous travel in order to start new lives in Oregon. Perils of the long trail included difficulties in finding adequate food and water, hostile Indians, and the danger of being trapped by snow in the mountains. The joint occupation of Oregon Country would not end until 1846, under President James K. Polk, when a treaty was signed setting the boundary at the 49th parallel between British Canada on the north and Oregon to the south of that line.

Another destination of western-bound emigrants was California. South of Oregon, California had once been a sparsely populated province of New Spain and then of Mexico, but by this time it was an American territory whose population was poised to explode. The 1848 discovery of gold near present-day Sacramento attracted huge numbers of people to California's gold fields in 1849 and 1850. Few of the newly arrived gold seekers ended up striking it rich, but many a personal fortune was made during the **Gold Rush** by those who owned the saloons, hardware stores, restaurants, and other businesses that sprang up in order to cater to the needs of the miners. In addition, many people lured to California by the chance to find gold instead discovered fertile lands and decided to settle there permanently with their families. Unfortunately, many parties of overland emigrants met with disaster. Such was the case of the **Donner Party**, members of which set out for California from their homes in Illinois in 1846. Trapped by high snow deep in the Sierra Nevada for an entire winter, some of these desperate people resorted to cannibalism in order to survive.

The Republic of Texas

Texas had been explored and settled by the Spanish, and for many years it remained the northern frontier of Spain's New World empire. As was also the case in California, Spain's presence in Texas was primarily limited to scattered garrisons of soldiers and missions established by the Catholic Church. When Mexico won independence from Spain in 1821 the new country's hold upon these northern regions remained tenuous at best. In order to promote the settlement of its far northern province, the Mexican government began to welcome American settlers who would swear allegiance to the government of Mexico and promise to convert to Catholicism. But by the early 1830s, the population of Texas had begun to swell with Americans who had no intention of becoming loyal citizens of Mexico. Indeed, the newly arrived Americans soon united in a rebellion of Texans against **Santa Anna**, the president of Mexico and the commanding general of that nation's army, declaring the independence of the **Republic of Texas** in March of 1836. Already, in response to the Texans' declaration, Santa Anna marched northward at the head of a force of some 6,500 soldiers intent on squashing this upstart rebellion. After defeating an interracial group of Texans amassed at the **Alamo** (an old mission in San Antonio) in a thirteen-day siege ending in a crushing assault, the Mexican general and his army were ultimately defeated by General **Sam Houston** and his Texas forces at the **Battle of San Jacinto** (near present-day Houston, Texas) in April of 1836. In a matter of months Texas had won independence from Mexico and established the Republic of Texas. Sam Houston, the hero of San Jacinto, was elected the first president of the Lone Star Republic.

Annexation and the War with Mexico

Many of the original American settlers in Texas had arrived in the Mexican territory with designs on making the region a part of the United States. Indeed, soon after the Texas Revolution, Texans began to explore the possibility of joining the Lone Star Republic with the United States. While Texas President Sam Houston had a friend and ally in President Andrew Jackson, in 1836 the time was not right for annexation. Due to internal disputes over slavery and continuing international arguments with Mexico, the United States did not annex Texas until December of 1845, under the direction of newly elected President **James K. Polk** of Tennessee.

The annexation of Texas ignited a new conflict between the United States and Mexico, this one over the new state as well as its boundary. Mexico disputed the annexation of Texas, having never officially acknowledged the breakaway province's independence or the Rio Grande border claimed by Texans and now the United States. By May 1846, fighting broke out between Mexican and American troops north of the Rio Grande, with President Polk signing a declaration of war against Mexico on May 13. The **War with Mexico** had begun.

Whig leaders such as John Quincy Adams voiced their strong opposition to the war. Many of them saw the conflict as a blatant act of aggression designed merely to acquire territory from a neighboring country, as well as a conspiracy among the southern aristocracy to expand the reach of slavery.

Ignoring his political opponents, the expansionist Polk selected General **Zachary Taylor** (known as Old Rough and Ready) to command a contingent of U.S. forces across the border and into Mexican territory. Soon thereafter, **Winfield Scott**, commanding general of the U.S. Army, arrived, courtesy of the U.S. Navy, with another fighting force at the east coast of Mexico and established a base at Vera Cruz before marching west to Mexico City, the capital. General Scott and his U.S. troops, after a series of victories along the way, entered Mexico City in September of 1847. The War with Mexico was over.

Meanwhile, in California, John C. Frémont had been instrumental in aiding a group in a rebellion against Mexican authority there, the movement's leaders proclaiming the creation of the Republic of California in June of 1846. In less than a month, the Bear Flag Republic (so named after the Rebel's battle flag) would also become a part of the United States. The northern provinces of Mexico had fallen to American expansion.

The Treaty of Guadalupe Hidalgo and the Aftermath of War

The **Treaty of Guadalupe Hidalgo** officially ended the War with Mexico. By the terms of this treaty, the United States acquired California and New Mexico, as well as settling the boundary of Texas at the Rio Grande. Mexico officially gave up all claims to Texas and recognized its annexation. In compensation, the United States was to pay Mexico $15 million. The U.S. Senate ratified the treaty on March 10, 1848. The War with Mexico had been won, but at a terrible cost. Over 12,000 American soldiers died in the war (mostly from disease), with the wounded adding more than 4,000 to the casualty list. Also, the war had cost the nation more than $90 million. Nonetheless, the military victories won and the huge expanse of territory gained as a result of the war contributed to a growing spirit of patriotic nationalism that increasingly characterized the American people. Ironically, despite these patriotic feelings, the territories acquired in the recent struggle featured prominently in the coming sectional conflict, one destined to embroil the nation in bloody civil war.

✤ Chapter Review

Identify

Manifest Destiny	Republic of Texas
Lewis and Clark	Alamo
Zebulon Pike	Sam Houston
John Charles Frémont	Battle of San Jacinto
mountain men	James K. Polk
Oregon Trail	War with Mexico
Gold Rush	Zachary Taylor
Donner Party	Winfield Scott
Santa Anna	Treaty of Guadalupe Hidalgo

Short Paragraph

1. Describe the Texas Revolution.

2. Describe the War with Mexico.

3. What is Manifest Destiny, and how does it relate to westward expansion?

7

Sectional Conflict

The Old South

From the earliest days of colonial America the South had developed differently than had the other regions of Britain's mainland colonies. Even as the struggle for independence gave way to a new nation, the South continued on its distinctive course. Increasingly cotton came to replace tobacco, rice, and indigo as the region's cash crop, a development that solidified the dominant position of planters and plantation agriculture in the society and economy of the Old South. While relatively few white southerners owned slaves, those who did (the planter class) remained as the social and political leaders throughout the southern states, with slavery playing an important role in sustaining this unique culture. While a significant number of free blacks lived in the South, most black southerners lived as slaves, the legally held property of other human beings.

Abolitionism

Even as slavery became more firmly entrenched in the southern states, **abolitionism**, the movement to abolish slavery, slowly gained momentum in the northern states. One early effort to free, or emancipate, slaves involved returning the freed people to Africa. This was the goal of the **American Colonization Society** (founded in 1817), the group responsible for the founding of Liberia in West Africa. The colonization movement, however, never resulted in widespread migration from anywhere in America to the new African-American republic. After all, as oppressive as conditions could be for free blacks at the time, the United States was their country of birth and the only home they had ever known.

Meanwhile, sentiment among supporters of the antislavery movement already had begun to shift, with calls going up for the immediate abolition of slavery. One leader in this militant branch of the movement was **William Lloyd Garrison** of Boston, editor and publisher of the abolitionist newspaper *The Liberator*. Black leadership in the antislavery protest included such famous figures as **Frederick Douglass**, an escaped slave whose autobiography, *Narrative of the Life of Frederick Douglass* (1845), is widely read to this day, and **Sojourner Truth**, who combined her support of women's rights issues with her crusade against slavery. Throughout the first half of the nineteenth century, groups such as the American Anti-Slavery Society raised the awareness of the American people regarding the inhumane treatment of those enslaved in the southern states.

Conflict and Compromise

To reduce the differences between North and South to the issue of slavery is to grossly oversimplify the complex difficulties that faced these two regions of the nation. While slavery often became the focal point of the interregional confrontations, the divisions went much deeper, down to the very core of each region's social, cultural, and economic identity. From the earliest days of the republic, North and South had been engaged in a pattern of conflict and compromise. As early as the Constitutional Convention and again during the controversy surrounding the War of 1812 and, of course, the showdown over the tariff, these two sections had squared off against one another with threats of secession followed by a grudging compromise to hold the union together, at least until the next crisis emerged. As the two regions continued to grow further apart, it became increasingly obvious that one or the other would either have to undergo a fundamental change or somehow separate itself from the other. In many respects, the coming of the Civil War must be viewed within the context of the ebb and flow of conflict and compromise that had sustained the union since the Constitutional Convention.

The ultimate secession of the southern states, then, was hardly a sudden split of a once healthy and whole nation, but rather the outcome of the continual inability of two distinctly different cultures and economies to coexist peacefully within the same government. By 1861, after the election of Abraham Lincoln as president, southern political leaders had concluded that the South must secede from the United States of America. After much discussion and debate, most southerners agreed.

The Road to Civil War

Following the controversy at the Constitutional Convention over how to count slaves in terms of representation (which resulted in the three-fifths compromise), the next major sectional conflict arose over the admission into the union of Missouri as a slave state, meaning a state in which slavery was a legal institution. While, once again, the focus was on slavery, the underlying cause of the issue was the struggle to maintain a balance of power between northern and southern (free and slave) states so that each region might continue to pursue its characteristic cultural and economic endeavors. In 1820, balance between the number of free and slave states had been maintained, and the union preserved, by the **Missouri Compromise**, a congressional agreement orchestrated by Henry Clay of Kentucky to admit Maine into the union as a free state, Missouri as a slave state, and to divide the remainder of the Louisiana Purchase territory at 36° 30′ N latitude, prohibiting slavery north of that line.

For many years this arrangement seemed to settle intersectional strife, but the conclusion of the War with Mexico and the land acquired through the Treaty of Guadalupe Hidalgo reopened the most controversial of the regional disputes. Even before the war had ended, Congressman David Wilmot of Pennsylvania had proposed the prohibition of slavery in any territories acquired from Mexico. This so-called **Wilmot Proviso** once again included bitter debate over the issue of slavery and the expansion of slave power into U.S. territories. Then, as people poured into California following the gold strikes of 1848 and 1849, conflicts over whether to permit slavery there were inevitable. By early 1850, both California and New Mexico were seeking entry into the union as free states.

Now the uneasy balance of power between North and South was poised to topple for good. At this point the aging Clay presented to the Senate a plan to compromise once again on the many regional differences. His complex **Compromise of 1850** was heatedly discussed and debated in the Senate by that great triumvirate of Clay himself, Daniel Webster of Massachusetts, and John C. Calhoun of South Carolina. President **Zachary Taylor**, popular hero of the War with Mexico, opposed Clay's compromise, as did Calhoun. Nonetheless, both Clay and Webster were undeterred, rising on the floor of the Senate to speak out passionately in an effort to save the disintegrating union. In the end, while Clay found it impossible to pass the compromise as a legislative package, he was able, with the assistance of Senator Stephen A. Douglas of Illinois, to guide individual measures through Congress. Then, with the sudden death of President Taylor and the support of the new President, **Millard Fillmore**, the Compromise of 1850 became reality.

Among other things, the Compromise of 1850 included the following provisions: the admittance of California into the union as a free state; a new fugitive slave law that favored slaveholders by empowering them to demand the return of runaway slaves living in any other state; the creation of the territory of New Mexico; the establishment of the current boundary between Texas and New Mexico; the creation of the Utah territory; and the abolishment of the slave trade (but not slavery) in the District of Columbia. Initially, people hoped that this ambitious agreement would end the controversy over slavery and save the union once and for all, but this proved wishful thinking. Indeed, the interregional conflict between North and South was opening anew, and on new fronts. The new fugitive slave act was largely unenforced in northern states, leaving southerners to harbor a bitter resentment towards the compromise. Meanwhile, a moving and vastly popular novel of the day worked to shift the arguments over slavery from the political to the social and moral arena. With the publication of her **Uncle Tom's Cabin** in 1852, **Harriet Beecher Stowe** stirred the antislavery passions of the general public in a manner and to a degree that no amount of political discussion or debate might have achieved.

Within this climate of growing tension came the debate over what to do with the Nebraska territory—which included present-day Kansas and Nebraska. In 1854, Illinois Senator Stephen A. Douglas proposed to Congress the creation of two new territories in his **Kansas-Nebraska Act**. Douglas courted southern support for his proposal by including in his bill a provision stating that these territories would be organized according to the principle of **popular sovereignty** (the idea that the people of a given territory should be able to decide for themselves whether or not slavery would be permitted within their borders). While the geography and location of Nebraska made it unlikely that slavery would ever flourish there, Kansas, located due west of the slave state Missouri, was a different story. Indeed, with the passage of the Kansas-Nebraska Act, Kansas literally became a battleground on which proslavery and antislavery forces engaged in open hostilities. Soon Americans were referring to the territory as **Bleeding Kansas,** a place where bitterly divided settlers actually established two separate constitutions, two separate governments, and two separate capital cities. In May of 1856, a group of proslaveryites raided the free-state town of Lawrence, killing several persons. Then, two days later, **John Brown**, a radical abolitionist, set out with a small band along Pottawatomie Creek, by the banks of which they brutally murdered five proslaveryites. The Pottawatomie Massacre sparked even more widespread violence in Bleeding Kansas.

Meanwhile, back east on the floor of the U.S. Senate, things were not much better. In May of 1856, Preston Brooks, a young congressman from South Carolina, came upon the ardent abolitionist Senator Charles Sumner of Massachusetts working at his desk. No sooner had Brooks begun to address Sumner than he proceeded to beat severely the older man with his gold-headed cane. Days earlier Sumner had made insulting comments about the congressman's uncle, the proslavery Senator Andrew P. Butler of South Carolina, in a speech entitled "The Crime Against Kansas." Sumner was so badly injured that he was unable to resume his senatorial duties for four years. With his seat vacant, Sumner became a symbol for his cause and stirred the sympathy of many northerners. Preston Brooks, meanwhile, was equally well received back in the South, where he was hailed as a defender of southern honor. Without question, relations between northerners and southerners were rapidly deteriorating.

The very next year, 1857, would bring the issue of the legality of slavery before the United States Supreme Court in the case of ***Dred Scott* v. *Sanford***. Scott formerly had been the slave of an army doctor, who had taken Scott with him as he moved about the country, specifically in free territory such as Illinois and Wisconsin. After the doctor died, Scott sued his new master, J. F. A. Sanford, for his freedom on the grounds that since he had once lived as a free man he was entitled, as an American, to remain free. After the state supreme court of Missouri ruled against Scott, he appealed his case to the United States Supreme Court. The high court decided that Scott should remain a slave and went on to rule that a slave owner could not be denied his right to property anywhere in the nation (a slave, of course, being considered one's legal property). While the South was delighted with the decision expressed by Chief Justice **Roger B. Taney**, the North was outraged by this stand.

Tensions already near the breaking point were even further aggravated by the economic depression known as the **Panic of 1857**. As times grew hard, each section blamed the other for the nation's financial crunch, so that the rift between North and South began to widen toward disunion.

In 1859 John Brown was back on the scene. For the past several years he had attempted to raise funds for a personal crusade against slavery. In October of 1859 the radical abolitionist, accompanied by a small force of men, attempted to seize the federal arsenal at **Harper's Ferry**, Virginia. Brown planned was to use the weapons housed at this facility to begin and then help spread a generalized slave revolt throughout the South. Instead, Brown and his followers were defeated in their efforts. Apprehended and arrested, Brown was convicted of treason and then hanged in December of 1859. Many in the North viewed the radical leader as hero, saint, and martyr to the cause of abolitionism, while most in the South saw John Brown as a dangerous enemy or devil.

The few ties still binding the nation together were quickly unraveling. It was the presidential **election of 1860** that severed the final cord.

The Crisis of Leadership and the Election of 1860

Soon after the Compromise of 1850, that great triumvirate of Clay, Webster, and Calhoun had passed away. These men had so clearly dominated the national political scene for so long that their absence was deeply felt within the federal government. While some struggled to fill the void, there was a crisis in leadership within the political circles of the United States. Those who held the highest office during the 1850s are prime examples of this significant weakness. After Taylor's death in 1850, Millard Fillmore became President, followed by **Franklin Pierce** (elected in 1852) and **James Buchanan** (elected in 1856). While these men served to the best of their abilities and were generally capable and competent, they lacked that ability to lead the nation through the series of crises, conflicts, controversies, and attempts at compromise that shook the United States in that last desperate decade preceding the war. A leader would emerge at last, in the person of Abraham Lincoln, but even before Honest Abe took the oath of office the time for further reason or compromise had passed.

The presidential election of 1860 was the final stop along the road to civil war. **Abraham Lincoln,** a congressman from Illinois, won the nomination from the relatively new Republican Party. The Republican Party had originated in Michigan in 1854 around the issue of Free Soil (antislavery) and was geographically a party of the northern states. Lincoln was a moderate candidate who took a firm stand on the containment of slavery within the areas where it currently existed, but otherwise he was not openly hostile to slavery or to the southern states. The Democrats nominated another moderate candidate, Stephen A. Douglas, but southerners unwilling to accept a moderate politician walked out of the Democratic convention, meeting separately and nominating their own candidate, John C. Breckinridge of Kentucky. Further dividing and confusing this important national election, other disenchanted politicians gathered themselves into the new Constitutional Union Party and nominated John Bell of Tennessee as their presidential hopeful. None of these four candidates was able to build a significant following outside of their regional loyalties, but by splitting their party, the Democrats had made it easier for the Republican candidate Abraham Lincoln to win the presidency in this chaotic contest.

Lincoln's victory soon proved bittersweet. He had gained the presidency without carrying the votes of a single southern state. Once the South had hoped to maintain a balance of power between itself and the North. After the Compromise of 1850, when it became obvious that the balance was disrupted, the South sought to maintain enough power and influence in the federal government to protect its unique culture and economy that had evolved since colonial days. With the election of Lincoln, it became obvious to southerners that they would no longer be able to play a deciding role in national politics. If the President of the United States could be selected without southern support, their cause was hopeless. Clearly the two regions could no longer peacefully coexist within the same government. For the South, the choice was fundamental: change or separate from the remainder of the country. While the choice was not easy, and probably not so clear for southern political leaders, secession from the union proved the most expedient answer to the confusing questions before them in 1860 and 1861. The union would soon be broken.

✢ Chapter Review

Identify

abolitionism	Kansas-Nebraska Act
American Colonization Society	popular sovereignty
William Lloyd Garrison	Bleeding Kansas
Frederick Douglass	John Brown
Sojourner Truth	*Dred Scott* v. *Sanford*
Missouri Compromise	Roger B. Taney
Wilmot Proviso	Panic of 1857
Compromise of 1850	Harper's Ferry
Zachary Taylor	election of 1860
Millard Fillmore	Franklin Pierce
Uncle Tom's Cabin	James Buchanan
Harriet Beecher Stowe	Abraham Lincoln

Short Paragraph

1. What were the origins and goals of the abolitionist movement? Who were its leaders?

2. What was the crisis of leadership leading to the election of 1860? What happened next?

3. Describe the causes of sectional conflict; that is, what were the issues, and how did they lead to secession?

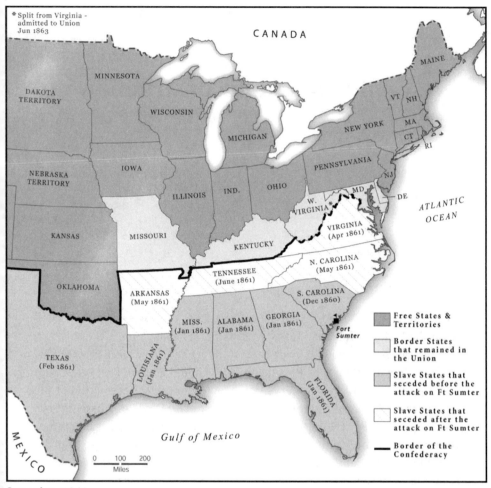

* Split from Virginia - admitted to Union Jun 1863

CANADA

MAINE

DAKOTA TERRITORY

MINNESOTA

WISCONSIN

MICHIGAN

VT NH

NEW YORK

MA
CT
RI

NEBRASKA TERRITORY

IOWA

ILLINOIS

IND.

OHIO

PENNSYLVANIA

NJ

KANSAS

MISSOURI

KENTUCKY

W. VIRGINIA *

MD

DE

VIRGINIA (Apr 1861)

ATLANTIC OCEAN

OKLAHOMA

ARKANSAS (May 1861)

TENNESSEE (June 1861)

N. CAROLINA (May 1861)

S. CAROLINA (Dec 1860)

TEXAS (Feb 1861)

MISS. (Jan 1861)

ALABAMA (Jan 1861)

GEORGIA (Jan 1861)

Fort Sumter

LOUISIANA (Jan 1861)

FLORIDA (Jan 1861)

MEXICO

Gulf of Mexico

0   100   200
Miles

Free States & Territories

Border States that remained in the Union

Slave States that seceded before the attack on Ft Sumter

Slave States that seceded after the attack on Ft Sumter

Border of the Confederacy

Secession, 1861

CHAPTER

8

Civil War and Reconstruction

Disunion and War

After the election of Abraham Lincoln in 1860 the lower South seceded from the Union. Alabama, Texas, Mississippi, Florida, Georgia, Louisiana, and South Carolina had all made their stand by February 1861 (before Lincoln actually took office as President of the United States). Delegates from these states met in Montgomery, Alabama, to declare the formation of the **Confederate States of America**, selecting **Jefferson Davis** of Mississippi as their president. For two more tense months the upper South attempted to remain within the Union and negotiate yet another compromise, but the Republicans in Congress still wanted assurances that slavery would be contained where it currently existed. Very soon, stubborn political debate would lose out to war.

Overlooking the entrance to the harbor at Charleston, South Carolina, **Fort Sumter**, a federal installation and garrison, became the first site of military action in America's Civil War. First, southerners opened fire to turn back a ship sent to resupply this federal fort. Having succeeded in this endeavor, the South Carolina militia encircled the fort, opening fire on the night of April 12, 1861. The next day Sumter was surrendered. Electrified by the news, the upper South, North Carolina, Virginia, Arkansas, and Tennessee, seceded from the Union to join the Confederate States of America. Meanwhile, Lincoln moved military forces in to occupy the **Border States**, slave states that bordered the Union and Confederate states—Delaware, Maryland, Missouri, Kentucky, and an area that later became West Virginia (a Unionist stronghold that had been looking for a reason to break with Virginia). Across the North, popular enthusiasm for the war spread with a patriotic zeal. Meanwhile, Lincoln put out a call for the formation of a 75,000-man volunteer militia to put down the insurrection.

The Two Sides

Historian James M. McPherson has noted that when the war began each side saw itself as fighting for freedom. It is important to understand that at the outset of hostilities, neither side focused on the various political conflicts and compromises that had brought them down the road to civil war. Instead, both were convinced they were fighting for the cause of freedom, to uphold the basic principles of the Declaration of Independence—life, liberty, and property. Also, both sides believed that the war would be a brief affair. Indeed, each thought the other would tire of the conflict in a matter of months, then give in to the demands placed upon them. Finally, each side had unique advantages that gave it hope for ultimate victory. The Union strengths included: a population advantage of about three to one over the South; far greater industrial development; diverse agricultural output; much stronger financial resources; an organized government; an existing military; and the able leadership of the new president, Abraham Lincoln. The Confederacy felt that its edge lay in: fighting a defensive war (the defender in Civil War–era combat could repel a numerically superior force); an aggressive willingness to fight on the part of white southerners; excellent military leadership; hope for foreign assistance, namely from England or France; and the belief that the northern public, whom they perceived as a squeamish lot of clerks and manual laborers, would quickly grow weary of the violence and willingly agree to allow the South to secede in peace.

Of course, the South's hopes would be dashed. Under Lincoln's adroit leadership, the Union would persevere in the war effort and the nations of Europe would opt to stay out of America's Civil War. And even as Jefferson Davis and the Confederate States of America attempted to organize a government and a military, they were actively fighting a war for their new nation's survival, the strain of which would ultimately be too much. Neither Davis, the Confederate government, nor the Confederate military would be equal to the challenge. For the first few years of the conflict, however, the outcome was less than apparent.

War

Following the fall of Fort Sumter in April of 1861, the first major military engagement came in July at **Bull Run** in northern Virginia, some twenty-five miles southwest of Washington, D.C. While **Rebel** (southern or Confederate) troops chased the **Yankee** (Federal, Union, or northern) soldiers from the field of battle, they failed to follow up on this victory by advancing on the capital city. Already, however, perceptive observers began to realize that the nation faced a long struggle.

As 1861 gave way to 1862, the war in the West began to take center stage in this growing conflict. In February, Union General **Ulysses S. Grant** won a major victory over the Confederates at **Fort Donelson** (on the Kentucky-Tennessee border) that brought him to the attention of President Lincoln. By April, Grant and his Federal troops won another hard-fought victory, this one at **Shiloh** in the southwestern corner of Tennessee. Back in the East, Lincoln was having trouble with his generals, particularly his general-in-chief, **George B. McClellan**, who proved overly cautious in his conduct of the war. Having drilled his large Army of the Potomac for months, McClellan had failed to move his men into battle, straining Lincoln's patience to the breaking point. Meanwhile Confederate forces under the command of General **Thomas J. "Stonewall" Jackson** were successful in using Virginia's Shenandoah Valley as a place to obtain food and a convenient corridor to advance north toward Washington. When, in June of 1862, at Lincoln's prompting, McClellan and his army finally made an advance toward Richmond, Virginia, the Confederate capital, he was pushed back by the brilliant Confederate General **Robert E. Lee** at the head of his Army of Northern Virginia. This victory established Lee as the preeminent southern general and led to a change in leadership for the Union army in the East. Lincoln, now disgusted with McClellan, went through a variety of commanders before eventually settling on General Grant as the commander of all Union forces in 1864.

In the meantime, as the war continued, a narrow northern victory at **Antietam**, Maryland, in September of 1862 gave Abraham Lincoln, who had been waiting for a good opportunity to drop a bombshell of his own, the right moment to issue his **Emancipation Proclamation**, to take effect on January 1, 1863. The Emancipation Proclamation freed slaves in all states currently in rebellion (meaning that it did not free slaves in the Border States), bringing a new emphasis on and dedication to the Union war effort. The President also hoped that with slavery abolished, the southern people would be denied one more thing for which they were fighting. Finally, the Emancipation Proclamation served to keep England—which was at least somewhat sympathetic to southern independence—from allying itself with the Confederacy, as England was officially against slavery.

In May of 1863, Lee led his men to victory at **Chancellorsville** in Virginia, but this proved to be the beginning of the end for the Confederate armies. Still fresh from his Chancellorsville victory, Lee undertook a major offensive into the North in June and July of 1863: it ended in disaster. Pushing up into Pennsylvania, Lee's army was soundly defeated at the **Battle of Gettysburg**. This smashing Union triumph was reinforced by news from the western theater: the surrender of **Vicksburg**, Mississippi, to General Grant the same day. Once again, the aggressive Ulysses S. Grant had achieved a major victory, but he would soon be retested. In November of 1863, President Lincoln traveled to Pennsylvania to make remarks at the dedication of a soldiers' cemetery near the Gettysburg town center. The speech he delivered, the **Gettysburg Address**, served to uplift an American people devastated by the long war.

Before year's end, Grant had achieved yet another victory, this one at **Lookout Mountain** in Tennessee. While much hard fighting lay ahead, clearly the Union forces were coming to dominate the brutal struggle between North and South. In May and June of 1864, Grant took the offensive against Lee's army in such Virginia engagements as **the Wilderness, Spotsylvania Court House**, and **Cold Harbor**, though with mixed results. It would be difficult to call these battles Union victories, but they certainly took a very heavy toll on the exhausted Confederate forces. Now Lee became committed to the defense of the Confederate capital at Richmond, with Grant pushing against his lines at every opportunity. On all remaining fronts, Union armies were advancing. On September 1, 1864, Union General **William T. Sherman** captured the city of Atlanta, Georgia. Soon thereafter Sherman began his infamous **March to the Sea**. Like Grant, Sherman believed in the concept of total war, meaning waging war against an entire enemy people, as opposed simply to fighting battles against the enemy military. Indeed, General

Sherman would implement total war against the southern population by burning Atlanta and then marching his troops on to Savannah, destroying everything in his path. Sherman figured correctly that making war upon the civilian population of the South would have a devastating impact upon both the southern will and ability to fight.

Meanwhile, Grant had continued to hammer Lee's forces in northern Virginia until, finally, even General Robert E. Lee could see that surrender was unavoidable. On April 9, 1865, Lee and Grant met at **Appomattox Court House** (in Virginia), where Lee surrendered his army. Some sporadic fighting continued for a time in various locations, but for all practical purposes the Civil War had ended. In this, America's most devastating conflict, over 350,000 Union soldiers had lost their lives, with more than 275,000 wounded. The South had lost over 250,000 men, with about 250,000. wounded. The long, bloody war had bitterly divided the nation. The awesome task of healing these sectional wounds now lay in the hands of President Abraham Lincoln.

Lincoln, Johnson, the Radicals, and Reconstruction

With the grueling war finally over, Lincoln hoped to restore the southern states to full participation within the federal government as quickly, easily, and painlessly as possible. Less interested in punishing the South and southern leaders than in rebuilding the war-torn region and restoring the Union, Lincoln's plan for **Reconstruction** (rehabilitating the former Confederate states and integrating them back under the U.S. government) was generous and forgiving. But only days after Lee's surrender at Appomattox, the assassin **John Wilkes Booth** shot the President as he and his wife watched a theatrical performance in Washington's Ford Theater. Upon Lincoln's death, Vice President **Andrew Johnson** assumed the presidency.

Johnson, a unionist from Tennessee, now assumed control of the Reconstruction process. The new President had little sympathy with the old southern planter aristocracy, but, in general, he did hope to carry out much of Lincoln's approach to the postwar South. **Radical Republicans** in the United States Congress (those who wanted to blame and punish the South and its leaders for the Civil War) might have been brought under control by the skills of the charismatic Lincoln, but Johnson had none of the deceased

President's talent in artful negotiation and political diplomacy. Just the contrary, Johnson was a stubborn man with few social skills. He ended up alienating congressional leaders and aggravating the Radical Republicans. Under Johnson's liberal terms, former Confederate leaders quickly began to arrive in Washington as the elected representatives of the former Confederate states. Now the Radical Republicans as well as other northern leaders were shocked and alarmed that the southern population seemed intent upon returning to power the very people who had brought the region to civil war just a few short years before. Johnson and congressional leaders engaged in bitter disputes regarding his plans for Reconstruction that resulted in the President's ultimate impeachment by the House of Representatives in February 1868. While the Senate declined to remove Johnson from office, it became increasingly clear that the Radicals in Congress would take control of southern Reconstruction.

In the hands of the United States Congress, Reconstruction took on a completely different character. In short order the South was occupied by federal troops and divided into military districts, each of which was subjected to the authority of a military commander. Along with Sherman's March to the Sea, the Reconstruction experiences of the South would long serve to embitter the southern people towards northerners. The program of Reconstruction did not come to an end until 1877. The stage for Reconstruction's demise had been set in the prior year, in the presidential **election of 1876**. The election itself had ended in dispute, but a deal was made in which the Democrats withdrew their objections to allowing the Republican candidate, **Rutherford B. Hayes**, to claim victory over the Democrat Samuel J. Tilden on the condition that all federal troops be withdrawn from the South and that Reconstruction policies be terminated. With this, any further efforts at Reconstruction effectively ended.

North and South in the Reconstruction Era

The most difficult problem facing the South during Reconstruction was how to assimilate the newly freed African-American population into southern life and society. As black southerners struggled to find a place for themselves in the workforce, white southerners searched for ways to keep the former slaves in subordinate positions. While the **Freedmen's Bureau**, a government agency created to assist the newly freed persons with the transition from slavery to freedom and an independent lifestyle worked with southern blacks, southern whites devised a variety of means to control and manipulate the freed people. One such vehicle was the **Black Codes**, laws passed by southern states to legalize an inferior status for African Americans. With very few opportunities available to them, many former slaves ended up working on farms and plantations as **sharecroppers** or **tenant farmers**. These positions involved dependent relationships with the landowner, whereby the worker leased a small parcel of land, either by giving over a share of the harvested crops or a cash payment after selling the harvest. Often at harvest time there was not enough surplus to pay the required rent, so the tenants, many of them African American, became indebted to the landowners and, hence, legally obligated to remain on the property in order to work off the incurred debt.

In addition to political and economic insecurities, African Americans also faced a growing culture of violence designed to perpetuate white supremacy through terrorist acts (lynchings and burnings) against the black population of the South. The newly organized Ku Klux Klan, an elaborate secretive organization, was the best-organized leader of these horrific racial attacks, but even whites unsympathetic to the KKK often gave, at least, tacit compliance to group's goal of white dominance in the deep South. In this social climate, African Americans not only suffered discrimination but feared for their lives and property.

In spite of these hardships, there was progress on some fronts during this time. The influence of poor whites and newly freed blacks in the state legislatures brought about advances in such areas as public health, public roads, and public schools throughout the South following the Civil War. In the North, the war had brought economic prosperity. Innovations in industrial technologies had multiplied business opportunities, while wartime expenditures had increased available capital. This combination of opportunity and capital brought about an economic boom throughout much of the Northeast. **Mark Twain**, popular author and social critic, called this age of prosperity and materialism **The Gilded Age**, implying that it only appeared shiny or attractive on the surface. Business and industry thrived in the postwar economy, with the trend toward a more urban and industrial base in the Northeast accelerating.

The Grant Administration

Andrew Johnson's presidency had been significantly marred by his impeachment trial early in 1868, another presidential election year. Former commander of the United States Army, General Ulysses S. Grant, won the Republican nomination and the presidency in 1868, taking office in 1869. Grant would serve two terms as President, his administration marked by scandal and corruption among his subordinates. In spite of these incidents, Grant remained popular with the American people and even considered running for a third term in office. Instead, in 1876 the Republicans chose to nominate Rutherford B. Hayes for the top spot. As mentioned, it was the dispute over that election that made Hayes the president to end America's experiment with Reconstruction.

Chapter Review

Identify

Confederate States of America	Lookout Mountain
Jefferson Davis	the Wilderness
Fort Sumter	Spotsylvania Courthouse
Border States	Cold Harbor
Bull Run	William T. Sherman
Rebel	March to the Sea
Yankee	Appomattox Court House
Ulysses S. Grant	Reconstruction
Fort Donelson	John Wilkes Booth
Shiloh	Andrew Johnson
George B. McClellan	Radical Republicans
Thomas J. "Stonewall" Jackson	election of 1876
Robert E. Lee	Rutherford B. Hayes
Antietam	Freedmen's Bureau
Emancipation Proclamation	Black Codes
Chancellorsville	sharecroppers
Battle of Gettysburg	tenant farmers
Vicksburg	Mark Twain
Gettysburg Address	The Gilded Age

Short Paragraph

1. How would you characterize both the North and the South at the beginning of the Civil War?

2. Briefly describe Reconstruction.

3. Describe Sherman's March to the Sea and Reconstruction, especially with regard to their impact on the South's attitude toward the North (Union).

9

The West (Post–Civil War)

Turner and the Frontier

In 1893 historian **Frederick Jackson Turner** delivered a paper to the American Historical Association titled "The Significance of the Frontier in American History." Turner's essay was, in part, a response to the news from the 1890 census that there was no longer a frontier. While many of Turner's ideas have been debated over the past hundred years, his basic premise remains an important thesis of American history. Turner claimed that the frontier experience had been the single most important influence on American life and culture. Further, he argued, the frontier had provided a safety valve for the pressures of American life; that is, a place of escape for those who could not or would not fit into the structure of civilization. More than one hundred years after the closing of the American frontier, the study of the West remains an important key to understanding our nation's past.

The Plains Indians

The **Great Plains** cover a vast expanse from the southern border of Canada down to central Texas. Early travelers crossed these rolling grasslands in order to reach their destinations in Oregon and California, but most whites had little interest in these wide-open spaces nicknamed the Great American Desert by the explorer Major Stephen H. Long in 1820.

For thousands of American Indians, however, the Great Plains was home. Such groups as the Sioux, Cheyenne, Crow, Pawnee, and Comanche roamed the plains in loosely defined regions. These **Plains Indians** were nomadic and often followed the great bison herds from early spring until late fall, then settled down to wait out the cold winter in a secure camp. As mentioned earlier, the American bison (buffalo) provided the Plains Indians with food, clothing, shelter, and tools. Letting no part of these great shaggy beasts go to waste, the Indian people used the animal's meat, bones, hide, hooves, and various internal organs.

These buffalo-hunting groups maintained warrior cultures. Long before the arrival of the Europeans and Americans, the various Indian groups of the plains had fought among themselves, with young men seeking honor and respect through bravery and military exploits. With the arrival of significant numbers of Americans on the plains following the Civil War, the plains tribes were thrust into a struggle for control of the lands they had traditionally roamed at will. Some, like the Crow and the Pawnee, would often fight on the side of the Americans against their hated enemy, the Sioux. Others, such as the Sioux and Cheyenne, engaged in bitter battles against the intruding whites. The warriors of these Plains Indian cultures fought with great personal valor in order to protect their homes and families. Unparalleled as horsemen, they were difficult to engage in battle and even more difficult to pursue. Often the plains warrior, finding no particular merit in standing firm against an obviously superior force, would choose to flee in order to live to fight another day. Following the migratory bison herds, carrying out pony raids on rival cultures, and making war on their traditional enemies, these Indians dominated the Great Plains prior to the Civil War. After the war, when a reunited nation resumed its Manifest Destiny, the Plains Indians' days of nomadic freedom were numbered.

Miners and Boomtowns

While the first big gold strike had come in 1848 in California, bringing a flood of prospectors to the West Coast territory in 1849, this was far from the last time that gold and silver would play an important part in luring people from the East to the frontier. The discovery of gold in the Pike's Peak region of Colorado in 1858 brought thousands of prospectors to the Denver area.

Gold and silver strikes in Nevada, Idaho, Montana, Dakota, and other parts of the West also would attract miners and build fortunes. For the most part, the fortunes ended up in the hands of wealthy investors and business owners while the prospectors and miners ended up with little to show for their labor. Shortly after gold or silver was discovered, a boomtown would explode upon the scene; within days or weeks tents and buildings would be erected. While boomtown businesses were dominated by saloons (establishments that housed gambling and prostitution), such enterprises as hardware and general merchandise stores and restaurants prospered as well. But the influx of large numbers of miners to the western frontier served to aggravate relations with the Plains Indians, peoples who saw these lands as their own.

Cattle and Cowboys

Following the Civil War, conditions in the Northeast and Midwest created a great new demand for beef. Prosperity and growing urban populations (owing largely to a massive wave of immigration) helped spur the growth of the newly invigorated cattle business west of the Mississippi River. In the early days of the cattle boom, wild longhorn cattle in south Texas were rounded up in large numbers and then driven to a point where they could be sold and shipped east on the railroad. This pattern of marketing gave birth to the era of the **open-range** cattle business, a time in which ranchers simply laid claim to and then grazed their cattle on vast expanses of rangeland without legal authority to do so or fences to enclose their stock. The open-range days are probably most famous for the **long drive**, during which cowboys drove thousands of cattle hundreds of miles north to newly sprung cowtowns such as Wichita, Kansas City, and Dodge City, Kansas. After the cattle were sold at auction, they were loaded into boxcars and shipped to eastern markets. Their herds delivered, the cowboys might take a day or two to relax in town, often spending their wages in local hotels, bars, and brothels. After ten to twenty years, the invention of barbed wire meant fences belonging to both ranchers and farmers increasingly closed in the open range.

Although he sparked a romantic myth, in practice the cowboy worked long hours, from sunup until sundown, usually six or seven days a week. Cowboys worked most often from horseback (tending to the cattle) but also took part in fencing, branding, and various other chores. Gunplay was not a normal part of a cowboy's day: he was a laborer, and a heavy, dangerous six-gun was neither convenient nor safe to carry while on the job. As the open range gave way to large, fenced-in ranches, fewer and fewer cowboys were needed, and a way of life practiced by a small number of workers gave way to an enduring symbol of the American West that continues to fascinate people from all parts of the nation and world.

The Plains Wars

Americans had been fighting Indian Wars since the 1600s. American Indians had been in conflict with white settlers from the coasts of Virginia and Massachusetts all the way into the Ohio River Valley, Alabama, and beyond. Nonetheless, the most intense and visible segment of this centuries-long conflict was the final one, which played out in the post–Civil War era on the Great Plains.

As more and more whites (trappers, troops, and settlers) began to spill out on to the plains from the east, the Indian peoples increasingly resented the intrusions on their lands. Among the Sioux, for example, famous leaders such as **Red Cloud** were among the first to speak out against continuing to allow whites to cross traditional Sioux lands. Later it was Red Cloud who planned a brilliant strike against the United States Army in 1866, led by the young Sioux warrior **Crazy Horse**, that resulted in the death of Captain William Judd Fetterman and eighty of his men in present-day Wyoming.

But as the Plains Wars ran their course, Indian victories were relatively infrequent, for the United States Army had been quick to employ a new military strategy—a variation of the total war they had used with great effectiveness against the South in the recent Civil War. Initially the army had great difficulty locating large bands of Plains Indians to engage in battle, and, once finally located, most bands of Indians would simply fight a delaying action before escaping, having no desire to formally engage the frontier military. Frustrated time and again, the army added a new twist on their total-war strategy: the **winter campaign**. The winter campaign involved sending soldiers out to find the Indian bands settled in their winter camps, then launching a surprise attack (usually in the early morning just before dawn) in order to drive everyone from the place. Then the bluecoats would move in and destroy everything the Indians owned (including their pony herds), in order to leave the Indians no choice but to move onto **reservations**, the small parcels of land the federal government had partitioned for the Indians' use. The winter campaigns had a devastating impact on the Plains Indians.

Still, the Indians continued to fight and even managed to pull off a few more victories. One of the best-known battles in all of American history took place in June of 1876 in present-day Montana. There, in the valley of the greasy grass along the Little Bighorn River, Lt. Colonel **George A. Custer** and the soldiers of the Seventh Cavalry under his command were massacred when they attacked what they had failed to realize was an overwhelmingly superior force of allied Sioux and Cheyenne warriors. **The Battle of the Little Bighorn** was the last great Indian victory, but even its leaders, brave men such as **Sitting Bull** and Crazy Horse, quickly came to see that their people's days of freedom on the Great Plains were all but over. For even if the Indians could somehow manage to stave off the U.S. Army a little longer, the white settlers had already partitioned their land and decimated the great bison herds on which their culture and lifestyle depended.

The final battle of the Indian wars came in 1890 at **Wounded Knee** in present-day South Dakota. There, on a cold winter day, the Seventh Cavalry slaughtered two hundred Indian people (men, women, and children) as they attempted to leave the Pine Ridge Indian Agency. On that tragic day, the Indian wars finally came to an end. Never again would the Plains Indians live free to roam the vast seas of grass west of the Mississippi.

Settlers

Due to improvements in farming technology (such as the steel plow) increasing numbers of settlers began to move onto the Great Plains in the years following the Civil War. Attracted by the promises of the **Homestead Act of 1862** (generous terms under which the federal government offered free land to those who would agree to live on the land and improve it) farmers came west hoping to improve their lot in life. In short order, however, fencing off farmland, starting smaller ranches, and claiming land alongside chief sources of water put these newcomers into conflict with both the Indians and the old ranchers who depended on the wide-open spaces and easy access to water to support their huge herds of cattle. In spite of Indian wars and range wars (between the small farmers and the older, larger ranchers) more settlers continued to arrive. Eventually, due to their increasing numbers, this second wave of settlers not only persevered but overwhelmed those who had come before them. Through the influence of the middle-class farmer, the Wild West was tamed, with towns, schools, and churches dotting the countryside by the turn of the century.

The Wild West

A large portion of our nation's self-image is caught up in our myth of the **Wild West**. In fact, much of that so-called myth was a reality, and because this era of our past was so uniquely American, it remains transfixed in the American mind. To a large extent the West was an extralegal society (one that operated outside of the law) that gave people a freedom to act upon their moral convictions that is almost lost in the modern world. In the absence of convenient law, a person's word and a community's standards became the functional law. An individual was free to live according to his or her own code, so long as this did not interfere with the rights and freedoms of anyone else.

While the cowboy has become the cultural icon of the Old West, no other man did more to keep that tradition alive than **William F. "Buffalo Bill" Cody**. Born in 1846 in Iowa, Cody was a freighter, fur trapper, Pony Express rider, soldier, army scout, buffalo hunter, hunting guide, and, finally, actor and showman. Cody created his Wild West show (a huge circus-like production that recreated scenes and events from western life) in 1883 and toured the United States and Europe with it, keeping the heritage of the Wild West alive until his death in 1917. By that time, much of what Cody had loved about the Old West had passed from the scene as well. The census of 1890 had announced the closing of the American frontier, and already historians such as Frederick Jackson Turner were analyzing the phenomenon. The world was changing, and America was becoming an urban, industrial power.

✢ Chapter Review

Identify

Frederick Jackson Turner

Great Plains

Plains Indians

open range

long drive

Red Cloud

Crazy Horse

winter campaign

reservations

George A. Custer

The Battle of the Little Bighorn

Sitting Bull

Wounded Knee

Homestead Act of 1862

Wild West

William F. "Buffalo Bill" Cody

Short Paragraph

1. Describe the culture of the Plains Indians.

2. What was the cowboy culture of the Old West?

3. Describe the part that miners played in the westward movement.

10

The Gilded Age and Imperial America

In 1873 Mark Twain co-authored with Charles Dudley Warner **The Gilded Age**. Although the novel proved to be less successful than other of the pithy Twain's books, its title stuck with historians as a handy label for post–Civil War America. In other words, the gilded United States appeared golden and shiny on the outside, but a closer inspection revealed decay, corruption, and vulgarity inside. Gilded Age presidents, for example, included likable but undistinguished men such as Rutherford B. Hayes, James A. Garfield, Chester A. Arthur, and Benjamin Harrison. Even better-known chief executives such as Ulysses S. Grant and William McKinley hardly inspired poetry and reverence, as had Washington, Jefferson, and Lincoln in prior times. Gilded Age presidents were Republicans with one exception, Grover Cleveland (Democrat), who likewise is not customarily listed among the most remarkable occupants of the White House. The key to understanding the Gilded Age, then, lies not in politics, but in business. For in the years between the end of the Civil War and the dawn of the twentieth century, business transformed the United States in many meaningful ways.

The Corporation

Various sorts of companies have existed in America since colonial times, but the Gilded Age produced business arrangements that were truly revolutionary. The new way to do business became **corporate consolidation**. Instead of an individual or small group of partners risking personal assets to set up a company, states began to legally permit companies to sell shares of stock to virtually any interested buyer. The obvious attraction of such an arrangement was that now vast sums of money could be raised, for no longer did all of the investors have to know each other. Giant railroad companies were the first to advocate the legalization of such schemes. Even more appealing was a new proviso for limited liability, under which shareholders still risked their investment capital, but faced reduced legal responsibility for debts should the corporation be sued or go bankrupt.

But while corporations in theory offered anyone the chance to purchase shares, the Gilded Age witnessed an unprecedented amount of combination into fewer and fewer hands. This consolidation took many forms (**pools, holding companies,** or **trusts**), but each arrangement was an attempt to squeeze out all competing firms, to establish a **monopoly**. Some corporations combined by **horizontal organization**—by organizing companies in the same field (imagine all gasoline stations owned by the same company and agreeing to sell gas at the same high price); or **vertical organization**—by controlling the many steps in producing a single commodity. A vertical monopoly over oil, for example, controlled the exploration, drilling, refining, and marketing of the product. While either form of corporate organization was difficult to achieve, at least one man was able to effect both arrangements in his industry: **John D. Rockefeller**.

Captains of Industry and the American Dream

Today the name *Rockefeller* is almost synonymous with wealth. A bookkeeper by training, John D. Rockefeller built the powerful Standard Oil Company, establishing the first trust, a legal device allowing him to own vast holdings and stifle competition without violating existing antimonopoly statutes. The trust became the prototype of other industries. Soon Americans were talking of the tobacco trust, the sugar trust, or the steel trust. Eventually many also worried about the growing influence of banks, since the money trust was, by all appearances, also dominated by a handful of ruthless profiteers such as **J. P. Morgan**. Overwhelmed by the speed of these developments, governments seemed powerless to combat the vast wealth and power of these consolidated companies. Indeed, one of the hallmarks of the Gilded Age was a seemingly high tolerance for corruption at the city, state, and federal levels of government. Corporations, with alliances in the banking industry (one of Rockefeller's partners was the Chase Manhattan Bank), wielded great political influence.

Admirers called corporate leaders of great wealth **captains of industry**, but their critics called them **robber barons**. While many of the so-called Captains of Industry amassed great wealth through inheritance or other in-born advantages, one man came to personify the rags-to-riches promise of the American dream. His name was **Andrew Carnegie**. As a poor lad of eleven, Carnegie had come to the United States from Scotland in 1848, when political upheavals and famine drove millions of Scots, Irish, and Welsh to American shores. He first found work as a telegraph boy in Pittsburgh and began to save his money with fierce determination. In 1873 he risked all his considerable assets in the development of the first steel mills in America, sensing correctly that the steel industry was destined for magnificent growth in an industrial age.

After meeting Sir Henry Bessemer, who recently had invented new techniques and equipment for producing steel cheaply from pig iron, Carnegie tirelessly promoted the **Bessemer converter**, and in so doing became the richest man in the world. Taking inflation into account, some authorities say he is the richest American who ever lived. But there is another side to Andrew Carnegie. In 1901 he abruptly sold out his stake in his corporations and spent his remaining years as a philanthropist, giving away $350 million to back up his belief that the wealthy owed a responsibility to society. In an essay called "**The Gospel of Wealth**," Carnegie declared that "the man who dies rich dies disgraced." But his gospel did not instruct the wealthy simply to toss money to the poor. Indeed, most beneficiaries of his generosity were institutions that helped people better themselves: universities, hospitals, music halls (including the famous site in New York City that bears his name), baseball parks, and libraries (many of which are still used today). Carnegie was not the only captain of industry known for philanthropy. John D. Rockefeller also gave away millions, most notably in founding the University of Chicago.

To many, men such as Rockefeller and Carnegie were champions of the American dream, having risen to success through their own business sense and hard work. But perhaps the most potent force in shaping this new mythology known as the American dream came in the form of fictional characters. To this day the name **Horatio Alger** remains synonymous with the rags-to-riches tale of American success, an image reflected in the immensely popular novels he penned during the Gilded Age. In more than 100 of these books the hero, named Ragged Dick or Tattered Tom, quickly rises to great prosperity in the business world through a combination of hard work, thrift, optimism, and clean living. (Careful readers also notice that luck is usually involved in the hero's meteoric rise too, as in one lad's good fortune in saving a rich man's daughter from drowning.) Ironically, Alger himself was a Unitarian minister who had fled Massachusetts after a sex scandal. When he got to New York, he discreetly cranked out his all-American-boy stories to earn a living—hence becoming both promoter and beneficiary of the American Dream.

Survival of the Fittest?

Achieving success in the modern industrial world presumably involved intense competition in the marketplace. This, the essence of the American economic system, is often called **capitalism**. In spite of the fact that the captains of industry often worked hard to squelch competition through monopolistic practices, the idea of competition was celebrated almost everywhere.

To many this notion of inevitable economic winners and losers began to resemble the law of the jungle, the popular assessment of a biological theory put forth by Englishman **Charles Darwin** in his monumental work, *On the Origin of Species* (1859). Darwin concentrated mostly on plants and animals in formulating what became known as the Theory of Evolution. Why does a giraffe have a long neck? Because over millions of years the species gradually evolved into long-necked creatures capable of reaching the leaves of tall trees. Those with longer necks could reach food better than could other giraffes, which improved the long-necked giraffes' chances of producing healthy offspring. By the late nineteenth century, **survival of the fittest** (a term not actually used by Darwin himself) was a prime topic of conversation among educated people all over Europe and America.

Eventually a school of thought arose that applied the biological theory of evolution to modern social relations. It was known generally as **social Darwinism**. British and American intellectuals theorized that the economic marketplace found in capitalism was one such example of survival of the fittest in action. By extension, men such as Rockefeller and Carnegie were simply more fit than were other businesspeople who had failed to prosper. Carnegie himself became devoted to this principle (one can easily see its attractiveness to the rich and powerful), arguing that unrestrained competition advanced society by weeding out the unfit. He saw no contradiction between this view and his Gospel of Wealth, since his generosity had always been directed at helping people help themselves, not simply keeping them afloat with handouts. Social Darwinism provided a scientific justification for another cherished economic myth, that of *laissez faire* (from the French to "let it alone") for the government. Proponents of laissez faire argued that when government interferes with private enterprise—even through well-intentioned reforms such as the minimum wage to help the lower classes—it disturbs the so-called fundamental laws of nature and inevitably saps healthy commerce. Finally, social Darwinism had applications outside the business world. Obviously, many Americans were uncomfortable with the *religious* implications of evolutionary theory. In addition, social Darwinism won adherents from those who argued that certain races of people were naturally superior to others. Those with racist views now claimed to have scientific evidence to support their prejudiced beliefs.

The New Immigration

As the United States continued to industrialize, there was an acute demand for new labor in the factories, steel mills, and coal mines of the nation. This in turn caused the rapid growth of cities, or **urbanization**, as more and more Americans forsook traditional occupations such as farmer, trapper, and blacksmith to work in the booming factories. This labor shortage also propelled the most massive waves of immigration in U.S. history. The numbers were staggering. Twenty-five million immigrants arrived between 1856 and 1915—over four times the total of those who came during the preceding fifty years.

Also significant were the new immigrants' places of origin. Prior to the closing years of the nineteenth century, most immigrants to the United States had come from England, Ireland, and Northern Europe. Whatever religious and ethnic differences had existed (and there were plenty, particularly between old-stock Protestants and the Catholic Irish), the new pattern of immigration was much more unsettling to resident Americans. Now, newcomers were streaming in from Southern and Eastern Europe—from exotic places such as Italy, Greece, Poland, and Russia—speaking a variety of languages, practicing a multitude of faiths, and deriving from mysterious and, in the eyes of established Americans, alien cultures. But whether or not anyone liked it, America was starting to look different. Most of the new immigrants flooded into teeming cities such as New York, Philadelphia, or Chicago, while railroad laborers from China poured into California. There, racially charged prejudice and hysteria helped produce support for a series of federal **Chinese Exclusion Acts** during the Gilded Age, as Congress tried to limit further immigration from China and then Japan. Many such laws stayed in effect through much of the twentieth century.

By 1890 most of the population of the major urban areas consisted of immigrants. Almost 90 percent of the people in Chicago, for example, were not U.S.-born. While the promise of the American Dream still loomed large in the hopes of countless newcomers (by 1886 the Statue of Liberty beckoned in New York harbor), the life that immigrants experienced in their new country was often harsh and bitter. For one thing, most of these people had grown up in rural homelands. Those who did not adapt quickly to city life could perish. The words *tenement* and *ghetto* are used to describe the residential areas of big cities crowded with immigrants clinging to old traditions and native languages. The rickety, wooden, multistory apartment buildings into which many poor immigrants crowded could, and often did, become hellish firetraps.

Various immigrant groups handled the problems they encountered upon arrival differently. Scandinavians and Germans tended to save their money and head west to start farms, perhaps seduced by railroad advertisements touting the good life out on a homestead. Many Irish, on the other hand, quickly seized on urban opportunities, taking jobs digging canals, building bridges, or working as policemen or firemen. Many Jews from Eastern Europe focused on the needle trades in the garment district of Manhattan, or established retail outlets selling goods to other immigrants. Historians have speculated on why some groups tended to be more successful in America than others. One theory holds that Jews and Germans, for example, advanced more rapidly because they clung together in ethnic neighborhoods (whether in the city or in isolated farming communities) and took care of each other with more intensity than did other groups. Many who struck out on their own ended up simply failing. In any case, most immigrants wanted the same thing—the chance for their sons and daughters to have a better life. And all immigrants to America faced agonizing decisions regarding **assimilation**: whether to cling to old ways or become Americans in the fullest sense. Some have called America a melting pot of ethnic blending, while others say it more closely resembles a salad bowl, with each ingredient tossed in while keeping its own identity. It is a debate that continues today.

One point beyond debate is the fact that the new immigrants permanently shaped American culture. Their contribution goes well beyond providing a source of labor. Men and women of talent in all fields of human enterprise such as business, religion, science, education, athletics, music, art, theater, and film, transformed the meaning of the term *American*. Patterns of behavior as basic as daily diet and as symbolic as a list of holidays have been affected.

The Rise of Big Labor

While statistics say the average standard of living for American workers *improved* during the Gilded Age, this does not tell the whole story. During the period wages still lay below commonly accepted levels of comfort (averaging less than $500 per year in 1900) and job security was practically nonexistent. With no national minimum wage, cuts in wages were common during downward slides in the business cycle. Because they could be hired for less money, women and children were routinely employed in hazardous occupations, which at the time was perfectly legal. Six ten-hour days a week was the norm in factories, with twelve-hour days common practice in the steel industry. As the United States continued to transform from a rural to an urban society, highly skilled artisans became obsolete, for machines and **mass production** ushered in new kinds of jobs that were monotonous, repetitive, and impersonal.

Eventually, laborers began to fight back, attempting to unify into consolidated organizations, just as business management had done. The first major attempt at a national labor organization was the **Knights of Labor**, which originated in 1869 as a secret fraternal organization but grew to a membership of 700,000 by 1886. The goals of the Knights were never well defined, but its main success was in the railroad industry. Then, a series of strikes in defiance of its own leadership failed, and scattered outbreaks of violence soured public opinion of the union. By 1900 the Knights had completely disbanded.

The labor movement, however, was not finished. In the wake of the Knights' demise another group, the **American Federation of Labor (AFL)**, tried a different strategy. In attempting to organize independent **craft unions** of *skilled* workers, the AFL became the most important labor organization in American history. The AFL also benefited from capable leadership under **Samuel Gompers**, whose approach involved the open acceptance of capitalism and private ownership of property. Using collective bargaining and occasional strikes, the AFL simply wanted a better deal for its members. The **eight-hour day**, for example, became one of the union's top priorities.

Although organized labor had taken its first steps in the era, the Gilded Age is notable for the failure of American unions to become as powerful as their counterparts in Europe. Several reasons explain this. For one, American companies had formidable resources in controlling their workforce, including the full support of the state and federal government in most cases. In numerous instances work stoppages were broken as state governors used the National Guard to escort strikebreakers (known as **scabs** by the unions) across picket lines. In addition, big companies often hired the Pinkerton Detective Agency as a private army to break the back of organized labor. The hated **Pinkertons**, with their blue uniforms and striped pants, were held in disgust by union organizers. Those workers whom management deemed radicals were often **blacklisted**, with their names shared among employers to ensure that they would not get another job. Finally, American union leadership was hampered by the frequent inability of diverse immigrant groups to cooperate because of differences in language and culture.

Most important, well-publicized violence turned American public opinion against the agitating workers. In Chicago, a city swarming with new immigrants and violent radicalism, seven policemen were killed in 1886 when someone threw a bomb during a protest over the killing of a worker in a strike urging the eight-hour day. The incident, which came to be known as the **Haymarket Bombing**, frightened people all over the country and dampened support for organized labor. The American public was outraged at the apparent lawlessness of the crowd as portrayed in the generally antilabor newspapers. Eight **anarchists** (radicals and visionaries who advocated the abolishment of most government) were rounded up, put on trial, and convicted with little evidence. Four of them were executed. Undoubtedly the foreign appearance and accents of the defendants had prejudiced people against them.

In 1892 a long standoff between the Amalgamated Association of Iron and Steel Workers and Andrew Carnegie's steel plant in Homestead, Pennsylvania, riveted public attention. A war-like atmosphere prevailed for weeks, once again pitting the hated Pinkertons against strikers and resulting in over a dozen deaths from gunshots and dynamite. The **Homestead Strike** was finally put down with the help of 8,000 state militia troops who escorted strikebreakers into the plant. Whatever natural sympathy the public had initially felt for the strikers evaporated when a lone radical tried to assassinate Carnegie's chief lieutenant, Harry Frick, stabbing him repeatedly and shooting him twice in the neck. Amazingly, Frick survived to keep on working, becoming a hero to many.

The labor confrontation with the greatest—if nonviolent—impact occurred in 1894. The **Pullman Strike** was mounted by **Eugene V. Debs** and his American Railway Union (ARU) against the Pullman Palace Car Company, maker of sleeping and parlor railcars. Pullman, Illinois, near Chicago, was a **company town**, built and maintained by the Pullman Company, which proclaimed that it provided an orderly, clean, and humane living and working environment for its workers. George M. Pullman himself referred to his employee residents benevolently as his children. Then during an economic depression known as the **Panic of 1893**, Pullman abruptly slashed wages, which persuaded Debs and the ARU to refuse to handle all trains with Pullman cars and equipment. Within days, rail transportation between Chicago and the Pacific Coast was paralyzed, as workers in twenty-seven states and territories succeeded in halting business in much of the country. This time, Federal troops were called in by President Grover Cleveland (under the legal pretext of protecting mail delivery), and a court order was evoked to end the strike. When Debs and his men held firm, they were arrested and imprisoned. The Pullman Strike collapsed.

Against the formidable weapons of state and federal troops, Pinkertons, court orders, and a hostile press igniting public opinion against its leaders, the U.S. labor movement suffered one defeat after another during the Gilded Age. Furthermore, unions were mostly unsuccessful in helping African Americans and other minorities into the mainstream of American life. (By 1902 blacks constituted only 3 percent of AFL membership.) Reform legislation regulating labor conditions showed up first in western states, with Utah and Oregon winning Supreme Court approval that would pave the way for future changes. Slowest to improve, however, were conditions among agricultural workers, particularly Hispanics in the West and Southwest. At the turn of the century, for instance, over half of the Mexican-American population of Texas was classified by the Census Bureau as unspecialized labor.

Meanwhile, working women all over America faced nearly impossible odds in what was still a male-dominated world.

The American Empire

In 1898 the United States became an imperial nation. The country had been expanding since its origins, of course, but always within the natural confines of North America. *Imperialism* is a word that traditionally disconcerts Americans because the United States itself was born in a revolution against imperial Britain. Indeed, to suggest that this same nation could fight a war for expansionist purposes outside its borders, or to acquire colonies, would have seemed absurd during the late eighteenth century. But only 100 years later, it became an open question—and soon a reality. One of the most effective advocates of American imperialism was **Alfred Thayer Mahan**, a naval officer who wrote the influential book, *The Influence of Sea Power upon History* (1890). Mahan's argument was simple: great nations are those that control the oceans. In order for the United States to become great it must have vast naval power and colonies to serve as strategic outposts in both the Atlantic and Pacific. Expansionist-minded politicians (especially the influential Theodore Roosevelt of New York) treated Mahan's arguments as gospel.

The most dramatic episode of expansionism was the **Spanish-American War**. The Spanish Empire, which had once claimed vast holdings in the Americas, was in fatal decline by 1898. Among its remaining possessions near the United States were Puerto Rico and Cuba. Cuba especially was of paramount importance in igniting what Secretary of State John Hay once called a "splendid little war" with Spain. For years the Spanish government had tried to put down revolutionary movements in Cuba, often resorting to brutal atrocities. Cries of *Cuba Libre!* (Free Cuba!) were heard throughout America, generating heartfelt sympathy for the cause of Cuban independence. After all, America itself had been founded in a swirl of revolutionary rhetoric directed against a European power. And the atrocities committed by the Spanish in Cuba were real: 100,000 Cubans died, many of them in wretched prison camps, between 1896 and 1898.

It is impossible to understand the reasons for the Spanish-American War without mentioning an important contributing factor: the rise of **yellow journalism**. Fierce competition between newspaper magnates such as

Joseph Pulitzer and **William Randolph Hearst** produced a rabid sensation-alism directed at the new urban readership that mushroomed in the late 1800s. Publicity stunts, comics (*yellow* referred to a comic strip character, *the Yellow Kid*), crime stories, and gigantic headlines captivated millions. Part of the lure of this new journalism was emotional sympathy for the un-derdog, and dramatic reports of the Cubans' desperate situation helped de-monize the Spanish in American minds.

In January 1898, the U.S. battleship *Maine* steamed into Havana harbor with no military objective, except perhaps a small show of force. Certainly President McKinley was determined at this point to avoid war. Suddenly the *Maine* exploded, killing 266 Americans. While the cause of the explosion was probably spontaneous combustion in a hot powder magazine, Ameri-cans were quick to respond with the battle cry of the Spanish-American War: **"Remember the Maine, to Hell with Spain."**

Before the war was formalized with declarations, Congress passed the Volunteer Army Act, which included provision for a First Volunteer Cav-alry, dubbed by the yellow press as the **Rough Riders**. As a chief instigator of the war, **Theodore Roosevelt** resigned his position as assistant secretary of the Navy and accepted a commission as lieutenant colonel of the First Cavalry, a unit consisting of Ivy League thrill seekers, Texas cowboys, and assorted misfits. The daring charge up San Juan Hill (actually Kettle Hill and San Juan Heights) personally led by Roosevelt became the most famous epi-sode of the war, making him a hero—and ultimately President. Significantly, African Americans fought in several combat regiments, including those en-gaged in the famed charge. While most such units were strictly segregated, many saw fierce action in Cuba, with five black soldiers winning Congres-sional Medals of Honor.

The other principal site of the war was the Philippines, a Spanish out-post off the coast of China and Southeast Asia. Commodore **George Dewey** (under secret orders from then–assistant secretary of the Navy Roosevelt) attacked Spain's aging fleet in Manila harbor the very instant war was de-clared. The fighting was completely one-sided, with more than 300 Spanish killed and only one American sailor dead (of heatstroke). Spanish authorities quickly surrendered. The "splendid little war" ended after only four months of actual fighting, with the following terms of peace (the Treaty of Paris): independence for Cuba, U.S. control of Puerto Rico in the Caribbean and control of Guam and the Philippines in the Pacific. In the entire war, there were 5,462 American deaths, only 379 of which were combat related. Yellow fever, malaria, and other tropical diseases were the chief killers.

Occupation of the Philippines proved to be a nasty and persistent problem for the victorious United States. A vicious guerilla war between American troops and native revolutionaries lasted for years, as U.S. soldiers found themselves oppressing the people they had supposedly come to liberate. Indeed, the **Philippine Insurrection** foreshadowed (at least to some historians) another quagmire in another distant jungle: Vietnam. Interestingly, the United States learned valuable lessons of command, mobility, and infiltration during the insurrection, all of which were apparently forgotten by 1965. At any rate, the United States had become an imperial nation, acquiring territory and responsibility for foreign populations in distant lands.

The Spanish-American War boosted nationalism and unified Americans in a way they had not experienced since the Civil War. Southerners, including former Confederate General Joseph Wheeler (who once in the heat of battle referred to the Spanish soldiers as "Yankees"), fought alongside the descendants of slaves, northerners, and cowboys from the West. The war also produced the first hero for a new generation and a new century: Theodore Roosevelt.

✤ Chapter Review

Identify

The Gilded Age	Bessemer converter
corporate consolidation	"The Gospel of Wealth"
pools	Horatio Alger
holding companies	capitalism
trusts	Charles Darwin
monopoly	survival of the fittest
horizontal organization	social Darwinism
vertical organization	*laissez faire*
John D. Rockefeller	urbanization
J. P. Morgan	Chinese Exclusion Acts
captains of industry	tenement
robber barons	ghetto
Andrew Carnegie	assimilation

mass production
Knights of Labor
American Federation of Labor (AFL)
craft unions
Samuel Gompers
eight-hour day
scabs
Pinkertons
blacklisted
Haymarket Bombing
anarchists
Homestead Strike
Pullman Strike
Eugene V. Debs
company town

Panic of 1893
imperialism
Alfred Thayer Mahan
Spanish-American War
yellow journalism
Joseph Pulitzer
William Randolph Hearst
Maine
"Remember the *Maine*,
   to Hell with Spain"
Rough Riders
Theodore Roosevelt
George Dewey
Philippine Insurrection

Short Paragraph

1. Why did workers have difficulty organizing during the Gilded Age?

2. Why did the United States fight a war with Spain in 1898?

3. Why was immigration important during the late 1800s and early 1900s? Who were the old and new immigrants?

CHAPTER

11

Populism, Progressivism, and the Great War

In 1890 the population of the United States was almost 63 million, as compared to only 4 million 100 years before. The nation had become an industrial giant with global ambitions. But the excesses, abuses, and corruption of the Gilded Age had produced great discontent.

Populism

The word *Populist* today is used to refer to almost any popular political movement, particularly one involving discontented people, but in the late nineteenth century it meant something quite specific. After the Civil War, disgruntled farmers began to organize out of frustration with low crop prices, monopolized railroads that charged whatever shipping rates they wanted, banks that parceled out the loans that farmers continually needed to buy supplies and equipment, and the perceived capture of government on the local, state, and federal levels by the moneyed interests.

Unlike industrial laborers, farmers were handicapped in their efforts to unite by physical distance from each other and a rural individualism that hindered union-style solidarity. An early successful agrarian organization was the Patrons of Husbandry, generally known as the **Grange** (from an old word for grain). Grangers tried to fight the rigged marketplace by establishing **cooperatives** for selling their crops in a pool—just like, they reasoned, the business monopolies. Believing the major parties (Democrats and

Republicans) were controlled by the influence of eastern money, the allied farmers helped spawn independent, or third parties, urging them to adopt into their platforms Granger laws intended to impose regulation over the railroads and crop distributors, whom farmers resented as parasitic middlemen. While most of these early efforts failed, those that succeeded, such as in Illinois, led to the recognition by the U.S. Supreme Court in **Munn v. Illinois** (1877) that state governments could indeed regulate businesses that affected a public interest. This ruling, in turn, spurred a flurry of state legislation creating railroad commissions charged with regulating the rates railroads could legally charge to transport freight as well as passengers.

By 1890 there were two main farmers' **alliances** in the Northwest and South, including a **Colored Farmers Alliance** in the Deep South, which claimed over 1 million African-American members. Eventually, the membership of the various farmers' alliances formed the **People's Party**, which was shortened in common language to **Populists**. Whatever their differences (regionalism and race would always plague them), these agrarian radicals shared a bitter resentment toward big business, especially railroads and banks. Such an atmosphere produced colorful and charismatic leaders. In Kansas, **Mary Elizabeth Lease** urged farmers to "raise less corn and more hell," warning the "bloodhounds of money" to beware. **Tom Watson** of Georgia urged black and white farmers to unite, citing a common enemy, the rich landed aristocracy. Not surprisingly, the upper classes and many city dwellers labeled populist leaders as rabble rousers.

The Populist Party was just getting started as a viable alternative to the two major parties when a devastating depression, the **Panic of 1893**, gripped the nation. What seemed to be complete economic collapse fueled angry strikes and protests all over the country. As usual, farmers were hit hardest during the downturn, as crop prices hit rock bottom. While today we have a tendency to view low prices as healthy, farmers saw things differently. First, to someone in debt—and virtually all farmers carried debt—inflation can be construed as good news, since one's debt could then be paid off with dollars worth increasingly less. Second, farmers wanted high prices because their livelihood depended on *selling* goods, while their costs of labor remained constant, at least in their own eyes.

In this atmosphere the **currency issue** caused a striking split between Populists and the proponents of more conservative economic theories. At the time, U.S. currency was backed (in complicated formulas) by two metals: gold and silver. Since gold was less plentiful, it was favored by some as the only true basis for a sound currency. Those in favor of retaining the gold standard, so-called **Gold Bugs**, tended to be eastern conservative businesspeople, while **Silverites**, who pushed for the use of silver in the hopes of deflating the value of the currency, tended to hail from the West, where farmers (and silver-mining interests) were more prominent. In the last presidential election of the nineteenth century, the Populists hoped to ride the free-silver issue to power. All they needed was a champion.

In the **election of 1896** the Democrats threw in with the Silverites behind a crusading, charismatic Nebraskan named **William Jennings Bryan** to oppose the Republican nominee, **William McKinley**. The dignified and conservative McKinley not surprisingly endorsed a gold-standard platform. Bryan received the Democratic nomination after giving one of the most famous political addresses in American history: the **Cross of Gold Speech**. Using emotional rhetoric, Bryan raised the roof with an endorsement of the free coinage of silver, attacking the gold bugs with Biblical imagery: "You shall not press down upon the brow of labor this crown of thorns. You shall not crucify mankind upon a cross of gold." The Populists quickly sensed their interests were with Bryan, but by endorsing the Democratic candidate they sealed the fate of their movement. As the Democrats absorbed the key Populist issue, they robbed the third party of its reason to exist.

After the convention, Bryan conducted what many consider to be the first modern presidential campaign, traveling the country and openly soliciting votes. Prior to 1896, presidential candidates typically let other people do such things on their behalf. For his part, McKinley ran a traditional campaign, literally from his front porch (letting interested parties come to him), while his campaign manager, Mark Hanna, shrewdly portrayed Bryan as a radical with a "communistic spirit." Apparently, this imagined threat to capitalism was effective. One factory owner told his employees, "Men, vote as you please, but if Bryan is elected . . . the whistle will not blow Wednesday morning." In the end, the strategy of fear worked, and McKinley won

the presidency. And while Bryan, at the age of thirty-six, was far from finished politically, the agrarian movement known as Populism had been dealt
a blow from which it would never recover.

Why Progressivism?

Like Populism, *Progressivism* is a word commonly used without much precision. When historians refer to the **Progressive Era** (1900–17), they generally allude to a period in which widespread political and social reform
was achieved—or at least attempted. Progressivism's focus was more urban
than rural, and it was a much more broadly based and successful movement
than Populism. Progressivism is also linked with the growing middle class,
in which it became increasingly fashionable to be a do-gooder and social
reformer.

And there was much in need of reform. Cities such as Boston, New
York, and Chicago had become cesspools of filthy living conditions and political corruption. Many cities were totally controlled by **political machines**,
highly disciplined party organizations that traded favors and jobs for votes.
Machines thrived on new immigrants, who could be recruited and given
work or a government contract, as long as the neighborhood (often called a
ward) voted correctly. The modern stereotype of the Irish beat cop or fire-
man, for instance, exists because many Irish got their first step up the ladder
with jobs doled out to them by machine politicians. The most famous political machine of all was the **Tammany Hall** organization in New York, which
began as a fraternal lodge in the 1700s. The leader of a political machine,
whether he held elected office or not, was called the **boss**. In some ways
machines performed needed services for lower-class immigrants, building
streets, sewer systems, and magnificent city bridges. Nonetheless, Tammany and similar organizations were extremely wasteful and corrupt, with
jobs and money changing hands in order to buy votes and keep the machine
alive. Reformers wanted the machines "cleaned up."

One of the reasons progressive reform became a national goal was a
new kind of journalism. Whereas the yellow journalism of the previous era
focused on publicity stunts and sensationalism, the new wave of progressive reporters saw themselves as chroniclers of social ills. For example, Ida
Tarbell's *History of the Standard Oil Company* documented the abuses of
the nation's largest monopoly. Danish immigrant Jacob Riis exposed slum

conditions in *How the Other Half Lives*. Lincoln Steffans wrote *The Shame of the Cities* to expose municipal corruption. Most of these lengthy works appeared first as serials in reformist magazines such as *McClure's* and were later put into book form. Theodore Roosevelt, while a reformer himself, thought that some journalists went too far in exposing evil, dubbing such writers **muckrakers**, after a character in the novel *Pilgrim's Progress* who would rather rake the muck than look at the positive things in life.

Even Roosevelt was reportedly impressed, however, with the best-known work of fiction in the muckraking tradition, **The Jungle**, by Upton Sinclair. Published in 1906, the novel graphically exposed the abuses and unsanitary practices of the meatpacking industry through the trials of a family of poor Lithuanian immigrants. In the narrative, women are forced into prostitution, old men are left to starve, children die needlessly, poisoned rats are ground up into sausage, and workers who fall into vats end up as lard sold to the public. While Sinclair's goal was to convert people to socialism, the book's practical impact was in helping to garner popular support for the passage of federal legislation that remains in effect to this day, the **Meat Inspection Act**.

The Progressive Agenda

The catalog of progressive reforms is long. Some involved direct political action, while others were more broadly focused. All, however, reflected a characteristically American attitude of optimism—the belief that human improvement is possible through collective action. As such, Progressivism is within the liberal tradition but cannot correctly be called radical. Progressives for the most part accepted the capitalist system, organized religion, and the Constitution of the United States—perhaps with a few amendments.

Some authorities believe Progressivism began in Chicago with the founding of **Hull House** by Jane Addams and Ellen Gates Starr in 1889. Hull House and similar facilities were part of the settlement movement, which sought to provide shelters and training for immigrants and the poor. The movement was particularly interested in Americanizing the foreign-born. Another early sign of reform was the **Social Gospel**, an expressed attitude of many church leaders and laypersons that the best way to serve God was to reach out to the members of the lower classes, who often felt out of place in middle-class congregations. Organizations directed toward youth such as the Young Men's Christian (and Hebrew) Association were founded and quickly grew in popularity, as did the Salvation Army. Churches acquired gymnasiums, libraries, and lecture halls to attract working people off the streets and men out of saloons.

Quite a few reformers saw alcohol as the main culprit in a host of social problems: the abandonment of children, wife-beating, and uncivilized blood sports such as boxing. Therefore the movement to make the sale or possession of alcoholic beverages illegal, **prohibitionism**, gained momentum during the Progressive Era, though it would not become national policy until the 1920s. Today, the turn-of-the-century prohibitionists might be thought of as conservative prudes, but it is important to note that the movement to ban alcohol was rooted in a genuine impulse to improve society. Rural fundamentalists also used Prohibition as a means to point the finger at immigrants, especially those who tended to be Catholic. Around 1900, prohibitionist groups such as the Women's Christian Temperance Union and the Anti-Saloon League broadened their efforts from reforming the behavior of individuals to influencing the political arena by agitating for women's right to vote.

This push for women's voting rights, the **Woman's Suffrage Movement**, also gained momentum during the Progressive Era after decades of valiant efforts by pioneers such as **Susan B. Anthony** and **Elizabeth Cady Stanton**. Interestingly, the western states were the leaders (with Wyoming the first) in granting women the right to vote. New York did not do so until 1917, shortly before women's suffrage became national policy in 1920, with the ratification of the Nineteenth Amendment to the Constitution. But even at the end of the nineteenth century, progressive-minded men supported the entrance of women into the political arena, partly because men believed women were inherently less corrupt and that society might become more humane and decent with their involvement.

One goal of the progressives was to make society more efficient. In business, the theory of **scientific management** gained ascendancy, thanks in part to a self-proclaimed expert on the subject, Frederick W. Taylor, who advised companies on how to restructure their organizations to avoid waste and duplication of tasks. When Galveston, Texas, was wiped out by a massive hurricane and subsequent flood in 1900, the city's leaders reorganized the municipal government with elected specialized commissioners. Soon cities all over America switched to the so-called **Galveston Plan** of efficient local governance. Eventually, city governments developed a completely new profession, **city manager**, an official charged with overseeing professional and rational city services. All this stood in direct contrast to the operation of the corrupt and wasteful political machines that had ruled cities virtually unilaterally.

At the state level, experimentation with government reform proliferated as well. In this area, the state of Wisconsin attracted the most attention. Indeed, the **Wisconsin Idea** became something of a slogan among progressives, as other states were urged to adopt Wisconsin-like policies hailed as progressive and modern. For instance, the Wisconsin legislature was staffed for the first time with professional analysts to study issues before the body and make recommendations for action based on evidence and statistics, as opposed to the interests of powerful lobbyists. At the same time, Wisconsin's charismatic governor, **Robert "Fighting Bob" La Follette**, achieved nationwide fame as a progressive politician worthy of emulation by others who sought reform. La Follette and other progressives advocated the **initiative, referendum,** and **recall**—three ways for voters to enact laws and remove politicians directly, bypassing the special interests. An *initiative* allows citizens to officially propose laws to the legislature. A *referendum* is a method of passing a law by a vote of the people after getting a certain number of signatures on a petition. A *recall* allows voters to remove an elected official before his or her term has expired. All three are used today in some states, especially in the West. Similarly, the **direct election of U.S. senators** (who were then still chosen by state legislatures) was urged by progressives. This became reality with the ratification of the Seventeenth Amendment in 1913.

The Progressive Presidents: Roosevelt, Taft, and Wilson

In September 1901, Theodore Roosevelt took the presidential oath of office at the age of forty-two, the youngest man to do so in history. In a sense he was an accidental president, having been picked as McKinley's vice president largely on his exploits in Cuba during the Spanish-American War. After McKinley was assassinated at the Pan-American Exposition in Buffalo, New York, by anarchist Leon Czolgosz, Roosevelt was thrust upon the scene as a youthful, charismatic president for a new century.

Conservative Republican party leaders were alarmed by his progressive reforms in New York and his reputation for independence and tenacity. Party leader Mark Hanna, who had warned McKinley about selecting Roosevelt as his running mate, remarked, "Now look, that damned cowboy is president of the United States!"

Roosevelt's presidency became known for its **trust busting**, but in fact Roosevelt's main approach toward business was in the regulation, not the destruction, of monopolies. In management's disputes with labor, he saw himself as an honest mediator between the two sides. Though his promise of a **Square Deal** for the American people increasingly alarmed business leaders, the general public loved the man. In foreign policy he aggressively arranged the construction of the **Panama Canal** ("I took Panama," he later boasted), and assumed the so-called **Roosevelt Corollary** to the Monroe Doctrine, purportedly giving the United States the license to intervene in all affairs of the Western Hemisphere, namely Latin America. Perhaps his most lasting legacy is as the first genuine environmentalist president. A famous outdoorsman and hunter, he persuaded Congress to set aside 125 million acres as forest preserves, national parks, and wildlife refuges.

At his friend Roosevelt's urging, **William Howard Taft** ran for president in 1908, handily defeating William Jennings Bryan, whom the Democrats had nominated once again. Taft saw his role as consolidating, but not extending, Roosevelt's reforms. Taft might be called a moderate progressive, but he clearly lacked Roosevelt's gift for politics. In fact, Roosevelt and Taft suffered a major falling out during Taft's administration, provoking Roosevelt to run as a presidential candidate of the **Progressive (or Bull Moose) Party** in the election of 1912. On the stump, Roosevelt decried Taft's caution and called for a more aggressive role for the federal government in fighting for the American people. Now the former president called for a **New Nationalism**. This split in Republican loyalties, since a good number of loyal Republicans had backed Roosevelt, contributed greatly to the election of the first progressive Democrat president: Woodrow Wilson.

Woodrow Wilson was, in a formal sense, America's first scholar president, having been a political science professor and president of Princeton University. His progressive credentials had been impressive as Governor of New Jersey, and Democrats, realizing that they must get on the reformist bandwagon too, had selected Wilson as their choice to oppose Taft and Roosevelt. Calling his program the **New Freedom**, which was intended to contrast with Roosevelt's New Nationalism, Wilson envisioned an aggressive role for the federal government in tackling problems created by the big business trusts. While few business combinations were actually dismantled during Wilson's first term as President, he offered the nation a glimpse of what the presidency might become in the modern age.

Wilson swiftly organized the various coalitions of the Democratic Party in the House and Senate. Under his active leadership, Congress from 1913 to 1916 enacted the most comprehensive domestic program the federal government had ever undertaken. Banking policy was completely redirected into the **Federal Reserve System**, which remains today as the principal agent for control of the money supply through the adjustment of interest rates. Federal tariffs were examined and reduced, agencies for business oversight were created, and funds were appropriated for education and agriculture. Congress also approved a **graduated income tax** (authorized by the Sixteenth Amendment), with rates ranging from 1 percent to 6 percent on the highest incomes. Taxing the rich had been a goal of reformers for decades.

Wilson and the Great War

When war broke out in Europe in 1914, Wilson intended to keep the United States out of the conflict and concentrate on domestic policy. Although he was a sophisticated intellectual in many ways, the southern-born Wilson was also a highly moralistic and stern man with a religious sense of mission. He saw the European war that became known as the Great War (before it was numbered as World War I) as the product of imperialistic rivalries between Germany and Austria-Hungary (the **Central Powers**) and Great Britain, France, Russia, and (after 1915) Italy (the **Allied Powers**). In Wilson's view, the chief task was to protect American shipping.

Public opinion in the United States about the war in Europe often divided along ethnic and class lines. Recent immigrants, particularly those from Ireland (people with long-standing animosity toward anything British) and Germany, tended to be skeptical of British claims that Germany was the aggressor. More established Americans (largely of Anglo-Protestant heritage) leaned toward support for Great Britain. Wilson himself hoped to conduct free trade with all sides, but this became increasingly difficult as Germany began using an unconventional strategic weapon to disrupt the shipment of supplies to its enemies: the submarine. Nicknamed **U-boats**, these tiny, subsurface vessels torpedoed merchant ships without warning, violating the customary practice of boarding a suspect ship to search for contraband before commencing hostile action. When Germany's new tactic took the lives of Americans, as in the U-boat sinking of the British passenger liner *Lusitania* in May of 1915 with 128 U.S. citizens aboard, Wilson protested with great forcefulness and emotion. But the American public was still not ready to participate in what they still regarded as a foreign war. Indeed, Wilson was re-elected in 1916 partly on the slogan *"He kept us out of war,"* which would quickly prove to be one of the most ironical campaign statements ever made.

As the war in Europe reached stalemate in early 1917, Germany announced a policy of **unrestricted submarine warfare** against all ships headed for Britain. Wilson broke diplomatic relations with Germany, but stopped short of asking Congress for a declaration of war. As the pressure began to build, several American ships fell victim to U-boat attacks. Now Theodore Roosevelt and other militarists were clamoring for action, accusing Wilson of weakness. Then March witnessed the interception and publishing of the **Zimmerman telegram**, a document detailing a secret German proposal to form an alliance with Mexico. If Mexico agreed and thereby helped the Central Powers, the terms stated, it would regain the territory it had lost to the United States in the 1840s, which included Texas, New Mexico, Arizona, and California. Now all Americans were outraged. In April, Wilson asked for and received a declaration of war from Congress.

The Great War had already proven to be a virtual slaughterhouse. Unlike previous wars, it featured few battles that could be drawn on a map and analyzed, and few heroic charges or tactical maneuvers to surprise the enemy. Each side simply hunkered down and tried to grind its opponent down, fighting what is often called a **war of attrition** in which no clear winners or losers emerge. France was the site of the most horrible carnage, with **"trench warfare"** quickly added to the vocabulary of soldiers on all sides. Day after day, an attack whistle would blow to signal men to leave the safety of their trench and charge across no-man's land to the enemy's trenches, perhaps only to retreat to their original position a few hours later. And, coming as it did after the age of industrialization, World War I was the first armed conflict to feature the widespread use of highly effective, mass-produced weaponry. Air-cooled machine guns, massed artillery, and magazine rifles killed with great efficiency. A further development, poison gas, was used by the German army with deadly and debilitating effect. Day in and day out, both sides launched a constant artillery bombardment, with many soldiers experiencing a new type of battle trauma: shell shock. Ace pilots who battled in dogfights in the skies over Europe, often dropping bombs by hand from their propeller-driven wooden bi-planes, provided the only thing approaching glamour.

Wilson understood the importance of public opinion in fighting a war. As important as freedom of the seas was as an objective, it didn't have quite the ring to it as did what became the official explanation of why Americans fought in Europe: making the world safe for democracy. The fight was also hailed as the "war to end all wars." The U.S. government formed the Committee on Public Information, which distributed 75 million pamphlets and produced countless films to demonize the German enemy. One such film was entitled *The Kaiser: Beast of Berlin*. Most Americans responded to the government's propaganda with waves of patriotism—as well as hostility toward anything German. Sauerkraut became known derisively as "liberty cabbage" in American restaurants and grocery stores, and frankfurters transformed into "liberty sausage." Soon after U.S. entry into the war, federal agents—authorized under hastily passed legislation known as the **Espionage and Sabotage Acts**—hunted down suspected radicals and spies. Under these measures, which were later held to be unconstitutional, criticizing the government became illegal, and recent immigrants who spoke with foreign accents quickly learned to remain as quiet as possible.

Nicknamed Doughboys at home and abroad, the Americans who joined the armed forces (2 million) or were drafted, were hastily drilled for battle. Lads from the farm and city alike were gallantly preparing to go *Over There*, in the words of the popular song by Broadway showman George M. Cohan, which went on to assure the world that "The Yanks are Coming!" But U.S. forces were not battle ready until spring of 1918. The draft included African Americans as well as whites. Indeed, four black regiments were among the first sent into combat. Ironically, they were fighting for freedom overseas even as discrimination and segregation prevailed at home. No black soldiers were allowed to march in the victory celebrations in Paris when the war ended. In any event, eight months after the Americans' arrival in Europe, the war was over. Under the command of General **John J. Pershing**, Americans joined existing Allied forces in turning back a series of ferocious

German assaults, including a bloody fight at **Château-Thierry** near Paris. In a later counteroffensive, more than 1 million American infantrymen advanced against the Germans in France's **Argonne Forest**. Now faced with an invasion of their own country, German military leaders sought an armistice. On **November 11, 1918**, peace was declared, but most of the issues that had provoked the war stubbornly remained in place. In hindsight, a combination of weariness and American intervention had turned the tide.

With the Allied victory, Wilson the moral idealist had a vision for the future, which he had previously outlined in a speech before Congress on January 8, 1918, in **Fourteen Points**. Some of Wilson's points were specific proposals for the creation of new nations in the disputed territories of Central Europe. Others, however, were lofty objectives for free trade, a call for open rather than secret agreements between nations, and another for self-determination for all people. The most controversial of Wilson's Fourteen Points proved to be a proposal to establish a **League of Nations**, an international body to resolve disputes between member nations peacefully in the hope of preventing future wars. Wilson was intimately involved in the negotiations in Paris, but the treaty that emerged was difficult to explain to the American people. The **Treaty of Versailles** was a complex document incorporating many of the Fourteen Points. Wilson was especially proud of the proposed League, which he saw as the key to avoiding war in the future.

Back in the United States, however, isolationist Republican opponents of Wilson succeeded in blocking Senate approval of the Treaty of Versailles, which included provisions for the League of Nations. The president misjudged the political resistance back home, leading some commentators to speculate that he should have included a few Republican leaders in his triumphant peacemaking mission to Europe. Historians generally fault Wilson as well for being unwilling to accept compromises offered by the senators. He overestimated his ability to carry the day because of the rightness of his cause. It became his biggest failure. Many senators felt the treaty embroiled the United States in Europe's problems in a manner that could lead to another world war. After an exhausting nationwide campaign in defiance of doctors' orders, Wilson failed to mobilize public opinion and the Senate refused to ratify the treaty to join the League by the required two-thirds vote. In the process, the tired and stubborn president suffered a severe stroke, leaving him an invalid for the few remaining years of his life.

❖ Chapter Review

Identify

the Grange

cooperatives

Munn v. *Illinois*

alliances

Colored Farmers Alliance

People's Party

Populists

Mary Elizabeth Lease

Tom Watson

Panic of 1893

currency issue

Gold Bugs

Silverites

election of 1896

William Jennings Bryan

William McKinley

Cross of Gold Speech

Progressive Era

political machines

Tammany Hall

boss

muckrakers

The Jungle

Meat Inspection Act

Hull House

Social Gospel

prohibitionism

Woman's Suffrage Movement

Susan B. Anthony

Elizabeth Cady Stanton

scientific management

Galveston Plan

city manager

Wisconsin Idea

Robert "Fighting Bob" La Follette

initiative

referendum

recall

direct election of U.S. senators

trust busting

Square Deal

Panama Canal

Roosevelt Corollary

William Howard Taft

Progressive (or Bull Moose) Party

New Nationalism

Woodrow Wilson

New Freedom

Federal Reserve System

graduated income tax

Central Powers

Allied Powers

U-boats

Lusitania

"He kept us out of war."

unrestricted submarine warfare

Zimmerman telegram

war of attrition

trench warfare

Espionage and Sabotage Acts

John J. Pershing

Château-Thierry

Argonne Forest

November 11, 1918

Fourteen Points

League of Nations

Treaty of Versailles

Short Paragraph

1. What are some similarities and differences between Populism and Progressivism?

2. Why did the United States get involved in World War I?

3. Compare the presidencies of Theodore Roosevelt and Woodrow Wilson.

CHAPTER

12

Boom, Bust, and the New Deal

The period immediately following World War I marks the end of the Progressive Era. By 1920, Americans, tired of war, Wilsonian idealism, and world politics, craved a **return to normalcy**. But, as they would soon learn, World War I had wrought significant changes in American society. Meantime, the situation in Europe remained far from stable. The **Russian Revolution** of 1917 had eventually produced a communist regime in Russia under the Bolsheviks, led by V. I. Lenin. The new nation called itself the Union of Soviet Socialist Republics (USSR), with a mission to establish a classless society. Many now began to see communism as the wave of the future, particularly desperate, war-ravaged Europeans and a number of American intellectuals. To complicate matters, strikes and riots abounded in the United States, and acts of terrorism by radicals (including several bombing incidents) prompted the nation's first **Red Scare**. During the final days of the Wilson administration, Attorney General A. Mitchell Palmer unleashed a fury of federal agents to search people's homes without warrants, read their mail, and closely monitor suspected radicals and subversives. The so-called **Palmer Raids** eventually ceased as the level and incidents of violence subsided, but the perceived threat of the spread of communism became a theme that influenced U.S. policy, both foreign and domestic, for most of the rest of the twentieth century.

The Jazz Age

During what became known as the **Roaring Twenties**, many Americans saw the world turn upside down. Postwar prosperity in the urban areas unleashed a number of long-suppressed impulses. One of the most interesting changes this effected was in women's behavior. Gradually, the **flapper** replaced the **Victorian woman** as the American feminine ideal. The Victorian Woman (the Victorian age corresponds to the reign of Queen Victoria of England) had been the model of middle-class womanhood for several generations. Stylized portraits, family photographs, and newspaper advertisements of the age typically reveal a woman with long hair neatly pinned under a gigantic hat. She endured a tightly cinched waist and a stiff corset in order to make her bosom and hips appear larger. Her dress reached all the way to the floor. The 1920s flapper, on the other hand, wore a dangerously short, sack-like dress, often adorned with long beads that twirled as she brazenly danced modern steps such as the Charleston. The flapper generally tried to appear as flat-chested as possible, and she wore no corset. Her hair was cut short (**F. Scott Fitzgerald**, the best-known writer of the Jazz Age, explores a young woman's feeling of exhilaration in his short story "Bernice Bobs Her Hair"). Moreover, the flapper danced, smoked, and drank—just like the guys! It was positively shocking—and fun. Even more shocking to some was the founding by **Margaret Sanger** of the American Birth Control League, which opened a free clinic to educate women about contraception and family planning.

During the first two decades of the twentieth century, the prohibition movement had been gaining support, with increasing numbers of so-called Dry candidates reaching Congress. Finally, in January 1919, the sale, manufacture, and transport of alcohol were outlawed after the ratification of the **Eighteenth Amendment**. But despite the nationwide prohibition during the 1920s, one could always find a way to get booze, illegally that is, especially in the cities. Indeed, **gangsters** such as Al Capone of Chicago became rich and powerful by providing liquor to a thirsty public. The spree of organized crime that ensued was undoubtedly helped by the automobile, useful for quick getaways, as well as by the devastatingly effective Thompson submachine gun, a technology developed during World War I. Historians have pointed out that per capita drinking did indeed decline during the so-called noble experiment of prohibition, but there is little doubt that lawlessness and corruption was the price of sobriety. In this fast-paced, seemingly free-and-easy climate, parents especially worried that they were losing control of their children. Kids were smoking, drinking, driving automobiles (the number of mass-produced cars rose from 8 million to 23 million during the 1920s), attending huge high schools far from home, and sneaking out to "petting parties" at night. Older folks yearned for simpler times.

It is only natural, therefore, that the 1920s witnessed a resurgence of religious **fundamentalism**. Old time religion, with its literal chapter-and-verse interpretation of Scripture, gave a renewed comfort to many, particularly those in rural areas. Fundamentalists felt threatened by the teaching of Darwin's theory of evolution in the public schools, a practice that spread as evolutionary theory became more accepted within the scientific community. Indeed, some states began to outlaw its teaching altogether. One such state was Tennessee, where the stage was set for one of the most famous trials in American history: the **Scopes "Monkey" Trial** of 1925. Teacher and football coach John T. Scopes accepted an offer from the American Civil Liberties Union (ACLU) to conspicuously violate the law to create a test case for the courts. Dayton, Tennessee, became the site for a frenzied gathering of evangelists, curiosity seekers, journalists, hot dog venders, and stuffed-monkey salesmen (the toys signifying the theorized evolution of man from ape). Dayton civic leaders fully supported the idea of a trial as a means to put their town on the map and, they hoped, attract tourists. They got their wish. Celebrated liberal trial lawyer **Clarence Darrow** agreed to defend Scopes, while none other than **William Jennings Bryan**—the three-time presidential hopeful—appeared for the prosecution, as lead counsel and also as an expert witness on the Bible. The significance of this trial is not in its unremarkable verdict (Scopes was convicted and fined $100, but the case was overturned later on a technicality), but in what it symbolized. Americans listening to the proceedings on the radio or following along in the newspapers often took sides, revealing deep divisions between modern, sophisticated urban dwellers and rural fundamentalists.

Fear of change was probably also responsible for a resurgence in the **Ku Klux Klan**, not only in the South but in many areas of the North as well. Racism and fear of the alien menace of immigration had always been present in America, but the sight of hooded Klansmen marching in Washington, D.C., or holding a rally in Indiana was deeply disturbing—and not just to African Americans, the traditional targets of the Klan's intimidation and violence.

Catholics and Jews were also cited in Klan speeches and pamphlets as the cause of the moral deterioration of the real America, meaning an America governed by and for white Protestants.

On the issue of race, perceptive Americans could not help noticing what commentators called the emergence of the **New Negro**. The most significant factor in this change was the massive migration of blacks from southern farms to cities in the North. World War I had started the trend as jobs were left vacant by departing soldiers. From 1920 to 1930, the South lost 8 percent of its black population, as people tried to escape segregation and poverty by getting jobs in cities such as Chicago and New York. Conditions were not always ideal in the new locations, but a sense of freedom and hope prevailed during these years. In the East, a literary and cultural movement called the **Harlem Renaissance** witnessed the rise of black artists, journalists, and poets such as **Langston Hughes**. Musically, **jazz**, with its roots in rural black America, flourished in the cities. With its individualistic improvisation and seeming lack of rules, jazz became a uniquely American sound, one celebrated all over the world. Unfortunately, black artists such as trumpeter Louis Armstrong, bandleader Duke Ellington, and blues singer Bessie Smith were often treated better in Europe than in their native America, where racism frequently dictated that these talented musicians could not even stay in the hotels at which they were performing.

Politically the National Association for the Advancement of Colored People (**NAACP**), founded in 1910 by white progressives and the black scholar-publisher **W. E. B. Du Bois**, made slow but real gains during the 1920s. While the **separate but equal** doctrine upheld by the U.S. Supreme Court still protected segregation (or **Jim Crow**) laws, the NAACP drew the nation's attention to lynching (thirty blacks were lynched in 1926 alone) and succeeded in passing the first federal antilynching law in the House of Representatives. While southern senators filibustered the bill to death, the heightened awareness contributed to a decline in lynching and mob violence against blacks. America was not yet ready to discuss racial equality under the law, but these early efforts to defend the civil rights of African Americans were a harbinger of things to come.

The first radio commercial aired in 1922, and soon almost all Americans with electric power were tuned in. Before the end of the 1920s, silent films became "talkies," the first of which was appropriately titled *The Jazz Singer*. These and other developments allowed Americans to connect with one another in ways never dreamed of before. In this media-rich environment, celebrities became national figures. Undoubtedly the most celebrated hero of the period (some would say any period) was **Charles A. Lindbergh**, a shy aviator who flew the first solo flight across the Atlantic ocean in 1927. Significantly, **Amelia Earhart** later became the first woman to do the same.

Three Republican Presidents: Harding, Coolidge, and Hoover

Warren G. Harding was elected President in 1920 promising normalcy. Americans liked how the Republican from Ohio described himself as "just a plain fellow," so unlike the intellectual and moralistic Wilson. Progressivism was clearly over as a public mood, though many of its reforms (such as women's suffrage) became commonplace. Harding, who enjoyed politics until he got to the White House, was soon overwhelmed, admitting to a friend, "I don't think I'm big enough for the job." To the extent that Harding had a philosophy, it coincided naturally with the probusiness Republicanism for which the 1920s are noted. Harding's administration was also plagued by corruption, most notably the **Teapot Dome scandal**, which involved an oil deposit on federal land. Harding's crooked appointees, known as the **Ohio Gang**, used the opportunity to enrich themselves at public expense. Before the scandal broke completely, however, Harding died of a heart attack in 1923. At his death he was still enormously popular, and Americans mourned Harding as deeply as they had Lincoln.

With Harding's death, the presidency passed to **Calvin Coolidge**, who was soundly elected in his own right in 1924. A quiet New Englander, Coolidge wore a pinched expression that prompted one observer to quip that he must have been "weaned on a pickle." The unflamboyant chief executive reportedly slept twelve hours a day, not including an afternoon nap. In other times, Silent Cal, might have been downright unpopular, but in the 1920s Americans responded to such a man with affection. In any event, more than any other President since the Gilded Age, Coolidge believed that "the business of America is business." Government, particularly the president, should stay out of the way and let free enterprise flourish. Sure enough, the boom years were on, and those who complained that Americans were taking too many financial risks were treated as cranks. Characteristically, Coolidge decided not to run again in 1928, returning to Vermont to write a newspaper column titled, "Thinking Things Over with Calvin Coolidge."

The economic boom was still going strong when the Republican **Herbert Hoover** was chosen as President in the election of 1928. Raised a Quaker in rural Iowa, Hoover became a millionaire by the age of forty as an engineer. After World War I, he put his engineer's mind to good use by organizing relief efforts in Europe, and he served with distinction in the cabinets of Harding and Coolidge. Unlike his immediate predecessors, Hoover was a moderate progressive who believed in the good use of government. Unfortunately for his reputation, however, the name "Hoover" will always be associated with the Great Depression, which began just a few months after he took office. Indeed, the shantytowns of the homeless were bitterly referred to as **Hoovervilles** all across America. Many of Hoover's attempts at dealing with the depression foreshadowed government programs that would be popularized later, such as the Reconstruction Finance Corporation, public works, and aid to agriculture. But it was too little, too late for Hoover, as he was swept from the White House in 1932.

The Great Depression

Historians and economists still debate the causes of the **Great Depression**, which lasted through the 1930s and up to the start of World War II. Americans had experienced downturns in the economy before, such as the Panics of 1873 and 1893, and many believed such episodes were a normal part of the business cycle. It might also be noted that America had been in a farm depression since 1921, but an increasingly urban America had failed to notice. Low crop prices had created deplorable conditions, particularly among migrant workers in the Southwest. In San Antonio, Texas, for instance, Mexican Americans had among the highest rates of death from tuberculosis (a disease that goes hand-in-hand with poverty) in the entire nation. Such statistics never made the newspapers, as the stock market continued to grab the headlines.

As a national and worldwide phenomenon, the Great Depression proved far longer and deeper than previous panics. Unemployment in the United States rose to 25 percent, 9,000 banks failed or were closed down, and the value of farm products declined by half. In diagnosing the Great Depression's cause, most scholars today point to the overheated economy during the boom times of the 1920s, coupled with the government's lack of will to step in as soon as the bottom dropped out. Also, the **Hawley-Smoot Tariff** of 1930, legislation intended to stimulate the economy by taxing imports, only made things worse by raising prices beyond the reach of consumers. It must be remembered, however, that the Great Depression was a global phenomenon, not an incident subject to a quick fix by the U.S. government.

The **Stock Market Crash of 1929** did not cause the Great Depression, but it certainly revealed the underlying economy as very shaky. During the 1920s the stock market had been bullish (with rising share prices) beyond anyone's wildest dreams. People who had never before considered investing in stocks did so enthusiastically, often buying shares **on the margin** with credit. Brokers seduced buyers with outlandish advertisements, persuading many people to invest their life savings. In hindsight, the collapse of the Florida Real Estate Boom in 1926 should have dampened the speculative mania, but investors simply diverted their money into stocks. When **Black Tuesday** occurred on October 29, 1929, the worst single day in market history up to that date, thousands of people were ruined. Some committed suicide.

One underlying cause of the Great Depression was the simple fact that incomes were poorly distributed: wages were low in comparison to corporate profits, and one-third of the nation's personal income was going to only 5 percent of the population. It must be remembered also that at the time there were few regulations on the way business was conducted. For instance, one's life savings, presumably stored safely in a bank, could disappear forever in a matter of minutes. Indeed, one of the most fearful scenes in America during the early days of the depression was the sight of **a run** on a bank, in which people lined up to withdraw their money—money that might no longer be there.

Soup kitchens, bread lines, Hoovervilles, and hobos riding freight trains aimlessly around the country were just a few of the prominent scenes in America during the 1930s. *Brother Can You Spare a Dime?* was a poignant song of the period. Families were broken up, as children were sent to live with more fortunate relatives or put into orphanages. Strong and proud men who had worked hard all their lives stood around idly staring at closed factory gates. Women told neighbors their husbands were away on business when in reality they were riding the rails or in a hobo camp.

On the farm, a severe drought in the early 1930s created the **Dust Bowl** in the heartland, the dust getting so thick that one looking out the kitchen window could not see the back-yard fence. Some farmers pulled up stakes and headed west along Route 66 to California in the hope of finding work. John Steinbeck's novel *The Grapes of Wrath* chronicles the journey by a family of *Okies* (the derisive term for migrants from Oklahoma) to the West Coast, where they were greeted by cruel bosses and violence at the hands of local residents. In the entire history of the United States, there is only one brief period during which more people left the country than entered it—the early 1930s. Some went to the Soviet Union, which seemed to be the only place in the world where jobs were guaranteed. To many observers, the United States stood on the brink of revolution.

In this charged atmosphere the **election of 1932** was shaping up as one of the most significant in U.S. history. Herbert Hoover was running for re-election, and there were signs of possible recovery as Republicans predicted prosperity just around the corner. Unfortunately for Hoover, such predictions turned into grim jokes as the depression continued relentlessly, demonstrating to all that this was not just another normal downturn in the business cycle. To make matters worse, in the spring a **Bonus Army** marched on Washington. This crowd, composed mostly of WWI veterans seeking a cash bonus promised by Congress in 1924, quickly grew to more than 15,000 desperate people camped out near the Capitol. When the crowd began to resemble a dangerous mob, the secretary of war directed the U.S. Army to evict them. There was one fatality from the use of tear gas—an infant born in the shanties. A bitter public blamed Hoover.

Democrat **Franklin Delano Roosevelt** (a distant cousin and admirer of the Republican Theodore Roosevelt) was swept into office in 1932 along with a huge majority of his party in Congress. Affable, charismatic, and inspirational, FDR previously had impressed many as a progressive governor of New York and with his courageous bout with polio as an adult—a disease that permanently denied him the use of his legs. A hero for the times, Roosevelt would be elected to four terms as President, violating the two-term tradition started by George Washington. For an entire generation, millions would look upon FDR as a second father, and his wife, **Eleanor**, as a mother figure. Whatever else one can say about Franklin Roosevelt (and his critics are numerous), most agree that he was the most important and influential president of the twentieth century.

The New Deal

FDR took office with only a vague notion of what to do about the Great Depression. He simply knew that the people wanted him to do something. After stating in his inaugural address that, "the only thing we have to fear is fear itself," he declared, "This nation asks for action, and action now!" Roosevelt's sweeping legislative package, the **New Deal**, is best described as pragmatic trial and error. FDR was not an intellectual. He did set out, however, to surround himself with the best minds in the country, and soon his advisors, including economists, professors, and experts in various fields, were labeled the **Brain Trust**.

One of Roosevelt's first goals was to restore Americans' faith in banks. If people remained afraid to deposit their money in banks, funds would not be available for loans to rebuild the economy. Declaring a four-day **Bank Holiday**, Congress responded quickly with rules for troubled banks to reopen under sound management. One of FDR's great skills was in communicating with the average American, using the medium of radio with great skill to hold **fireside chats** with the public. In these addresses he assured the audience at home that their money would be safe in the restructured banks. Later, Congress created the Federal Deposit Insurance Corporation (**FDIC**) to insure bank deposits. This agency performs the same duty today.

Much of the New Deal involved the creation and maintenance of a confusing **alphabet soup** of federal agencies. Congress willingly gave FDR what he wanted during the **first 100 days** of his term in 1933, a time widely regarded as the most intense period of Congressional action in history. Soon the flurry of activity in Washington had a psychological effect as well, as Americans began to think of the government more in national terms, as opposed to state and local.

Before long, a strange assortment of abbreviations dotted the front pages of the nation's newspapers. The Civilian Conservation Corps (**CCC**) was created to provide useful jobs for young men in national parks and forests. Another jobs program, the Works Progress Administration (**WPA**), built bridges, roads, airports, and schools, many of which are still standing. The WPA (critics tagged it "We Poke Along") also employed artists, writers, and actors to use their talents in the public sector. The Agricultural Adjustment Administration (**AAA**) began an allotment of crop commodities to reduce crop surpluses and therefore raise prices. Most controversially in a time of widespread hunger, some crops were plowed under to take them out of the market. The Tennessee Valley Authority (**TVA**) was created to provide hydroelectric power and flood control in the South, which was by far the most impoverished region of the country. The National Recovery Administration (**NRA**) attempted to enlist businesses to subscribe to fair codes of wages and working standards. This particular experiment largely failed, but a common sight during the 1930s was a blue eagle sticker on storefronts proclaiming, "We Do Our Part." The depression continued, but people sensed improvement. Perhaps the program with the most lasting significance was a modest pension plan for the elderly called **Social Security**. Where did the money come from for these programs? Largely through deficit spending, the expenditure of public funds raised by borrowing, instead of taxation. Modern economists said creating the deficit was necessary to prime the pump to get things going again.

Not everyone liked the New Deal (business and powerful newspapers were its perennial enemies), but FDR was re-elected in 1936 by a landslide. The so-called **Second New Deal**, which commenced in 1937, was less stunning than the first, but equally controversial. Naturally, conservatives disliked what FDR was trying to do. What is sometimes forgotten, however, is that many Americans thought he was not going far enough. Chief among these critics was the Louisiana governor and senator **Huey P. Long**, the "Kingfish," whose motto was "Every Man a King." Long devised a program called Share Our Wealth, which would confiscate the surplus wealth of the rich to establish homesteads and guarantee annual wages for the poor. Although Long was assassinated in 1935 by a mentally unstable man, FDR and his advisors were well aware that programs more radical than the New Deal were appealing to millions of poor Americans. Perhaps because of Long and other critics, Roosevelt began to attack big business and openly support organized labor.

One of the New Deal's chief obstacles was the U.S. Supreme Court, which struck down several New Deal measures as unconstitutional. Many of the justices on the Court had been appointed during the Gilded Age and were unyielding in their laissez-faire interpretation of the powers of Congress to regulate the economy. In a bold move, FDR devised the so-called **court-packing plan** in 1937, which would allow a President to appoint a new justice for each one over the age of seventy. Had Congress approved the plan, the number of Supreme Court justices would have risen from nine to fifteen, giving FDR (he hoped) a majority of New Deal supporters on the bench. Perhaps because many democracies in Europe were transforming into dictatorships during this time (and the Court began upholding a good deal of New Deal legislation anyway), Congress refused to adopt the court-packing plan, delivering FDR one of his most significant defeats. Roosevelt was also unsuccessful in the attempted purge of Congress in the elections of 1938, in which he would have liked to replace southern conservative Democrats with more liberal New Dealers.

Throughout his presidency FDR's most important ally was his wife Eleanor. She became the President's eyes, ears, and legs, traveling the country to meet the people, going into coal mines and factories, speaking frequently in public, and writing in the newspapers about the problems facing America during the depression. Many times she urged her husband to take actions he might not otherwise have taken. In one memorable 1939 episode, the First Lady quit her membership in the Daughters of the American Revolution to protest their refusal to allow black opera star **Marian Anderson** to perform at Constitution Hall in Washington. Because of politics in the South and elsewhere, the New Deal did not accomplish much for blacks. Segregation still ruled in one form or another almost everywhere. But the reverence for Eleanor Roosevelt and the stands she took showed the potential for change.

The New Deal did not end the Great Depression. It would take World War II to do that. Nevertheless, the era of Big Government was here to stay. Many programs born in the 1930s, most notably Social Security, have become so established in the modern American mind that few politicians of either party dare openly criticize them. Social problems are thought of as national problems now, unlike before the rise of FDR. And political commentators for several decades have referred to the New Deal Coalition of Democrats, consisting of the solid South, urban areas, organized labor, and liberal reformers.

✷ Chapter Review

Identify

return to normalcy	Roaring Twenties
Russian Revolution	flapper
Red Scare	Victorian woman
Palmer Raids	F. Scott Fitzgerald

Margaret Sanger

Eighteenth Amendment

gangsters

fundamentalism

Scopes "Monkey" Trial

Clarence Darrow

William Jennings Bryan

Ku Klux Klan

New Negro

Harlem Renaissance

Langston Hughes

jazz

NAACP

W. E. B. Du Bois

separate but equal

Jim Crow

Charles A. Lindbergh

Amelia Earhart

Teapot Dome scandal

Ohio Gang

Calvin Coolidge

Herbert Hoover

Hoovervilles

Great Depression

Hawley-Smoot Tariff

Stock Market Crash of 1929

on the margin

Black Tuesday

a run

Dust Bowl

election of 1932

Bonus Army

Franklin Delano Roosevelt

Eleanor Roosevelt

New Deal

Brain Trust

Bank Holiday

fireside chats

FDIC

alphabet soup

first 100 days

CCC

WPA

AAA

TVA

NRA

Social Security

Second New Deal

Huey P. Long

court-packing plan

Marian Anderson

Short Paragraph

1. What made the Roaring Twenties distinct?

2. What made the Great Depression so severe?

3. How did the New Deal address the Great Depression?

4. Why is Franklin Roosevelt regarded as such an important president?

13

World War II and the Origins of the Cold War

❖

After President Woodrow Wilson failed to get the Treaty of Versailles ratified by the Senate following World War I, the United States retreated into **isolationism** through most of the 1920s and 1930s. Most important, the United States refused to participate in the League of Nations, which Wilson had hoped would usher in a new era of peaceful resolution of disputes. The victorious European powers insisted on punishment in the form of financial **reparations** from the defeated Germany—a nation already reeling financially. It was by all accounts a disastrous situation, with Britain and France resenting U.S. efforts to collect $10 billion in war loans to the Allies. Germany sank into chaos. Unemployment, severe inflation, strikes, and the rising tide of communism alarmed many middle-class Germans, who began to see the anticommunist National Socialist Party (**Nazis**)—an upstart working-class group with a thuggish reputation—in a different light. After the Nazi Party became the second most popular party in Germany, **Adolf Hitler**—a previously obscure rabble-rouser—was invited to take the post of Chancellor. Germany would rise again as the **Third Reich**, Hitler promised, and unite all Germanic peoples. Hitler also capitalized on latent fears and suspicion of Jews, who were seen by the Nazis as dominating the financial markets.

Germany was not alone in moving toward dictatorship during the 1930s. In Italy, the **fascists** had become powerful under the charismatic **Benito Mussolini**. Fascism became the principal movement opposing radicalism, especially communism. Nonetheless, nazism and fascism shared many characteristics and soon blended in the public mind. Both movements can be seen as ultraconservative, antidemocratic, highly nationalistic, and expansionist. The **Spanish Civil War** in 1936 similarly brought a fascist regime to power in Spain as loyalist republican forces were defeated by troops led by **Francisco Franco**, who quickly assumed the role of dictator. On the other side of the world, the **Japanese Empire** fell into the hands of military warlords, men who oversaw Japan's brutal invasion and subjugation of much of the rest of Asia, especially China. But the world's democracies, including the United States, were in no mood to resist these disturbing trends.

The Road to Pearl Harbor

Under Hitler's influence Germany had reinvigorated its military in violation of the Treaty of Versailles. With Hitler firmly in control of a newly rearmed Germany, a chain of events began that was to have tragic consequences. In 1936, Germany reoccupied the **Rhineland**, a German-speaking region taken away from it by the Treaty of Versailles. As the world watched closely, England and France took no action against Germany in the hope that Hitler would now be satisfied. In 1938, Germany forced Austria into the *Anschluss* (union) with it, and moved into the **Sudetenland** region of Czechoslovakia. Both areas were Germanic in culture, which fortified Hitler's argument that they all belonged together under one Germany. In the meantime, a conference had been held at Munich, where the leaders of England and France adopted a policy of **appeasement** toward the German dictator, calculating once again that Hitler would now be contented with his newly regained territory and halt his expansionist designs. For generations after the fateful meeting, the very word *Munich* symbolized this misguided strategy, placing a burden on future leaders never to engage in appeasing a potential enemy. The last straw was Hitler's **invasion of Poland** in September 1939, after which England and France at last (and as promised) declared war on Germany. World War II had officially begun in Europe.

Franklin Delano Roosevelt, at the time of his unprecedented election to a third term as President in 1940, was deeply concerned about Hitler's actions, and the American formed a close relationship with the new British Prime Minister, **Winston Churchill**. The American public, however, remained determined this time not to get involved in Europe's conflict, and the national mood prevented FDR from officially taking sides. Indeed, in the

1930s Congress passed a number of **Neutrality Acts** to enforce this isolationist attitude. American isolationism reached its peak just as Hitler's troops were seizing new territory, and soon the public felt justified as stalemate appeared to slow things down in Europe for a time. Some Americans now hailed the conflict in Europe as the **Phony War**. Isolationists began to organize, most notably in the **America First Committee**, which included many celebrated figures such as aviator-hero Charles Lindbergh. America First argued that, while Hitler's conquests were alarming, it was not in the national interest of the United States to get involved in Europe's problems.

The tide finally began to turn as Hitler stepped up his aggression against America's traditional allies. FDR was pleased as Americans took a sympathetic interest in the desperate **Battle of Britain** in 1940, wherein German war planes mercilessly bombed the British Isles for weeks on end. The first to die in the Battle of Britain were the courageous women firing anti-aircraft artillery at the powerful German air force, the **Luftwaffe**. Radios across the United States tuned in to American journalist Edward R. Murrow's broadcasts ("This . . . is London," he would intone grimly with the sound of sirens and falling bombs in the background). Churchill's heroic voice ("We shall never surrender") also inspired Americans and persuaded many to alter their feelings toward involvement. British courage and resolve ultimately convinced Hitler to abandon the air attack and concentrate instead on intensifying Germany's campaign of submarine war in the Atlantic. A desperately concerned Roosevelt was finally able to help Britain by convincing Congress to pass the **Lend Lease Act**, which bypassed the Neutrality Laws to help "any country whose defense the President deems vital to the defense of the United States." FDR clearly made it appear that the $7 million appropriation was simply a loan to a neighbor, comparing it to innocently loaning someone a garden hose to put out a fire. But the Lend Lease program ensured Britain access to American war materials. The United States was clearly taking sides, whether it admitted it or not.

Roosevelt was increasingly concerned as well about Japanese aggression in Asia. Furthermore, Japan had signed a **Tripartite Pact** with Germany and Italy, with each signatory pledging to declare war on any nation that attacked any of the three. In response to Japan's announcement establishing a protectorate in French Indochina, Roosevelt froze all Japanese assets in the United States and restricted oil exports to the island empire, which in turn drove Japan to attack oil-rich British and Dutch colonies in Southeast Asia. At this point Roosevelt sent U.S. Army General **Douglas MacArthur** to the Philippines as commander of American forces in the Far East. Shortly thereafter Japan's government was completely absorbed by fanatical military warlords under Premier **Hideki Tojo**. Apparently they were not even afraid to strike at the United States. Theirs was a miscalculation that changed the world.

On Sunday morning, **December 7, 1941**, Japanese airplanes attacked **Pearl Harbor** in Hawaii, destroying much of the American Pacific fleet and killing over 2,000 armed personnel and civilians. American military intelligence had broken the Japanese code, and knew an attack was imminent; they just didn't know *where*. Calling December 7 a day that will "live in infamy," President Roosevelt asked Congress for a declaration of war the next day, which was approved almost unanimously. On December 11, Germany and Italy declared war on the United States. Congress reciprocated shortly thereafter. American isolationism was over.

The War in Europe

The principal **Allies** in World War II consisted of the United States under Roosevelt, Great Britain under Churchill, and the Soviet Union under Josef Stalin, who had come to power there in the 1930s. FDR, Churchill, and Stalin constituted what was called the **Big Three** by the popular media. France by this time had been occupied by Nazi troops. A pro-Nazi French government was established in Southern France at Vichy, while a government-in-exile was headed by **Charles DeGaulle** commanding the so-called **Free French** in coordinating resistance. The German *blitzkrieg* or lightning war—an effective use of combined air and ground forces featuring the use of tanks—had been extremely successful in Germany's rapid invasion and occupation of Poland, France, Denmark, Norway, Belgium, and the Netherlands. The desperate task of the Big Three was to roll back German and Italian forces, but they needed an effective strategy. Mindful of the murderous trench warfare of World War I, the Allies decided against immediately invading the European continent across the English Channel, in favor of hitting what Churchill called the "soft underbelly" of Europe. This meant striking from the south. **North Africa** became the site of the first joint effort by American and British forces, who successfully united in May of 1943 to push back Germany's *Afrika Korps* and leaving the entire African continent under Allied control. The North Africa campaign was noted for vicious

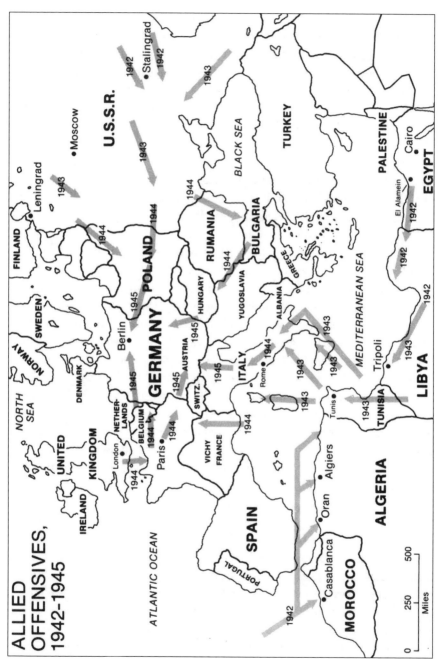

ALLIED OFFENSIVES, 1942–1945

North African and European Campaigns

tank warfare and the union of two colorful personalities: U.S. Major General **George S. Patton, Jr.**, and British Field Marshall **Bernard Montgomery**. Politically, FDR and Churchill felt this joint effort was necessary to convince Stalin of their commitment, since the Soviet Red Army was enduring horrendous casualties fighting Germany alone on Europe's Eastern Front.

Next, Patton's forces landed on Sicily and, after heavy fighting, captured the critical city of **Palermo**. The Italian army was quickly disintegrating, but Germany poured reinforcements into the Italian Peninsula. As the Allies advanced up the boot of Italy, bloody fighting in miserable conditions made Italian place-names such as **Salerno, Anzio,** and **Monte Cassino** the stuff of headlines all over Europe and America. American forces finally took Rome in June 1944. Eventually Mussolini was killed by Italian rebels, his corpse hung upside down in the street for all to see.

While American G.I.s fought their way through Italy, preparations for the ultimate Allied invasion of Europe across the English Channel proceeded. The operation would amass the largest invasion force in human history. Everyone, including Hitler, knew it was coming. The mystery was *when* and *where* the amphibious landing would strike along the hundreds of miles of French coastline. The man in charge of the operation was Supreme Allied Commander **Dwight D. "Ike" Eisenhower**, a plain-spoken Kansan gifted with political and military skill. Ike's job not only involved the logistics of invasion with U.S. troops, but also coordinating the efforts of the British and Free French forces, as well as landing resistance fighters behind enemy lines. The entire effort had to be organized and put into motion without Hitler knowing when or where. A vast armed metropolis gathered in England, as American factories worked twenty-four-hour days to produce landing craft, gliders, parachutes, tanks, ammunition, and artillery shells.

The most likely and favorable spot for the invasion was near Calais, the spot on the French coast that would require the shortest trip across the treacherous waters of the English Channel. Ultimately, Eisenhower and his advisors decided on **Normandy**, calculating that the Germans would be less likely to expect an invasion there. Meanwhile, strategic bombing of German industrial centers by U.S. planes and those of the Royal Air Force attempted to neutralize Nazi manufacturing capacity and reduce German morale. The **Air War** was relentless, but Germany still remained strong at the time of the Allied cross-channel invasion code-named **Operation Overlord**.

After unfavorable weather conditions caused one delay, **D-Day**, June 6, 1944, had arrived. Historian Stephen Ambrose called it the most important single day in the twentieth century. Hours before dawn, 4,000 ships and a force of 150,000 men, including 57,000 Americans, left England's shores headed for Normandy. Eisenhower's German counterpart, Field Marshall **Erwin Rommel**, had left his post to visit his family in Berlin, feeling confident that the Allies would not venture an invasion in foul weather. He was mistaken. Amazingly, the crucial element of surprise worked for the Allies, but the beaches on which they landed were still well fortified. And there were many deadly mistakes, aggravated by treacherous seas that dumped troops ashore at the wrong location. As German machine guns opened fire on the tiny landing craft, casualties on some boats reached 90 percent before the Allied soldiers even reached dry land. Many paratroopers and glider pilots missed their landing zones. Naval bombardment was misdirected frequently. More than a thousand men drowned before hitting the beach to aim their rifles. Seasickness on the small craft was rampant, as frightened soldiers vomited into their helmets. At several key moments it appeared the invasion would fail completely. Eisenhower carried a note in his wallet to read to the press if it did, prepared to take full responsibility. The bloodiest fighting for Americans was at **Omaha Beach**, where bombardment failed to take out German defenders. On June 6 alone, 5,000 Allied troops were killed or wounded at Normandy, but within two weeks a million men were ashore. The climactic battle of World War II was won.

Germany made one last push in the **Battle of the Bulge** (so named because the counteroffensive created a bulge in Allied defenses) in December 1944. In desperate winter fighting, exhausted and freezing American forces refused to surrender and daringly held the German troops back at **Bastogne**, Belgium. Meanwhile, the Allied Air War pounded the interior of Germany, most notably in the firebombing of **Dresden**, which destroyed 75 percent of the city and killed 135,000 people, mostly civilians. In later times, such an episode would cause controversy, but Americans accepted atrocity as the price of winning the horrific war. On April 30, with westward-pushing Soviet forces on the outskirts of Berlin, Hitler committed suicide. Less than two weeks later, the pitiful remnants of the German government surrendered.

The Pacific War and the Nuclear Age

After the attack on Pearl Harbor, General Douglas MacArthur was ordered to abandon the Philippines and go to Australia to take command of Allied Pacific forces. His famous remark upon leaving U.S. and local forces there, "I shall return," became the most inspiring words of the Pacific war. And American troops would need all the inspiration they could get, as Japan gobbled up territory in the region to expand its empire. In April 1942, 75,000 U.S. and Philippine troops finally surrendered after tenacious resistance. The Japanese drove the chained captives over 100 miles in the infamous **Bataan Death March**, during which thousands died or were brutally executed on the route to prison camps.

An early turning point in the Pacific theater was the naval engagement known as the **Battle of the Coral Sea**, which prevented a Japanese invasion of Australia. For the first time in naval history, ships did not fire directly upon each other, since the entire battle was waged by planes launched from aircraft carriers. A new age in warfare had begun. Another crucial American naval victory was the **Battle of Midway**, in which four Japanese aircraft carriers (essential craft for waging battle on the vast seas) were wiped out, greatly reducing the enemy's advantage. An early strategic victory for U.S. Marines and naval forces came in finally capturing the island of **Guadalcanal**, where the Japanese planned to construct an important air base. The Allied strategy in the Pacific necessarily involved **island hopping**. Once an island was secured, the Allies moved north to the next one in a bloody path toward the Japanese home islands. Tarawa, the Marshall Islands, Saipan, and Okinawa all involved daring and costly amphibious assaults by U.S. Marines and naval forces directed by Admiral **Chester Nimitz**. The Battle of Iwo Jima attracted much attention in the newspapers because of the famous photograph of several Marines (including Ira Hayes, a Pima Indian from Arizona) raising the flag on the island's Mount Suribachi. Seven thousand Americans died fighting for the small volcanic island during an intense six-week battle. The taking of Okinawa proved even bloodier.

Now signs of Japanese desperation were everywhere, and American ships could roam freely in the Pacific. MacArthur had finally returned to the Philippines amidst great celebration and relief. The Japanese began to resort to suicide attacks by *kamikaze* (divine wind) pilots who purposely crashed their planes onto the decks of Allied ships, inflicting devastating physical and psychological damage. Washington meanwhile had decoded secret Japanese transmissions, including an internal message from the Emperor to the Premier instructing him to seek peace. American leaders understood all too well that fighting all the way to Tokyo would be terribly costly, as Japanese troops rarely surrendered and had to be rooted out by infantry on tiny

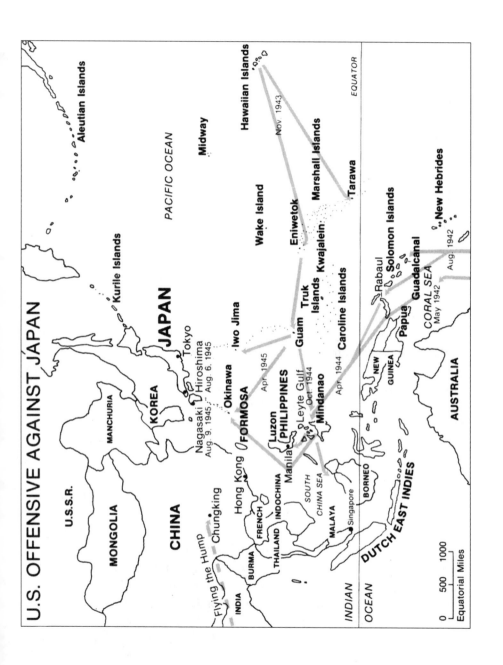

U.S. OFFENSIVE AGAINST JAPAN

U.S.S.R.

MONGOLIA

MANCHURIA

KOREA

CHINA

Chungking

Flying the Hump

Hong Kong

FRENCH INDOCHINA

BURMA

THAILAND

INDIA

MALAYA

Singapore

BORNEO

SOUTH CHINA SEA

DUTCH EAST INDIES

INDIAN OCEAN

JAPAN

Tokyo

Hiroshima
Aug. 6, 1945

Nagasaki
Aug. 9, 1945

Okinawa

Iwo Jima

FORMOSA

Apr. 1945

Luzon

Manila

PHILIPPINES

Mindanao

Leyte Gulf
Oct. 1944

Kurile Islands

Aleutian Islands

Midway

PACIFIC OCEAN

Hawaiian Islands

Nov. 1943

Wake Island

Eniwetok

Guam

Truk

Islands Kwajalein

Caroline Islands

Apr. 1944

Marshall Islands

Tarawa

EQUATOR

Rabaul

NEW
GUINEA

Papua

May 1942

CORAL SEA

Solomon Islands

Guadalcanal

Aug. 1942

New Hebrides

Aug. 1942

AUSTRALIA

0   500   1000
Equatorial Miles

islands stretching hundreds of miles. Such was the situation facing the new American President **Harry S Truman**, a former senator from Missouri who was suddenly thrust into office when Roosevelt died of a massive cerebral hemorrhage in April 1945.

FDR had been like a father to an entire generation of Americans—elected to an amazing fourth term in 1944—and many of them could not imagine anyone else as the chief executive. Indeed, Truman had been selected as FDR's new vice president with no regard to the Missourian's lack of foreign or military policy experience. Although a combat veteran of World War I and an avid reader of history, the new President had only a high school education. Yet it would be Harry Truman's decision whether to use the most formidable and sophisticated weapon ever conceived.

In 1939 physicist **Albert Einstein** sent President Roosevelt a letter alerting him about potentially dangerous German advances in the study of nuclear fission. FDR responded by quietly redirecting military funds into research that grew into the top-secret **Manhattan Project**, at a laboratory compound near Los Alamos, New Mexico. There, scientists led by Dr. **J. Robert Oppenheimer** conducted a test detonation of a nuclear device on July 16, 1945—a blast so powerful it cracked windows 125 miles away. President Truman wrote in his diary, "We have discovered the most terrible bomb in the history of the world." His advisors told him that if the "A-bomb" were used on Japan, the war would be over in a matter of days.

Truman's decision to use the atomic bomb is one of the most debated in American history. In July at the **Potsdam Conference**, the governments of the United States, Great Britain, and the Soviet Union issued a declaration that Japan surrender or face "prompt and utter destruction." Without hearing the Japanese reply to the ultimatum, on August 6 the first atomic bomb was dropped on the Japanese city of **Hiroshima** from a U.S. B-29 bomber named the *Enola Gay* (after the pilot's mother). Hiroshima had been selected as the target due to weather conditions and because it was a military center, but the blast killed from 50,000 to 100,000 people, mostly civilians. Exact figures were not possible to determine because of the magnitude of the bomb's devastation, and many victims took weeks to die a slow, agonizing death from the effects of radiation poisoning. After hearing no clear response from Japan's imperial government, three days later a second nuclear bomb was dropped on the city of **Nagasaki** instantly killing 36,000 people, although final death tolls are now considered about double that. On August 14, Japan's emperor announced surrender. It was formalized to General Douglas MacArthur on September 2 aboard the U.S.S. *Missouri* in Tokyo bay.

The Home Front

Americans have never been more united in a common purpose than they were during World War II. Wartime **rationing** programs to conserve gasoline, rubber, and metal (materials considered vital to the successful prosecution of the war) worked amazingly well in spite of occasional black marketeering. Unions agreed to a **no-strike pledge**, and most work stoppages were of the wildcat variety and did not last long. Perhaps most significant, during the war years the role of women transformed as men left factories and farms for the armed forces. **Rosie the Riveter** became a common sight in advertisements and patriotic literature, as women marched out of the home to take blue-collar manufacturing jobs previously reserved for men. With money of their own, women also began to exercise their new independence, shocking many a husband upon his return. Of course, women had been working in various jobs for years and also serving in all-women military units, but World War II put relations between the sexes on an entirely new scale. Due to family dis-locations, a number of unfortunate developments also occurred—things that did not show up in patriotic newsreels. The rate of juvenile crime rose rapidly. The arrest rate for prostitution (many of the perpetrators teenage girls) also went up, as did reported outbreaks of venereal disease.

After the attack on Pearl Harbor, resentment against Japanese Ameri-cans accelerated, particularly in California, where large numbers of Asians lived. The government, at the national and state levels, eventually ordered over 100,000 Japanese people (whether U.S. citizens or not) into **War Reloca-tion Camps**. Japanese-owned homes and businesses had to be sold hurriedly or abandoned, properties that some white neighbors were all too happy to confiscate. While the detention centers into which Japanese Americans were placed were clean and hardly brutal, they effectively were prisons in which patently innocent people were confined without trial. (A formal apol-ogy from the U.S. government to the surviving internees would not come until 1989.) Despite the internment, Japanese Americans had fought for their country in the Italian Peninsula in the 442nd Regiment, winning more decorations for valor than any other U.S. Army regiment in World War II.

The massive mobilization of the U.S. economy to supply the vast needs of the military during World War II ended the Great Depression, bringing a new prosperity to the American people, as well as considerable unease. Graphic depiction of the aftermath of the use of the atomic bomb had convinced many that war must never happen again if the human race was to survive. But even more disturbing were photographs from Nazi concentration camps, from which emaciated prisoners had been liberated by Allied troops toward the end of the war. It is a point of ongoing controversy exactly how much and when the Roosevelt administration knew about the **Holocaust**, which included the systematic murder by the German state of over 6 million Jews and at least 4 million Poles, communists, Gypsies, homosexuals, and assorted political prisoners. The Final Solution of the Nazi regime became official policy during the war, as labor camps such as **Auschwitz** and **Buchenwald** were converted into factories for mass execution. After the war, U.S. representatives participated in the international proceedings known as the **Nuremburg Trials** in which some Nazi leaders were tried, convicted, and executed for war crimes. At this time, the new state of **Israel** was created, with U.S. help, as a haven for Jews from all over the world. Israel was partitioned out of the ancient land of **Palestine**, aggravating tensions with Arab neighbors that continue to erupt into violence to this day.

The Long Cold War Begins

The **Cold War**, which most assuredly turned hot many times, refers to the almost fifty years of constant tension between the United States and the Soviet Union after World War II. In many ways it began during the war, as Stalin seized territory in Eastern Europe from the Nazis while the U.S. and British forces pushed toward Germany from the west and south. Right before Roosevelt's death, the Big Three met at **Yalta** on the Black Sea, where FDR reluctantly accepted Soviet demands for the new territory. Realistically, he had little choice but to do so, since the Red Army already controlled these regions and the United States still had a war to wage in the Pacific. The Soviets lost 20 million people fighting the Nazis—a far greater sacrifice than any of the other Allies had made, and they were constantly suspicious of western intentions. By the war's conclusion, the Soviets occupied Poland, Romania, Czechoslovakia, Hungary, the eastern half of Germany, and a host of other **satellite nations**. President Truman was concerned but remained

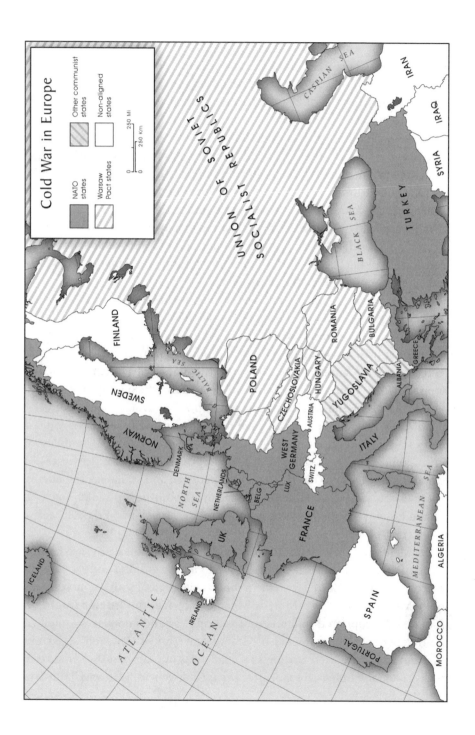

Cold War in Europe

NATO states

Warsaw Pact states

Other communist states

Non-aligned states

0   250 Mi
0   250 Km

optimistic that differences between the United States and the Soviet Union, nations that had emerged from the war as superpowers, could be worked out peacefully. The creation of the **United Nations** in 1945, which was (unlike the earlier League of Nations) enthusiastically endorsed by Congress, seemed to signal some promise.

Nonetheless, both the United States and the Soviet Union distrusted each other for a host of reasons. The United States had been hostile toward communism since the Bolshevik Revolution in 1917, refusing to recognize the new regime until the 1930s. And Stalin did not think twice about the use of deception, such as in his promise of democratic elections in the newly seized territories—a pledge that would immediately prove empty. One early critic of Soviet behavior was Winston Churchill, who spoke eloquently of an **iron curtain** in Europe, behind which a new tyranny was emerging that was every bit as oppressive as that of the Nazis.

Now Truman was in the hot seat. Some, including General George S. Patton, advocated war with the Soviets while they were still weak from fighting Germany. But America was in no mood for another war. Others trusted Stalin, or at least did not feel that the communists provided a threat to U.S. security. In 1946 an expert on Russia in the State Department, **George F. Kennan**, wrote a long memo, followed by a 1947 article published anonymously (as "X") in the periodical *Foreign Affairs*. The article spelled out what had already become policy, but gave it a name: **containment**. The United States had no choice but to accept the current level of Soviet domination, but it could contain the spread of Soviet control elsewhere. Advocates of containment believed further that, with patience and vigilance, the enemy would eventually weaken due to communism's built-in contradictions. The remainder of the Cold War is best understood as based upon the U.S. strategy of containment.

Incidents in Greece and Turkey provided an early test. By 1947 communist-led factions in both countries were gaining ground, and the Soviets clearly wished to acquire territory in this crucial region, with its open access to the Mediterranean Sea. In what became known as the **Truman Doctrine**, Congress appropriated millions in economic aid and supplies to stabilize the independent governments of Greece and Turkey. An even larger aid program to war-ravaged Europe as a whole was put forward the same year; it was called the **Marshall Plan**, after the former general who was Truman's secretary of state. Ingeniously, under the Marshall Plan the United States offered aid to the Soviets as well as other European nations to rebuild their economies, but the Russians, deeply suspicious, turned down Washington's offer. The Marshall Plan cost the United States billions of dollars, but this gesture helped Western Europe recover and remain democratic. Economic stability and prosperity proved a formidable enemy of communism, and much less expensive to maintain than waging war. Getting Congress to reject a retreat to isolationism on the heels of an especially brutal war was a significant political achievement by President Truman.

Perhaps the most visible symbol of the Cold War was Berlin, a divided city situated well within Soviet-held eastern Germany. In the uneasy atmosphere after the Nazi surrender, the nation of Germany was partitioned by the Allies. East Germany was occupied and controlled by the USSR. The crucial city of Berlin was also split in two. In 1948 the Soviets stopped all traffic into West Berlin, the free half of the city, isolating it from other democracies. After considering a variety of alternatives, Truman chose what seemed to many a foolhardy risk, the **Berlin Airlift**. For almost a year, Allied planes flew in supplies, providing 1.5 million tons of coal, food, and other necessities to the citizens of West Berlin. Eventually the Soviets lifted their blockade, but the nation of Germany remained divided between East and West for over forty years. Western nations formed the North Atlantic Treaty Organization (**NATO**) in 1949 to provide collective security in case any member nation (in Western Europe) were to come under Soviet attack. The Soviet counterpart to NATO was called the **Warsaw Pact**.

In the **election of 1948** Truman held on to the presidency even though the experts had predicted he would lose to Republican **Thomas Dewey**. Truman's domestic program, called the **Fair Deal**, was basically a consolidation and extension of FDR's most popular New Deal policies. Truman relished the campaign trail, blaming the "do-nothing" Republican Congress for its failure to pass his agenda. Shouts of "Give 'em hell, Harry!" became one of Truman's trademarks. In a moment filled with future ramifications, the **Dixiecrats** (disaffected southern Democrats who bolted from Truman) walked out of the 1948 Democratic convention, nominating their own candidate, Strom Thurmond, for president. They were angry over the Democratic platform's endorsement of civil rights for African Americans—a position that had been a long time in coming and would take longer to achieve.

✤ Chapter Review

Identify

isolationism

reparations

Nazis

Adolf Hitler

Third Reich

fascists

Benito Mussolini

Spanish Civil War

Francisco Franco

Japanese Empire

Rhineland

Anschluss

Sudetenland

appeasement

Munich

invasion of Poland

Winston Churchill

Neutrality Acts

Phony War

America First Committee

Battle of Britain

Luftwaffe

Lend Lease Act

Tripartite Pact

Douglas MacArthur

Hideki Tojo

December 7, 1941

Pearl Harbor

Allies

Big Three

Charles DeGaulle

Free French

blitzkrieg

North Africa

George S. Patton, Jr.

Bernard Montgomery

Palermo

Salerno

Anzio

Monte Cassino

Dwight D. "Ike" Eisenhower

Normandy

Air War

Operation Overlord

D-Day

Erwin Rommel

Omaha Beach

Battle of the Bulge

Bastogne

Dresden

Bataan Death March

Battle of the Coral Sea

Battle of Midway

Guadalcanal

island hopping

Chester Nimitz

kamikaze

Harry S Truman

Albert Einstein

Manhattan Project

J. Robert Oppenheimer

Potsdam Conference

Hiroshima

Enola Gay

Nagasaki

rationing

no-strike pledge	iron curtain
Rosie the Riveter	George F. Kennan
War Relocation Camps	containment
Holocaust	Truman Doctrine
Auschwitz	Marshall Plan
Buchenwald	Berlin Airlift
Nuremburg Trials	NATO
Israel	Warsaw Pact
Palestine	election of 1948
Cold War	Thomas Dewey
Yalta	Fair Deal
satellite nations	Dixiecrats
United Nations	

Short Paragraph

1. Describe the nations and leaders involved in World War II.

2. What were the causes of the Cold War?

3. What was the impact of World War II and the Cold War on American women and racial minorities?

4. How was the United States home front affected by World War II and the Cold War?

CHAPTER

14

Postwar America:
The Fifties and Sixties

Two key events of 1949 shaped the consciousness of the next generation of Americans. In China, communist rebels under **Mao Zedong** (Mao Tse-tung) overthrew the nationalist Chinese government headed by **Jiang Jieshi** (Chiang Kai-shek), who along with his forces fled to the offshore island of Taiwan, where he set up the Republic of China, a bone in mainland China's throat for many years to come. Jiang's regime had been pro-Western and a faithful bulwark against Soviet expansionism. Now it appeared communism was unstoppable, as a furious debate raged in Congress and the media over "Who lost China?" Truman's defenders responded that the world's most populous country was not ours to lose in the first place, but such statements held little weight as apprehension over the perceived threat of communism mounted. Another key event was even more alarming. The Soviet Union successfully detonated a nuclear device in a test explosion, which meant, at least potentially, that they now had the A-Bomb as well. "How have they gotten so far so fast?" many wondered. In response, Truman ordered the development of a new hydrogen bomb, a higher technology nuclear weapon far more lethal than anything dropped on Japan. The arms race was on.

The Cold War Gets Hot

While Cold War espionage and intrigue spawned a great number of novels and films, the fear of Soviet spies in America was not all fantasy. **Whittaker**

Chambers, an admitted former Communist Party member, accused former State Department official **Alger Hiss** of espionage. The evidence against the respected Hiss was strong and burst forth in widely broadcast perjury trials, resulting in his conviction. In critics' eyes, the Truman administration looked weak in fighting communism because of its early defense of Hiss. The president dismissed the initial charges as a "red herring," or distraction. Another highly celebrated spy case involved husband and wife **Julius and Ethel Rosenberg**, who were convicted of treason for passing secret information from the nuclear laboratory at Los Alamos to Soviet agents. Both Julius and Ethel died in the electric chair, though there is still dispute about just how damaging the information they passed really was to the national security. At any rate, America was in the grip of its second **Red Scare**.

Postwar Congressional committees fueled the atmosphere of fear. For many years the House Un-American Activities Committee (**HUAC**) conducted investigations into suspected subversives. One of the committee's favorite questions of those brought before it to testify was, "Are you now or have you ever been a member of the Communist Party?" The Committee also wanted to know about the friends and acquaintances of its many suspects, and even delved into their past activities as youngsters. In all the emotion, much of America forgot that being a communist had been perfectly respectable back in the 1930s and 1940s (especially when the Americans and Soviets were allies against the Nazis). But by the 1950s, some ex-communists were in prominent positions. Some of the most frequent targets of HUAC were those in the film industry. Tragically, many Hollywood artists, especially writers, were blacklisted by the movie studios, most prominently the so-called **Hollywood Ten**, who refused to cooperate with the Committee at great sacrifice to their careers. One of the most persistent members of HUAC was a young congressman from California, **Richard M. Nixon**.

One Red-baiting Senator from Wisconsin attracted the most attention. His name was **Joseph McCarthy**, and his high-handed tactics were eventually labeled **McCarthyism** (thanks to political cartoonist Herbert Block). In one speech McCarthy claimed to have in his hand a list of known communists within the State Department, holding up a piece of paper for emphasis. He refused to make the list public, however. He later began investigations into the U.S. Army, which he also claimed was infested with communists. Critics called McCarthy's bullying a **witch hunt**, but official Washington stayed largely silent. Interestingly, public opinion grew weary and suspicious of the senator, especially after seeing him on television for hours on end. Finally, after one respected witness asked him, "Have you no decency, sir?" and the influential journalist Edward R. Murrow devoted a TV program to challenging McCarthy, the U.S. Senate voted to censure him. He died a few years later of chronic alcoholism.

The **Korean War** (1950–53) is sometimes called the Forgotten War but it certainly is not forgotten by those who were involved in it. On June 25, 1950, North Korean forces crossed the **38th Parallel** (the line dividing pro-Soviet North Korea from pro-Western South Korea), and captured most of the peninsula. In a clear test of containment, President Truman went to the United Nations Security Council, eventually getting a resolution authorizing U.S. military assistance to South Korea. Significantly, the Soviets at precisely this time were boycotting the UN Security Council over China policy and therefore were not able to veto UN military authorization. Although the fighting in Korea was technically called a UN *police action* or a *conflict* as opposed to a *war*, it is clear the United States bore the main responsibility for pushing out communist forces from South Korea. U.S. forces on the Korean Peninsula totaled 350,000, while the troops of all partner nations totaled about 50,000.

Debate was furious over U.S. goals and strategy in Korea, but the public was supportive when the UN named General **Douglas MacArthur** as chief commander. In one of the most inventive military victories in modern U.S. history, MacArthur landed a force behind the North Korean rear guard at **Inchon**, causing enemy forces to retreat back across the border. MacArthur eventually concluded that the war should be taken north all the way to the Yalu River bordering Chinese Manchuria. Truman, fearing the outbreak of World War III should the Soviets come to the aid of China, instructed MacArthur to maintain his position. The situation became desperately critical with the sudden entry into the fighting of thousands of Chinese so-called volunteers, an army that dealt heavy blows to UN forces. After repeated disagreements with the president, MacArthur went beyond his authority, among other things telling China to make peace or be attacked. In a decision that stunned the country, Truman fired MacArthur for insubordination. While Truman's popularity plummeted as a result of the move, subsequent investigations by the Joint Chiefs of Staff confirmed the wisdom of Truman's position. Truman later stated simply, "I fired him because he wouldn't respect the authority of the President."

The Korean War lapsed into stalemate—the kind of limited war Americans would learn to endure. The actual combat, however, was among the most brutal in history, often conducted in freezing temperatures. Names such as Heartbreak Ridge and Pork Chop Hill became part of the soldiers' vocabulary. President Truman decided not to run for re-election as peace negotiations continued. In the **election of 1952**, Republican candidate and military hero **Dwight Eisenhower** (who had been solicited by both major parties) promised, "I shall go to Korea," which impressed Americans, though it was always unclear what he would do when he got there. Ike's opponent, **Adlai Stevenson**, campaigned on traditional liberal Democratic programs. Eisenhower's election, the sudden death of Josef Stalin in the Soviet Union, and several key military successes all perhaps contributed to a truce between North and South Korea on July 27, 1953, ending the war almost precisely where it began, along the 38th Parallel. The boundary became one of the most durable divisions of the Cold War.

The Eisenhower Years (1953–1961)

Eisenhower and his vice president, Richard Nixon, seemed to give Americans a sense of security as the Cold War continued through the 1950s. Ike's military record spoke for itself, and Nixon had become famous in Congress investigating communists. But the decade also witnessed a powerful social upheaval totally unrelated to politics and war. **Suburbanization** cannot be overestimated in importance. A whole new way of life was developing. Previously suburbs were communities linked directly to a hub city by subway and light rail lines, but the new bedroom communities born in the 1950s were a product of the **automobile culture**. Widespread use of the personal automobile allowed people to live miles from work, in neighborhoods of mass-produced homes built on affordable land. The homes were often purchased by veterans with G.I. loans bearing low rates of interest, and paid for by newly educated vets who went to school thanks largely to the **G.I. Bill of Rights**, a program of generous educational benefits. The post–World War II **Baby Boom** (the largest population explosion of its kind in history) created a huge demand for new homes, schools, and more consumer goods than the world had ever seen. All these forces linked together, producing things that revolved around the use of cars such as drive-in movie theaters (perfect for taking small children), diaper services, and huge supermarkets with acres of parking spaces. The federally funded interstate highway system, with its many freeways and exits, made cross-country family vacations commonplace. Soon, rural and small-town America became known as nostalgic places where grandparents lived.

The impact of **television** was also profound. By the end of the 1950s, most Americans regularly watched network fare on television sets in their own living rooms. Popular shows included comedies such as *I Love Lucy* and adult westerns such as *Gunsmoke*. (There were so many westerns on the air that on some evenings it was hard to find anything else. Some observers wrote that Americans were subconsciously seeking earlier times when right and wrong were supposedly clearer.) But Americans also used television to tune into coverage of political conventions, congressional hearings, and the nightly news. While some complained that TV was offering a cultural wasteland or "chewing gum for the mind," it was often assumed that the medium would bring families together—quite literally in the living room. During the 1950s, families usually had one TV set, with spirited discussions ensuing over what to watch. Hence the advent of variety programs such as The *Ed Sullivan Show*, which offered comedians, acrobats, as well as something for the youngsters. When **Elvis Presley** sang "You ain't nothin' but a hound dog" on the *The Ed Sullivan Show*, it created a national sensation.

But American social life was more than just eating on TV trays and arguing over rock and roll. In May 1954 the United States Supreme Court issued the **Brown v. Board of Education** decision, which originated in Topeka, Kansas. In this landmark case the Court ordered that racial segregation in the public schools be ended "with all deliberate speed." It was a stunning announcement, particularly in the South, where politicians promised **massive resistance** to the federal order. The case overturned the **separate but equal** justification for segregation that had prevailed in American law since the nineteenth century. While enforcement of *Brown* was left up to the federal courts, occasionally the other branches felt compelled to get involved as well, as the issue of racial equality hit the front pages for the first time since Reconstruction. In 1957, President Eisenhower sent federal troops into Little Rock, Arkansas, to enforce a court order to allow nine black children to attend that city's Central High School.

During World War II and the Korean War, over a million African-American men served in the armed forces. They experienced discrimination but met the challenge and persevered, earning high praises and commendations from their commanders. When these individuals returned to civilian life, they encountered the same harsh treatment and policies that existed before the war. This was especially the case in the South. As African-American vets began to ask themselves, "What were we fighting for?", the long drive to obtain full civil rights began its final and climactic phase.

Two important African-American figures in the **civil rights movement** in the 1950s were **Rosa Parks**, often called the mother of the movement, and **Dr. Martin Luther King, Jr.** On December 1, 1955, Parks, tired after working all day as a seamstress, refused to give up her seat on a bus to a white person as required by law in Montgomery, Alabama. That night at the Dexter Avenue Baptist Church, black community leaders organized a boycott of the city's bus system. Dexter's pastor was the charismatic and courageous Martin Luther King, Jr.. The reverend Dr. King had been raised in Georgia, later obtaining a seminary degree from Morehouse College and a Ph.D. in Philosophy from Boston University. This important American was instrumental in merging the civil rights movement with Christianity, relying heavily on the nonviolent teachings of Jesus and the **civil disobedience** of Henry David Thoreau, who wrote in the previous century protesting slavery. King's principal twentieth-century inspiration was Mahatma Gandhi, who used nonviolent civil disobedience to achieve independence for India from its British governors. Without ever resorting to violence—even in the face of violent resistance—King organized and took part in boycotts, sit-ins, and other formalized protests to bring an end to **Jim Crow** segregation in the workplace and in lunch counters, restrooms, and other public facilities. The fight for the civil rights of minorities lasted all through the 1950s and 1960s, as King and other black citizens were beaten, jailed, and even killed. White racists once bombed King's home, and innocent children were killed in church bombings at the hands of reactionary whites, one of whom was finally prosecuted in 2005.

Thus, all was not well in America during the 1950s. In 1957 the Soviets launched the first artificial satellite to orbit the earth. They called it Sputnik. Although about the size of a basketball, **Sputnik** could be viewed by Americans in their own back yards with the aid of binoculars. Alarmed, Americans now demanded to know if this meant that the Russians were on the verge of launching weaponry from space. Lyndon B. Johnson, the powerful senator from Texas, announced gravely that he did not want to look up at the night sky and see a communist moon. The **space race** was on, driven by fear and competition more than scientific curiosity.

Concern spread through the educational system, as experts wondered whether the Baby Boom generation had grown lazy and indifferent from watching too much TV and listening to rock and roll music. Congress spent more money on science education, as parents worried that their kids would become **beatniks** who never held steady jobs, grew their hair long (the young men sported goatees), and hung out in coffee houses snapping their fingers to free-verse poetry. As with all counterculture movements, the beat generation was a small minority, but it seemed threatening to the placid suburban atmosphere the middle class hoped to cultivate.

The Eisenhower-Nixon ticket was easily re-elected in 1956, but there was still considerable Cold War anxiety. In the 1960 **U-2 incident**, a high-altitude American spy plane was brought down over the Soviet Union. At first Eisenhower disavowed the mission's purpose, claiming that the flight had been made for scientific purposes, but then grimly accepted responsibility. (The pilot, Francis Gary Powers, was ultimately exchanged for a Soviet spy.) A planned summit conference with the unpredictable Soviet Premier **Nikita Khrushchev** soon collapsed, as tensions mounted. Even more disturbing was a communist revolution in Cuba in 1959 led by **Fidel Castro**. Castro seemed harmless and even admirable at first. He had, after all, overthrown an oppressive dictatorship and could quote from America's Declaration of Independence better than most Americans. Very quickly, however, he formed an alliance with the Soviet Union, which now had its own puppet nation only ninety miles from U.S. shores.

The New Frontier

Senator **John F. Kennedy** defeated Vice President Nixon in the extreme-ly close **election of 1960**. Part of what helped him win was the televised **Kennedy-Nixon Debates**, watched by millions of Americans. The substance of the debates was quickly forgotten (people listening on the radio felt Nixon won), but Kennedy looked great on TV—tanned, relaxed, articulate, and, at the age of forty-two, youthful. Nixon, on the other hand, looked shifty and nervous, was perspiring heavily, and appeared pale and unhealthy due to a recent infection and the unfortunate application of too much makeup. The merger of TV and politics had arrived.

In some ways the American mood was optimistic by 1960 with the recent addition of Alaska and Hawaii as the forty-ninth and fiftieth states, but in other ways the public was not enthusiastic for upsetting the status quo. During the campaign, Kennedy chose not to emphasize the traditional liberal agenda of Democrats, instead vaguely promising to "get America moving again." As a Catholic, he managed to neutralize traditional prejudices by selecting Lyndon Johnson of Texas as his running mate, a choice that helped him in the conservative (and largely Protestant) South. The campaign also stressed JFK's war record as the legendary commander of a PT Boat in the Pacific. And it certainly did not hurt that his father, Joseph P. Kennedy, was extremely wealthy and well connected, or that his wife, Jacqueline, was smart, glamorous, and beautiful. Kennedy's vision of a **New Frontier** was hardly precise, but his style was infectious.

Before leaving office, President Eisenhower delivered what may be the most significant farewell address since that of George Washington. Eisenhower warned of too much reliance on material strength and wealth, and urged the country not to abuse its resources in living only for the present. Perhaps most prophetically, he warned of the dangers of the **military-industrial complex** and its influence on government. As a former military man himself, Eisenhower had enormous credibility in alerting the nation to beware of the political power of the military and defense industries. Ike's warning would echo through the remainder of the Cold War—and after.

A popular musical running on Broadway when Kennedy took office was *Camelot*, and the name stuck to describe the glittering social atmosphere surrounding the Kennedys in the White House. The world outside presented immediate challenges, however. A CIA plan for the invasion of Cuba by 1,500 U.S.-backed anti-Castro Cubans was already in the works, and Kennedy's military advisors recommended he approve it. The plan's ultimate success depended on the Cuban people rising up to join the invaders to overthrow Castro. When what became known as the **Bay of Pigs Invasion** occurred, however, it fell apart immediately. Kennedy was embarrassed by the failure, and he became permanently skeptical of advice from the military and the CIA. Still, the Cold War raged on as the Soviets abruptly erected the **Berlin Wall**, cutting off almost all movement between the two sectors of the symbolic city.

The most dangerous military confrontation between the United States and the Soviet Union was the **Cuban Missile Crisis** of 1962. In response to

U.S. attempts to invade Cuba, Castro requested nuclear missiles from the Soviet Union. When Kennedy learned through intelligence photographs that missile sites were indeed being established in Cuba, he immediately decided it was unacceptable. The only problem was what to do about it. Some advisors urged an immediate air strike of the missile sites, followed by an invasion of Cuba. A more moderate path was decided upon, a quarantine of Cuba, which meant in practice a naval blockade of the island. As Soviet supply ships steamed toward the area, the world watched anxiously. Finally a private offer was put forward by the Soviets to pull the missiles out of Cuba in exchange for a promise by the United States not to invade. A deal emerged, which included the removal of obsolete U.S. missiles from Turkey and several symbolic gestures. The fear of World War III took another break, and Kennedy's prestige rose, as the youthful president had proven himself decisive and competent in a crisis.

Domestically, however, Kennedy's New Frontier had a tough time in Congress. Bills seeking aid to education, health care, and civil rights legislation all languished on Capitol Hill, partly because southerners dominated Congress's most important committees. Kennedy was sympathetic to concerns expressed by Martin Luther King but was unable to steer the passage of laws mandating equal treatment of blacks. In a largely symbolic gesture, federal marshals (under the direction of Attorney General **Robert Kennedy**, the President's younger brother) moved aside Alabama Governor **George Wallace** as he stood in the door of the University of Alabama to block the entry of black students. To some it appeared civil rights legislation would pass in the 1964 session of Congress with Kennedy's urging, but southern leadership was once again hostile to civil rights, and the Democratic Party grew bitterly divided. To help shore things up, President Kennedy and Vice President Lyndon Johnson decided to take a trip to Texas.

The **Kennedy assassination** in Dallas on November 22, 1963, is one of those extraordinary events in history when people remember precisely what they were doing at the moment they learned of it. Suddenly, and brutally, Camelot had ended. With JFK's death, much of the nation's idealism died too. The sight of Jacqueline Kennedy in her blood-splattered dress standing next to a somber Lyndon Johnson taking the presidential oath made an unforgettable photograph. In a weekend filled with horrific images, suspected assassin **Lee Harvey Oswald** was gunned down at point-blank range, in full view of the Dallas police and with television cameras rolling. With Oswald dead and conspiracy theories (involving the Cubans, Russians, organized crime, and even the CIA) mounting, President Johnson directed the **Warren Commission** to conduct a systematic inquiry. To almost no one's satisfaction, the Commission concluded that Oswald acted alone in killing Kennedy.

The Great Society

Johnson's Texas roots plagued him during his entire presidency. For one thing, the assassination of JFK occurred in LBJ's home state. Furthermore, as head of an administration still filled with Kennedy loyalists and Harvard-trained sophisticates, Johnson often appeared crude and tasteless. He did not look great on TV as Kennedy had. To make matters worse, LBJ had a long-standing animosity with Attorney General Robert Kennedy. The two men simply hated each other. But Johnson was no amateur politician, having risen swiftly to the post of Senate majority leader during the 1950s. In most respects, he was better prepared to deal with Congress than was his predecessor. Events soon proved him more successful, too.

Moving cautiously at first, Johnson helped calm a nation still reeling from the assassination by retaining most Kennedy appointees and declaring his goals to be identical with "our martyred President." Much of JFK's agenda was stalled in Congress, and the new President contrived a scheme to pass it—and much more. Calling his vision a **Great Society**, in which equality, abundance, and justice for all would be achieved, he eased the fears of the Eastern Establishment liberals who were suspicious of the man from Texas.

By background and temperament, Johnson was actually more liberal than Kennedy had been. Coming from a populist heritage, Johnson had risen in Congress as an extremely loyal New Dealer. As president, he quickly passed a measure that had been promised for decades, the **Civil Rights Act of 1964**, the most far-reaching law on the subject of race since Reconstruction. The new statute outlawed discrimination in public facilities and put the power of the federal government behind it. After re-election on his own in the **election of 1964** against archconservative **Barry Goldwater**, Johnson set out to become the most successful President with Congress since FDR.

The list of laws passed in the mid-1960s under LBJ's direction is impressive. As a fellow southerner and personal friend of many of the committee chairmen, LBJ wheeled and dealed, promised and threatened, nursed tender egos, and ultimately convinced reluctant members that it was their patriotic duty to go his way. The **Voting Rights Act of 1965** gave special protection to racial minorities at the polls, increasing black voter turnout dramatically. This single law literally changed the face of southern politics. Johnson further declared an unconditional **War on Poverty**, with funding for the **Job Corps** and **Head Start** educational programs for youth in the poorest areas of the country. **Medicare** was also authorized, providing health insurance for the elderly. And there was more. Due to a booming economy during most of the 1960s, Congress could not argue that money was not available, and the public—at first—supported Johnson's efforts. While a generation later some of these programs would be eliminated, others (Head Start and Medicare, for instance) would ultimately get broad support from both parties.

The Mood Turns Sour: Vietnam and the Late 1960s

Vietnam was once a colony of France, part of a region known as French Indochina. After years of jungle warfare against a nationalistic independence movement led by **Ho Chi Minh**, France withdrew from Vietnam in 1954. Vietnam then became the staging area for a long contest between communistic revolutionary forces (who began to receive support from the Soviet Union and China) and the pro-Western regime based in South Vietnam. When Johnson came into office there were 16,000 U.S. military advisors in South Vietnam charged with bolstering the morale of the South Vietnamese and improving the combat readiness of its army. Soon U.S. forces became directly involved in the fighting, which many observers clearly saw was shaping up be a Korea-like confrontation between the communist North and the democratic South.

Johnson feared that a communist takeover of South Vietnam would jeopardize his domestic agenda and make him forever the president who lost Vietnam. He also wanted to avoid any negotiated settlement that resembled appeasement, the policy that had proved so tragic in dealing with the Nazis before World War II. Therefore, U.S. intervention in Vietnam's civil war was completely consistent with the long-standing strategy of containment and based on the premise (sometimes called the **domino theory**) that a victory for communism anywhere would eventually affect the United

States directly. Johnson became the president responsible for the **escala-tion** of the Vietnam War, turning it into the longest and most controversial military quagmire in U.S. history. Nonetheless, Congress clearly permitted Johnson to proceed by passing overwhelmingly the **Gulf of Tonkin Resolu-tion** in 1964, this after two American destroyers allegedly were fired upon by North Vietnamese forces. Johnson claimed that the attack was unpro-voked, but the United States had initiated military actions in the Gulf as well. The Gulf of Tonkin Resolution gave the president authorization, with-out a declaration of war, to use military force in the region. LBJ relied upon the resolution to escalate the war.

Soon America's involvement in Vietnam included the saturation bomb-ing of the North, called **Operation Rolling Thunder**, plus combat infantry based in the South. From the beginning, the goal was never to force North Vietnam to surrender unconditionally, but to prevent Ho Chi Minh's com-munist forces from achieving victory. This meant the communists, consist-ing of North Vietnamese regulars and guerrilla fighters in the South, called the **Vietcong**, simply had to outlast the Americans—a technique that had al-ready worked against the French. Johnson often personally and carefully di-rected bombing raids from the White House, fearful that totally unleashing American strength in Indochina would bring the Soviet Union and China directly into the fray. Meanwhile, North Vietnamese forces relied upon an elaborate tunnel system and, more important, a grim willingness to sacrifice lives in great numbers to expel yet another foreign invader.

Although tons upon tons of bombs had failed to break the spirit of the North Vietnamese, the ground war proved even more frustrating to Ameri-can troops, who numbered 385,000 in 1966. With no clear objective, pla-toons were sent on search-and-destroy missions into enemy-held territory, then returned to camp to rest up for another march through the hot, mos-quito-infested jungle. It was often impossible to tell who the enemy was, as Vietcong soldiers wore no uniforms and their forces included women and children. Booby traps, mines, tunnels, searing heat, and an invisible en-emy caused low troop morale as the war raged on. Perhaps most significant, Vietnam became a **living-room war**, as the American public watched tele-vised coverage of the carnage on the nightly news. Some observers (includ-ing President Johnson) felt it was a major turning point when respected TV journalist **Walter Cronkite** declared that the United States was not winning the war, and that the best thing to do was negotiate a withdrawal.

Cronkite's announcement in early 1968 had followed the so-called **Tet Offensive** (Tet being the Vietnamese New Year) in which communist forces launched surprise assaults on a wide range of targets in South Vietnam. The Vietcong even briefly occupied the grounds surrounding the American Embassy in Saigon. Although the attack was repelled and U.S. commander General **William C. Westmoreland** justifiably proclaimed Tet a U.S. victory, public opinion soured still further. Back in the states, antiwar protests reached their peak in 1968, as young men burned their draft cards and protestors chanted outside the White House, "Hey, hey, LBJ. How many kids did you kill today?"

Journalist and historian William Manchester called 1968 "The Year Everything Went Wrong." On March 31, President Johnson announced he would not seek re-election, voicing the hope that his decision, coupled with a pause in the bombing, would encourage the communists to settle favorably. But the war dragged on. In April, Dr. Martin Luther King was assassinated in Memphis by a white racist, setting off riots in dozens of American cities. To many, the **King assassination** meant the death of hope, as King's nonviolent resistance gave way to more militant voices such as those of the **Black Panthers**, whose young members openly advocated revolution. On June 6, presidential candidate Robert Kennedy was assassinated by a young Palestinian outraged by Kennedy's stand on Israel. In August, the Democrats, holding their convention in Chicago, nominated Johnson's Vice President, Hubert Humphrey, but the TV cameras were focused instead on riots and demonstrations on the streets outside, where antiwar protesters and assorted radicals were beaten by Chicago police as they chanted, "The whole world is watching!" Public opinion polls showed Americans supported the actions of the cops, but a later investigation called their tactics a "police riot."

The Republicans, meanwhile, nominated former Vice President Richard M. Nixon, who quickly capitalized on the backlash conservative mood. Running a campaign on the platform of law and order, Nixon criticized the U.S. Supreme Court for coddling criminals. He promised peace with justice in Vietnam, which seemed vague to many, but the public thought it suggested a more aggressive approach to ending U.S. participation in the Vietnam War. The **election of 1968** also produced the American Independent Party, under former Democrat and Alabama Governor George C. Wallace. Wallace urged a get-tough policy toward racial violence, in contrast to the antipoverty approach of the Great Society programs. Although Wallace appealed mainly to white southerners, the conservative message he preached was attractive to many blue-collar whites in the North as well. In a close election, Nixon won. Now the country waited for a new approach to its serious social problems.

As the 1960s drew to a close, many Americans felt the country's social fabric was unraveling. Sociologists wrote of a **generation gap** between old and young. "Sex, drugs, and rock and roll" eventually symbolized the entire decade for some. A new counterculture, featuring young people known as **hippies**, rejected traditional values, espousing free love, communal lifestyles, and "doing your own thing." Parents were horrified, of course, but it is important to note that most young people of the era never lived in a commune, protested the war, or dropped out of society. Certainly casual drug use increased, particularly that of marijuana and LSD, and there is little doubt that sexual activity was less restrictive, perhaps due to the newly available **birth-control pill**, an easy-to-use form of contraception. And then there was the music, which provided a constant anthem for rebellion. The music of Janis Joplin, Jimi Hendrix, the Doors, the Grateful Dead, and countless other artists blared from the stereos of the younger generation, which thought of itself as special (a line by songwriter Joni Mitchell said, "We are golden . . ."). Actually they were the post–World War II Baby Boomers, who now faced the challenges of adulthood as the turbulent 1960s sputtered to conclusion.

Chapter Review

Identify

Mao Zedong	Korean War
Jiang Jieshi	38th Parallel
Whittaker Chambers	Douglas MacArthur
Alger Hiss	Inchon
Julius and Ethel Rosenberg	election of 1952
Red Scare	Dwight Eisenhower
HUAC	Adlai Stevenson
Hollywood Ten	suburbanization
Richard M. Nixon	automobile culture
Joseph McCarthy	G.I. Bill of Rights
McCarthyism	Baby Boom
witch hunt	television

Elvis Presley
Brown v. *Board of Education*
massive resistance
separate but equal
civil rights movement
Rosa Parks
Dr. Martin Luther King, Jr.
civil disobedience
Jim Crow
Sputnik
space race
beatniks
U-2 incident
Nikita Khrushchev
Fidel Castro
John F. Kennedy
election of 1960
Kennedy-Nixon Debates
New Frontier
military-industrial complex
Bay of Pigs Invasion
Berlin Wall
Cuban Missile Crisis
Robert Kennedy
George Wallace
Kennedy assassination
Lee Harvey Oswald

Warren Commission
Great Society
Civil Rights Act of 1964
election of 1964
Barry Goldwater
Voting Rights Act of 1965
War on Poverty
Job Corps
Head Start
Medicare
Ho Chi Minh
domino theory
escalation
Gulf of Tonkin Resolution
Operation Rolling Thunder
Vietcong
living-room war
Walter Cronkite
Tet Offensive
William C. Westmoreland
King assassination
Black Panthers
election of 1968
generation gap
hippies
birth-control pill

Short Paragraph

1. What were the major social trends of the 1950s?

2. Why did the United States under President Johnson escalate U.S. involvement in the war in Vietnam?

3. Compare the accomplishments of Presidents Kennedy and Johnson.

4. What were the significant milestones in race relations in the 1950s and 1960s?

15

Retrenchment:
The Seventies and Eighties

When **Richard M. Nixon** took the presidential oath of office in January 1969, many hoped for a more stable and conservative atmosphere. Nixon, who was raised a Quaker and spent much of his political career opposing communism, seemed the exact antithesis of the radical counterculture of the late 1960s. Also, since he had plenty of experience as Eisenhower's vice president back in the 1950s, most of the country felt comfortable with him. On budgetary matters, however, Nixon proved to be more liberal than conservatives had hoped, for during his administration most of the Great Society programs remained in force and even increased in funding. Furthermore, Nixon proposed bold new initiatives in advancing the war on poverty. Increasingly, however, it was not the traditional bread-and-butter issues that gained Richard Nixon the most attention.

The Counterculture Fades—and Feminism Rises

By 1969 there were signs that young people were losing interest in the counterculture. Contrary to their appearance (typically in bell-bottomed jeans, sandals, and tie-dyed T-shirts), most hippies were from middle-class homes and adapted quickly to changes in fashion or vocabulary. Cynical attitudes began to replace idealism and social consciousness. The last burst of 1960s idealism was probably best represented by a rock festival known as **Woodstock** in upstate New York. For three days in 1969,

500,000 young people gathered to listen to rock music, smoke marijuana, and share food and kindred spirits. There was virtually no violence during the festival—a phenomenon that observers noted could never happen in a city of equal size back in the real world. Just a few months later, however, when promoters attempted to hold the same sort of event featuring a performance by the Rolling Stones in **Altamont**, California, a knife-wielding man was beaten to death by members of the Hell's Angels Motorcycle Club, who had been recruited as, of all things, security officers. After Altamont, few argued that the new generation was innately superior to the old. Many observers noticed as well that the counterculture had offered only traditional roles for women. In most hippie communes that sprouted across the country during the 1960s, the responsibilities of males and females were very distinct—with women often left to raise the children, cook, clean, and quietly perform other domestic duties.

The movement known as **feminism** has many roots. Certainly the woman's suffrage movement after the Progressive Era accustomed men to think about women in nontraditional ways. As noted earlier, during World War II, women worked at jobs that previously had been reserved for men. The Civil Rights upheavals of the 1950s and 1960s further alerted Americans to the similarity between the treatment of African Americans and other racial minorities and the inferior legal and social status of women. Finally, during the 1960s, the development and new availability of oral contraceptives for women (the pill) permanently changed attitudes regarding sexual behavior. With more control over family planning, career-oriented women opened new doors.

Modern feminism is sometimes traced to the publication of a bestselling 1963 book titled *The Feminine Mystique*. Its author was a former housewife and mother of three named **Betty Friedan**. Friedan, educated at Smith College, noticed throughout the 1950s that her women friends and acquaintances, in spite of having families and successful husbands, were deeply miserable. The mystique of the book's title refers to the popular image of suburban women portrayed in magazines and television—with women presumably interested only in shopping, PTA meetings, beauty secrets to please their husbands, and mindless activities of no social consequence. Friedan and others were instrumental in forming the **National Organization for Women** (NOW), which began to pressure Congress to end discrimination against women in the workplace, legalize abortion, and fund childcare centers. Feminism's time had come. Congress passed many such measures and even proposed the **Equal Rights Amendment** to the U.S. Constitution in 1972 (which barely failed ratification in the state legislatures).

In 1973 the United States Supreme Court struck a blow for women's rights that is still controversial today. The case of **Roe v. Wade** overturned laws making abortion a crime in all fifty states, based upon an implied constitutional **right to privacy**. The case marked the beginning of a bitter clash of opinion within American society, stimulating many into political action to elect presidents who would appoint judges who shared their own views. Some opponents of abortion resorted to acts of violence against doctors who performed abortions and the clinics in which they worked. In an economic context, the entire nation by the 1970s was transforming with regard to the role of women in the workplace. The gap in incomes between men and women was (and is) striking, but women began to perform in occupations and positions of leadership that would have been unthinkable just a few years before.

Nixon's Foreign Policy and the End of Idealism: Watergate

President Nixon faced liberal Democrat **George McGovern** in the **election of 1972**, defeating the antiwar candidate in a landslide. However controversial the war in Vietnam remained, it is clear that the American public did not favor unilateral withdrawal, as McGovern recommended. As it turned out, Nixon's plan for "peace with honor" involved **Vietnamization**, a gradual turning over of South Vietnam to its own troops and resources in fighting the communist threat. Nixon also established a military draft lottery system, replacing assorted college deferments and exemptions that tended to benefit the sons of the upper classes. Part of the controversy of Vietnam centered upon the fact that U.S. combat forces and casualties came disproportionately from the poorer classes—especially African Americans and Hispanics. Most controversially, in 1970 Nixon extended the war into neighboring **Cambodia**, presumably to destroy Vietcong military staging areas there. Congress and the public were unaware for many months of this secret war against a supposedly neutral nation.

On May 4, 1970, a domestic tragedy occurred that galvanized the country, demonstrating the deep division between hawks and doves on the issue of Vietnam. Four students at Kent State University, while participating in an antiwar demonstration, were shot and killed by Ohio National Guard troops, who had been called up to quell previous disturbances. Witnesses later noted that some protesters had thrown rocks and tossed back some of the tear gas canisters fired by the Guard into the crowd. Nevertheless, no direct cause of the shots was ever determined, and no one was ever prosecuted for the shootings. Subsequently, the lyrics to a popular song, "Ohio," by the rock group Crosby, Stills, Nash, and Young, became an anthem for younger Americans who felt they were now living in a police state.

By the early 1970s the Soviet Union and China began to exhibit considerable hostility toward one another. Long-standing grievances and border disputes fractured the communist alliance that had seemed so monolithic and formidable just a few years before. Working closely with his national security advisor **Henry Kissinger**, President Nixon suddenly announced in 1972 that he would visit China, which could be seen as a prelude to full diplomatic relations. Nixon could manage such a bold stroke (and openly infuriate the anticommunist people of **Taiwan**, a U.S. ally since the end of World War II) because his past as a cold warrior made him almost invulnerable to political criticism. The meeting was a great public relations success, which also helped propel Nixon to re-election. Indeed, all seemed well in the Nixon White House. In Vietnam, after the so-called Christmas bombings of 1972, a peace agreement was signed with the North Vietnamese in early 1973. Kissinger declared that "peace is at hand." American troops were rapidly withdrawn, leaving a number of questions unresolved, including the whereabouts of several thousand men who were missing in action. South Vietnam would be turned over to the South Vietnamese—or so everyone thought. One critic noted that the United States simply "declared victory" and went home. For the time being, the fate of the South Vietnamese was ignored.

During the summer of 1972, with the arrest of several men attempting to break into the Democratic National Committee's headquarters at the Watergate hotel and apartment complex in Washington, D.C., the so-called **Watergate scandal**, had begun. Those accused in the incident had former connections with the CIA and had money in their pockets from Nixon's re-election campaign. While no evidence exists that Nixon arranged or knew the details of the break-in (he called it a third-rate burglary), Senate and House investigations revealed a criminal conspiracy to cover up damaging information. The head of the FBI, for instance, admitted destroying documents. Even more harmful to Nixon was evidence of a campaign of dirty tricks against his political enemies, including the existence of an enemies list of political opponents and critics. The list included respected journalists and scholars, as well as a few Hollywood celebrities.

Many contend that Nixon could have survived the Watergate crisis if not for one startling revelation: for years the president had secretly taped all conversations inside his office. When news of the tapes' existence came out during a congressional hearing, a fierce battle between the White House and Congress ensued. Criminal defendants wanted access to the tapes for use as evidence in court, but the president refused to turn over the tapes. Finally, on July 24, 1974, the United States Supreme Court ruled unanimously (in a case appropriately named **U.S. v. Nixon**) that the tapes must be surrendered. As predicted, the taped conversations revealed concrete evidence of a cover-up, including the proposed use of hush money to keep witnesses quiet. Several days later, in televised proceedings, the **House Judiciary Committee** recommended three articles of impeachment against Nixon as the nation watched. Sensing certain removal from office, Nixon resigned the presidency on August 9, 1974. It was the first presidential resignation in American history.

The complicated events of the Watergate scandal captivated many and bored others. By the early 1970s much of the radicalism associated with the 1960s seemed in abeyance, and many Americans were visibly tired of controversy and confrontation. But at least one category of Americans—Native Americans—grew increasingly militant. On February 27, 1973, members of the **American Indian Movement** (AIM) took over the village of **Wounded Knee**, South Dakota, near the site of the tragic 1890 massacre of some 250 Indians by the U.S. Cavalry. AIM militants, who pressed for a variety of reforms, held the town for seventy-one days before surrendering to federal authorities. Although the stand-off gained little public sympathy, Congress in 1974 passed the **Indian Self Determination and Cultural Assistance Act**, giving individual tribes control over federal programs carried out on their reservations. Long-standing grievances remained among the Indian population, but with more autonomy some tribes began to make substantial progress in helping their people.

The Ford and Carter Years

Gerald R. Ford became President of the United States in 1974 having never run for any national office in his life. He was appointed Nixon's vice president in 1973 after Spiro Agnew had resigned amidst a separate scandal over alleged bribery and income-tax evasion. After taking the oath of office, Ford announced that the "long national nightmare" of Watergate was over. Ford was a well-liked congressional leader from Michigan who enjoyed broad public support at first. But only a month after taking office, his popularity plummeted when he used his powers as president to **pardon** Richard Nixon for any federal crimes he *may have committed* while in office. Americans were suspicious (without any real evidence) that a secret deal between the two men had led to Ford's appointment as vice president in the first place. Shortly thereafter, in the first congressional election since Watergate, the public responded in 1974 by electing the largest Democratic majorities since the New Deal.

Faced with formidable partisan opposition, Ford had the dubious distinction of casting more vetoes than any other president in such a short period of time. Two-thirds majorities overrode several of these vetoes, and commentators began to speak of a veto-proof Congress. The 1970s were also plagued by a new economic evil: **inflation**, which lurched into double-digit figures. Rejecting earlier attempts at wage and price controls, Ford launched a voluntary campaign, complete with lapel buttons reading **WIN** (for "Whip Inflation Now"). To compound Ford's problems, the buttons quickly became objects of ridicule. Finally, Ford, despite being athletic and fit for his age, was caught in several on-camera incidents bumping his head, tripping, stumbling, and looking vaguely foolish and clumsy. As Ford and other politicians would learn, in the age of television, even normal human behavior can be deadly to one's image.

In 1975 the nightly news featured the images of a more historic humiliation. North Vietnamese forces, despite their government's earlier promises, closed in on Saigon, the capital of South Vietnam. In an earlier time and in another place, such a bold incursion would have prompted quick U.S. intervention, consistent with the long-standing policy of containment. While some congressional leaders called for re-entry of American troops, there was little sentiment for combat among the American public. The **fall of Vietnam** to communist forces in 1975 drove home a fact Americans did not want to contemplate: the United States had *lost* a war. It had been the longest and most controversial war in the country's history, with 58,000 American men and women killed. Their names are now engraved on **The Wall**, the Vietnam Veterans Memorial in Washington, a simple granite wall that draws more tourists than any other site in the nation's capital.

In the **election of 1976**, Gerald Ford faced Democrat **Jimmy Carter**, who had surprised the experts by winning the Democratic nomination as a relative unknown. A former governor of Georgia, Carter possessed the added political advantage of being from the South—a region rapidly turning Republican in national elections. Just as important, he emphasized his outsider role, which appealed to post-Watergate America. Carter was also a born-again Christian who promised voters, "I will never lie to you." Whether the voters believed him or not, Jimmy Carter, a peanut farmer (and Naval Academy graduate) from Plains, Georgia, was elected over President Ford in a close race.

Economically the curious merger of high unemployment and inflation—**Stagflation**—plagued the 1970s. Its causes can be traced partially to the **Arab Oil Embargo of 1973**, which boosted gasoline prices in the United States drastically. Furthermore, the Baby Boomers of the 1950s were now young adults and in need of jobs, which put further strains on American industries already reeling from stepped-up foreign competition, especially from Japan. Long lines at gas stations and employment offices made life tough on all incumbent politicians of the day. Carter's approach to the **Energy Crisis** spurred by the oil embargo emphasized government-mandated conservation of energy by business and industry, but Congress rejected most of his plans. The president valiantly attempted to rally public opinion, calling the energy crisis the "moral equivalent of war," but few Americans saw it that way. Carter also spoke of an American malaise in which problems seemed insurmountable, rejecting the buoyant optimism that successful U.S. politicians usually convey. Before long, Americans grew weary of listening to dour sermons from the president, who appeared desperate and indecisive.

Carter's economic and political problems were somewhat muted by a stunning achievement in the strife-torn Middle East. In the **Camp David Accords** of 1978, the President managed over a grueling two weeks to persuade Egypt's President Anwar el-Sadat and Israel's Prime Minister Menachem Begin to conclude a fragile peace. The deal involved the withdrawal of Israeli forces from the Sinai Peninsula (which Israel had taken in 1967 in exchange for acceptance by Egypt of Israeli sovereignty). Then, in 1979, President Carter was blindsided by the most painful episode of his presidency, the **Iran Hostage Crisis**. It all started when the pro-American Shah of Iran was overthrown by Islamic fundamentalists led by Ayatolah Ruhollah Khomeini. When Carter allowed the exiled Shah to come to the United States for cancer treatment, a mob seized the American Embassy in Teheran, the capital of Iran, taking fifty-three Americans hostage.

For more than a year, Carter and the nation endured globally televised humiliation, as militant Iranians with full government support held the Americans, burned the American flag as they paraded through the streets, and referred to America as the "Great Satan." In desperation, Carter authorized a daring rescue operation, which had to be aborted after eight men were killed when a combat helicopter crashed into a transport plane in the middle of the Iranian desert. To much of the American public, Carter appeared hopelessly naïve and helpless. Getting support from allies during the entire hostage crisis also proved difficult because of the other nations' dependence upon Iranian oil. The hostages were ultimately released after Carter's defeat in the **election of 1980**.

The Reagan Years

Ronald Reagan offered an alternative vision for America in 1980. A former movie actor and conservative governor of California, Reagan promised an end to weakness and humiliation, a 25 percent tax cut for working Americans, and a buildup of the U.S. military to resist Soviet expansionism. Although surveys indicated that in voting for Reagan Americans were expressing anti-Carter attitudes rather than pro-Reagan conservatism, the likeable and optimistic Reagan became extremely popular. Reagan's successful bid was also helped by a new coalition among Republicans, a curious union of laissez-faire economics and religious fundamentalism. The goal of the so-called **Reagan Revolution** was to unleash business from government regulations ("government is not the solution, it is the problem") while supporting the conservative agenda of a newly emerging force known as the **Christian Right**.

Throughout the 1950s and 1960s, evangelical Christianity was associated with a liberal agenda—support for civil rights for blacks, opposition to the

Vietnam War, and generosity with welfare programs. By the 1980s, however, a new conservative evangelism was spreading rapidly, finding a home within the revamped Republican Party. The Christian Right's agenda included an emphasis on traditional family values, prayer in schools, and, most important, a firm opposition to legal abortion. Using umbrella organizations such as the Moral Majority and the Christian Coalition, conservative activists gathered their money and energies to support Reagan, who talked their kind of language (conveniently ignoring the fact that as governor of California, he had signed the state's first abortion-on-demand bill). At the same time, white southerners and blue-collar workers in particular abandoned their traditional support of the Democratic Party during the 1980s, becoming known as the **Reagan Democrats**.

Reagan's domestic program rested upon a faith in **supply-side economics**. In order to understand this theory, two terms must be understood. The *deficit* represents the amount of money borrowed each year by the U.S. government (through the sale of government securities, such as bonds, to investors). The *national debt* is the total amount of borrowed money (including interest) over many years that is still owed. As the budget deficit grew to alarming proportions during the 1970s, Republicans had been stifled by traditional economic theories that proclaimed that either taxes must be raised or popular programs cut in order to save money and reduce the deficit. Both approaches were deadly to politicians. Supply-side theory argued, however, that a drastic tax *reduction* would stimulate investment, create jobs, and hence bring in new revenues painlessly. In 1981, Reagan convinced Congress (while the House was still in Democratic hands) to pass a 25 percent cut in personal income taxes. Due to the graduated nature of income taxes, the cut gave a windfall to wealthy Americans but pitifully small sums for those with lower incomes. As the 1980s progressed, however, the deficit shot upward to alarming levels. Subsequent statistics revealed that tax revenues actually went up during the Reagan years due to a drastic increase in Social Security payroll taxes. Furthermore, during Reagan's two terms the national debt doubled, rising more under Reagan than under all previous presidents combined. But once inflation dropped dramatically, Americans soon forgot about the deficit, spending more and spurring the economy—and giving the Reagan Administration a political boost.

Part of Reagan's agenda included cuts in proportional spending on domestic programs. Public housing in particular experienced steep declines in funding. Most "entitlement" programs (such as Social Security and Medicare) remained untouched, however, and Reagan's pledge to abolish the Departments of Education and Energy also failed to materialize. Military spending increased dramatically during the Reagan years, as the post-Vietnam reluctance to fund armed readiness and weaponry all but disappeared. The Soviet Union's crackdown in Poland and Afghanistan during the 1980s also helped convince Congress that the Cold War was far from over.

Reagan's charisma and speaking skills earned him the popular label the "Great Communicator," while other observers dubbed him the "Teflon President" for his uncanny ability to disavow himself from political mishaps. For example, after Reagan had ordered U.S. Marines into strife-ridden **Lebanon**, an Islamic suicide bomber breached the U.S. compound, killing 241 Americans. Ultimately the tragedy forced the withdrawal of U.S. troops from the area. This was precisely the kind of episode that would have been devastating to President Carter, but Reagan's buoyancy and hawkish stance muted most critics. Soon thereafter, a quick and successful military action on the Caribbean island of **Grenada**, against a leftist government that had placed American medical students in peril, reinforced Reagan's image as decisive and firm. In the **election of 1984**, Reagan defeated Democrat (and Carter's vice president) **Walter Mondale** in a major landslide. This election is also notable because of Mondale's selection of a woman, U.S. Representative **Geraldine Ferraro**, as his running mate. While the Mondale/Ferraro ticket lost, it was the first time a major U.S. party had nominated a woman. The Democrats were attempting to exploit a **gender gap** in public opinion that many experts had begun to notice. Since the 1970s women's voting patterns differed somewhat from men's, with women supporting the Democrats in greater percentages than before.

Reagan's second term was less successful than his first. The skyrocketing deficit, coupled with the stock market Crash of 1987, made investors uneasy. The Democrats had regained control of both chambers of Congress in 1984, throwing cold water on conservative hopes for continuing the Reagan Revolution. Most significant, the administration was rocked by the **Iran-Contra Scandal**. Reagan's desire to support the anticommunist Contras in Nicaragua resulted in an unbelievable scheme in which money from the illegal sale of arms to Iran (who had of course recently held American hostages) was secretly shunted to the Contras in Central America. Once the deal was exposed, Congress was furious. Reagan's extremely loose management style came under attack as the president's popularity took a downturn. In delegating too much authority to others, Reagan showed he had little control (and sometimes scant awareness) of the people in his own administration. Still reeling from a post-Vietnam reluctance to get involved in the fight against communism with money and troops, Americans did not like the looks of another potential jungle quagmire. An uneasy truce was negotiated in Nicaragua as the Reagan years drew to a close.

❖ Chapter Review

Identify

Richard M. Nixon	inflation
Woodstock	WIN
Altamont	fall of Vietnam
feminism	*The Wall*
The Feminine Mystique	election of 1976
Betty Friedan	Jimmy Carter
National Organization for Women	Stagflation
Equal Rights Amendment	Arab Oil Embargo of 1973
Roe v. *Wade*	Energy Crisis
right to privacy	Camp David Accords
George McGovern	Iran Hostage Crisis
election of 1972	election of 1980
Vietnamization	Ronald Reagan
Cambodia	Reagan Revolution
Henry Kissinger	Christian Right
Taiwan	Reagan Democrats
Watergate scandal	supply-side economics
U.S. v. *Nixon*	Lebanon
House Judiciary Committee	Grenada
American Indian Movement	election of 1984
Wounded Knee	Walter Mondale
Indian Self Determination and Cultural Assistance Act	Geraldine Ferraro
Gerald R. Ford	gender gap
pardon (for Nixon)	Iran-Contra Scandal

Short Paragraph

1. What are some of the modern roots of the feminist movement?

2. What did the Watergate scandal involve?

3. Why was the Reagan presidency important?

16

Cold War Ends,
War on Terror Begins

❖

Reagan's vice president, **George H. W. Bush**, easily defeated Democrat Michael Dukakis of Massachusetts in the **election of 1988**. Nationally, the mood was optimistic, partly because the Reagan years witnessed a steady decline in inflation, as energy prices tumbled in world markets. But there was a catch. The budget deficit had grown to levels that deeply disturbed leaders of both parties. By this time, simply paying the interest on the national debt required massive amounts of money—funds that were siphoned from social programs. And with the Baby Boomers reaching middle age, the future of Social Security and Medicare seemed in jeopardy as well.

A New World

Bush came to the presidency with impressive foreign policy experience as Reagan's vice president, former director of the CIA, and ambassador to China. But experience alone did not prepare him or the rest of the world for the spectacle that quickly unfolded in 1989: the **end of the Cold War**.

Early that year Soviet troops abruptly pulled out of Afghanistan after nine years of intense guerrilla fighting against insurgent rebels. As the world watched in amazement, Soviet communism began to unravel in other areas behind the iron curtain as well. Poland, Hungary, and Romania successfully rejected the Communist Party, either peacefully or through revolution. Most spectacular, on November 9, jubilant Germans tore down the Berlin

Wall, as millions watched on television from around the world. A newly united Germany chose to remain in NATO, as the Soviet Union, their antagonist for the last forty-four years, completely disintegrated in a matter of weeks. It was a breathtaking series of events that almost no one foresaw.

Why did the Soviet Union collapse? In the United States, conservatives pointed to the defense buildup of the Reagan years, or the inherent superiority of free enterprise capitalism. Others wrote of the inevitability of democracy. The truth is probably complex. The policy of containment initiated under President Truman after World War II, backed up by bipartisan support in Congress (with some notable exceptions such as the nightmare in Vietnam), and persistent vigilance under both Democratic and Republican administrations over fifty years are likely responsible. Modern information technology also made it impossible for Soviet leaders to insulate their population from the knowledge of and desire for Western goods and freedoms.

Ironically, the relaxation of the iron grip of the Soviet communism unleashed dangerous cultural and ethnic forces around the world, upsetting stability and providing for new peril. One dictator, **Saddam Hussein** of Iraq, had been a client of U.S. intelligence in years past, as a counterforce to vilified Iran. When Saddam unexpectedly moved troops into tiny Kuwait in 1990, President Bush responded with Operation Desert Shield, sending thousands of combat-ready troops into nearby Saudi Arabia. Then, in January 1991, a historic twenty-eight-nation alliance launched **Operation Desert Storm** (also known as the **Persian Gulf War**), pushing Iraq out of Kuwait with tanks and troops, as well as high-technology missiles and smart bombs targeted with amazing precision by computers and laser guidance systems. It was a new kind of war.

Some were unhappy that the United States and its allies ended hostilities once Saddam withdrew his forces from Kuwait, allowing him to remain in power as a merciless dictator. Immediately after the Gulf War, however, President Bush enjoyed high approval ratings. Domestic politics, on the other hand, proved his undoing. Bush had been adamant during his presidential campaign that taxes would not be raised, once proclaiming (to his later regret) "Read my lips. No new taxes." While the statement made Republicans wildly enthusiastic, it was replayed endlessly when Bush was compelled to strike a deal with Democrats involving a major tax increase. This embarrassment, plus a troubling economic recession, made Bush vulnerable as his term concluded.

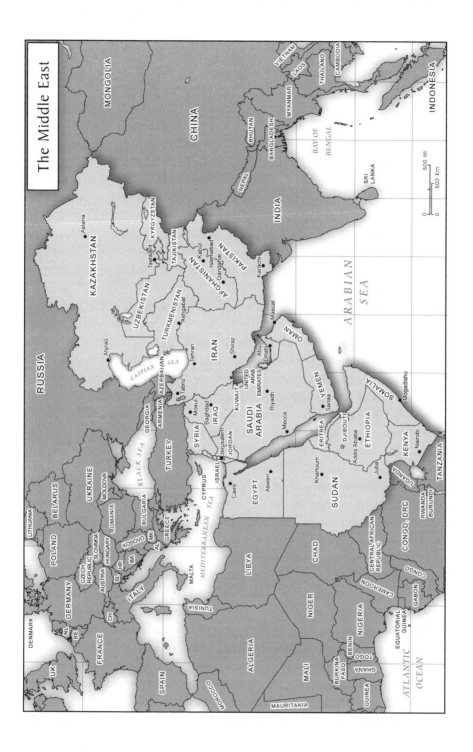

The Middle East

The Clinton Years

As the **election of 1992** approached, Democrats were hungry for the White House after twelve years of Republican control. **Bill Clinton**, former reformist governor of Arkansas, seemed like the New Democrat he promised to be. Rejecting the traditional liberal rhetoric of Democrats since Woodrow Wilson, Clinton moved decisively toward the center of the political spectrum. Also joining the campaign for president was Texas businessman **Ross Perot**, who tapped into growing resentment toward government and politics as usual. Although the independent candidacy of Perot failed to carry a single state in 1992, he garnered enough popular votes to get plenty of attention. Clinton won the close election in the Electoral College, but he was denied a popular majority.

The beginning years of Clinton's administration were shaky. Sensing public concern over health insurance (millions of Americans remained uncovered), Clinton proposed an ambitious overhaul of the health care system. It was a complicated mixture of public and private coverage that alarmed scores of corporate and health-related interest groups, with insurance and drug companies spending heavily on advertising to strike down the plan. First Lady **Hillary Clinton** (a successful attorney in her own right) took the lead in presenting the program to a skeptical Congress. Ultimately the **Clinton health care plan** went down in humiliating defeat, and Republicans sensed victory in the future. In one notable first-term success with Congress, Clinton won approval of the North American Free Trade Agreement (**NAFTA**), a controversial free-trade minded reduction in tariffs on goods from Mexico and Canada. Organized labor—a traditional Democratic constituency—had opposed NAFTA.

In the **congressional elections of 1994**, the Republican Party captured both the House and Senate for the first time since the 1950s. It was clearly an anti-Clinton vote, plus the fruits of an orchestrated strategy by Representative **Newt Gingrich** of Georgia, who was subsequently elected as Speaker of the House. Gingrich became the personification of Republican conservatism and the chief opponent of the Democratic president.

But the political life of Bill Clinton, who had a history of rebounding from defeat and scandal (mostly involving financial dealings in Arkansas and persistent charges of sexual misconduct), was far from finished. A number of factors worked in his favor as he faced re-election. Most important was the amazing performance of the American economy, which produced the most sustained period of full employment and inflation-free growth in several decades. This, in turn, virtually wiped out the annual budget deficit. Whether the good times were the result of government policy or not, the incumbent president reaped the benefits. Clinton's pledge to "Save Social Security First" also went over well with voters when contrasted with Republican promises of tax cuts. In the **election of 1996**, Clinton became the first Democratic president to win re-election since Franklin Roosevelt, easily defeating respected Senator Bob Dole of Kansas, the Republican candidate.

The 1990s Congress was increasingly partisan, as party-line votes became commonplace on a host of controversial issues. With a Democratic president in the White House and a fierce Republican-dominated Congress on Capitol Hill, the stage was set for one of the most bizarre episodes in political history. Special Independent Prosecutor **Kenneth Starr** (appointed under a Watergate-era statute) began to investigate the financial dealings of the Clintons while they lived in Arkansas. The alleged wrongdoing in question was tagged the **Whitewater investigation**, after a complicated real estate deal gone sour. In the course of his investigation, Starr's office also raised allegations of Clinton's sexual misdeeds, with little effect until a former White House intern named **Monica Lewinsky** was secretly taped by a friend while discussing her affair with Clinton. Starr called a Grand Jury. Under oath and on camera, President Clinton denied any sexual relationship with Lewinsky—a denial he later modified drastically (also under oath) to say the least. Starr presented several charges to the House of Representatives, as formal impeachment hearings commenced in the Republican-controlled Congress. Two articles of impeachment were approved by the House, formally charging the president with obstruction of justice and perjury. And so Clinton became the second President in history to be impeached (the first was Andrew Johnson in 1868). Nevertheless, the vote in the Senate fell short of the two-thirds necessary for the president's removal. The general public, as revealed in opinion polls, certainly disapproved of Clinton's behavior, but also believed that Starr's investigation had strayed too far into private matters, prompting talk of "sexual McCarthyism." All agreed it was a sorry and embarrassing spectacle. Clinton's presidency was saved, but at great cost.

In 1999 Clinton was tested as commander in chief. The **Balkans War** came in response to the brutal **ethnic cleansing** of Muslim Albanians by Serbian forces in the Yugoslavian province of **Kosovo**. Many experts believed a terrible holocaust was under way. Mass graves were uncovered, and Serbian troops were reportedly kidnapping and killing men and gang-raping women. Yugoslavian president **Slobodan Milošević** (a former communist official) was defiant. For the first time in history, NATO ordered military action within the borders of a sovereign nation. President Clinton, heading by far the largest power in the NATO alliance, ordered American forces to the region, which commenced bombing and missile attacks on Yugoslavian targets. Milošević, after weeks of unrelenting attacks from the air, finally gave in. Amazingly, there were no American casualties.

The **election of 2000**, pitting Republican Governor **George W. Bush** of Texas against Democratic Vice President **Al Gore**, proved to be one of the closest races in U.S. history. Bush promised tax cuts in the wake of the budget surplus, as Gore hammered home traditional Democratic themes. Interestingly, Bush's strategy of supporting health care and education while avoiding issues favored by Christian conservatives, may have helped him attract moderate voters. In a first, Gore chose as his running mate a Jewish vice presidential candidate, Senator **Joseph Lieberman** of Connecticut. Although Gore barely beat Bush in the popular vote, the Electoral College proved exceedingly problematic, with most of the disputed votes occurring in Florida.

After four weeks of indecision and acrimony, on December 12, the United States Supreme Court, in a case aptly titled *Bush v. Gore*, ruled 7–2 to overturn a decision by the Florida Supreme Court ordering recounts in some counties. The court split along party lines in requiring any new count to be implemented by a midnight deadline, effectively ensuring that it would be too late. Many thought the highest court in the land had succumbed to the tide of partisanship. The next day, the Florida Supreme Court rejected another appeal from Gore, sealing his fate. That evening he conceded the race to Bush, who promised to be "a uniter and not a divider."

Bush and the War on Terror

George W. Bush, as Governor of Texas, had impressed many with his willingness to cross party lines. As President, he at first exhibited the same traits, most notably in the **No Child Left Behind** Act, an education reform invoking national standards and testing for public school children. Although Democrats complained that the law was never funded as promised, the measure placed education as a national priority in new ways.

In most matters, however, the second President Bush took his cues from Ronald Reagan rather than his own father. "W" Bush persuaded Congress to cut income taxes dramatically, precisely when a stubborn recession was beginning. The policy mirrored the supply-side economic policies of Reagan, promising growth in the economy as a means to cut the deficit. The red ink, however, continued to grow wiping out the balanced budget Bush had inherited from Clinton. Since the tax cuts proportionately benefited wealthy Americans, the Bush administration remained open to charges of favoring the rich. The Bush administration also pleased social conservatives. Speaking frequently of his born-again Christian faith, he persuaded Congress to direct federal funds to faith-based initiatives, crossing the traditional line separating church and state. He also placed limitations on stem cell research, which uses cells from, among other places, discarded human embryos to develop potential treatments for chronic diseases.

September 11

On the fateful morning of September 11, 2001, two passenger airplanes crashed spectacularly into the twin towers of the World Trade Center in New York City. Shortly afterward, a third plane dove into the Pentagon, the Washington headquarters of the U.S. Defense Department. A fourth crashed in a field in Pennsylvania, apparently intended by the perpetrators for the U.S. Capitol. It soon became obvious that terrorist hijackers were responsible. President Bush was informed during an appearance at an elementary school: "America is under attack!"

The number of Americans killed was almost 2,500—more than at Pearl Harbor at the outset of World War II, and more than any single terrorist attack in any location. Before the day was over, as the horrific scenes of collapsing skyscrapers in the financial district of Manhattan were replayed incessantly on television, experts surmised that the perpetrators were Islamic (or Muslim) extremists with ties to **Osama bin Laden**, a millionaire Saudi fundamentalist who had openly declared war on the U.S., Israel, and the Saudi monarchy.

Bin Laden's network, **al-Qaeda** (the base), believed to encompass operations in more than sixty countries, was implicated previously in terrorist acts against Americans, including at U.S. embassies in Africa, and the USS *Cole* near Yemen. America had acquired determined enemies before, but these new combatants recruited and trained individuals eager to commit suicide for their cause, a *Jihad*, (holy war). Their doctrines opposed many aspects of modern culture—gender equality, religious pluralism, artistic freedom, etc.—and yet the terrorists were highly sophisticated in the use of the latest technology and communications.

Since the new threat involved airplanes used as missiles, one of the most noticeable changes in American life was increased airport security, resulting in long lines and more extensive searches of persons and property. Congress passed the **Patriot Act**, which gave the government unprecedented authority to investigate private communications and associations. (Portions of the Act were subsequently held to be unconstitutional by the Supreme Court.) A new Cabinet department was created, the Office of Homeland Security. Though violence was rare, Muslims in America were occasionally subjected to harassment. Hundreds of people were arrested, usually on immigration law violations. Some were convicted of collaboration with terrorists. Others were held without legal representation, most notably at the U.S. Naval base in Guantanamo, Cuba. The U.S. government even refused to release the names of some detainees, who faced military tribunals rather than civil courts.

The global War on Terror at first focused on Afghanistan. The **Taliban**, a Muslim faction controlling the government there, was believed to have harbored bin Laden for several years. On October 7, after the Taliban refused to turn over bin Laden, the United States and its close ally Great Britain began air strikes against Afghan military targets and reported terrorist training camps. The Taliban government fell two months after the bombing began. America sent troops to stabilize the new leadership. Bin Laden himself, however, remained elusive, along with many of his collaborators and supporters.

War in Iraq

"Today we focus on Afghanistan," Bush said, but "the battle is broader." Soon the focus of the war shifted remarkably to Iraq. Within the administration, officials began to argue that military action was needed in Iraq, despite no clear evidence of any Iraqi complicity in the attacks of September 11. Iraq, which was still ruled by Saddam Hussein, the man who had invaded Kuwait when President Bush's father had been in office, was believed to be sponsoring terrorists and, more ominously, developing and stockpiling **weapons of**

mass destruction (WMDs). These weapons, intelligence suggested, included a potential nuclear capability. Furthermore, Saddam had used biological weapons previously, against the Kurds in his own country, who had been rebelling against his authority.

President Bush, who had been elected with fewer popular votes than his opponent in 2000, soon commanded higher approval ratings than any president since polling began. His administration began to build the case for an invasion of Iraq. The United Nations was thwarted in its efforts to conduct thorough inspections for WMDs, but it still insisted that the process be completed before authorizing the use of force.

President Bush made it clear that the United States would not wait for UN approval, as nations of the world (and many Americans) began to voice opposition. Critics of the United States accused Bush of **unilateralism** in foreign policy, suggesting that the go-it-alone strategy was unnecessary, arrogant, and dangerous. The Bush administration, unable to obtain unanimous approval in the UN Security Council, announced that a "coalition of the willing" would topple Saddam to make the world safer.

On October 10, 2002, Congress adopted a joint resolution authorizing the president to deploy the U. S. military in Iraq should he deem it necessary. The vote was crucial but far from unanimous, reflecting a deep division among the public as well. UN weapons inspectors remained unable to determine the extent to which WMDs remained a threat, or if they even existed. The U. S.-led invasion began on March 19, 2003. Baghdad, the capital, fell on April 9.

Nevertheless, to call President Bush's celebrated appearance on the deck of an aircraft carrier under a "Mission Accomplished" banner premature is, at best, understatement. A determined Iraqi insurgency mounted by various cultural and religious affiliations fought the kind of guerrilla war that had plagued the U.S. military before, with the added hazard of suicidal bombers. Some nations in the coalition began to express reluctance for a protracted occupation.

The 2004 Election

The public's willingness to give the president wide latitude undoubtedly helped win support for the war on Iraq, in spite of the dubious link between the events of September 11 and Saddam Hussein. In fact, a bipartisan commission determined that there was no credible evidence of any such connection. Months after the commission's findings were published, however, public opinion polls revealed that a significant portion of the American population continued to agree with Bush that the war on terror and the war on Iraq were essentially the same thing.

President Bush presided over a nation more polarized than at any time since the 1800s. Democrats, still bitter from the contentious election debacle of 2000, were determined to nominate someone who could win, and eventually agreed upon Senator **John Kerry** of Massachusetts, a seasoned politician and a highly decorated Vietnam war hero. Kerry proved to be a formidable opponent, but he was plagued by charges of having flip-flopped on votes during his Senate career. The senator also had voted for the resolution giving the president authority to use force in Iraq, which made it harder for him to criticize Bush's war policies.

Despite polls indicating that the election would be close again, President Bush won re-election with room to spare, prompting the inevitable post-election theories of why voters make the choices they do. Many pointed to conservatives in the so-called **red states** (those with a tendency to vote Republican) who objected to social trends such as same-sex marriage, which was newly allowed by some state and local officials. While Kerry was opposed to same-sex marriage, many conservative and rural Americans associated Democrats (in **blue states** such as California and Massachusetts) with a lack of values. Democrats, of course, saw plenty of values in opposing the war, saving Social Security, and providing universal health insurance. It is clear that the president benefited from the fear enveloping the nation since September 11. In such times, voters tend to seek safety in continuity.

The Great Recession

President Bush announced that his second term would include bold new initiatives. One of his proposals included an attempt to privatize Social Security, to allow younger workers to invest a portion of their paychecks in the stock market rather than the Social Security fund. The move further illuminated concerns over the long-term solvency of the system. The proposal never gained traction in Congress, as the general public, particularly older Americans, exhibited their customary protective attitude toward established entitlement programs. The war in Iraq grew steadily unpopular too, even after a major surge in troop levels by the United States appeared to achieve the goal of increased stability there.

In 2006, the Democrats began an impressive comeback, ultimately winning majorities in the House and Senate. The House selected its first woman Speaker, **Nancy Pelosi** of California, as the pendulum began to swing away from the Republicans and their policies. The shift in mood reflected a dramatic decline in the popularity of President Bush. During his second term, the economy began to exhibit a profound sense of instability. By the fall of 2008, a major economic meltdown had begun.

The roots of the **Great Recession** (as experts began to call it) can be attributed to a number of factors, but all are agreed that it was the worst economic decline since the Great Depression. The debacle was driven, at least in part, by inflated housing prices in many areas of the country. Many thought the housing bubble would never burst, but in 2008 it did so spectacularly. As the price of homes tumbled, homeowners increasingly found themselves in "upside-down" mortgages, meaning that they owed more on their mortgages than their homes were worth. Significantly, the financial services industry—including well-respected commercial banks and Wall Street investment houses—had devised investment tools that "bundled" mortgages, a great many of which were classified as "sub-prime," meaning known to be poor bets, and sold them on the open market as well as in closed deals. Clearly these types of investments were extremely risky, yet they went virtually unregulated. In short, speculators had risked huge amounts of money on borrowers who had no ability to pay (some didn't even have jobs) their mortgages. They assumed, apparently, that housing prices would always continue to rise.

As the number of housing foreclosures reached unprecedented levels, the overall fragility of the national economy presented itself stunningly. The financial services industry almost collapsed, as the government and public finally realized that it was rife with "creative" accounting, with little or no underlying foundation of collateral. Banks closed. The stock market lost one-third of its value. Bankruptcies were epidemic. Unemployment rose to 10 percent. Pension plans became insolvent. As the meltdown played out, no nation in the world was spared its effects. Worse yet, no one knew where the bottom might be, as most of the experts had already been proven dead wrong.

President Bush had based his economic policies on an unquestioning faith in the free market's ability to correct itself when problems arose. But this time the market had fallen flat, with no way to mend itself. Bush's economic advisors, including **Ben Bernanke**, chair of the Federal Reserve Board (and a scholar of the Great Depression), urged massive, rapid government spending to avoid catastrophe.

In a series of emergency meetings, theBush team and Congress devised a plan. Most urgently, they believed, credit must start to flow again. The **Troubled Asset Relief Program (TARP)** was created to **"bail out"** the financial services industry, doling out hundreds of billions of dollars in loans to huge companies—some of which had been deemed **"too big to fail."** Infuriatingly, many of the firms taking the money were thought to be culprits in creating the problem in the first place by recklessly and greedily taking on too much risk. The public was also angered by reports that some of the taxpayer dollars were being awarded to Wall Street executives in the form of lucrative bonuses. Understandably, struggling individuals all over the country began to ask, "Where's *my* bailout?"

The 2008 Election and Barack Obama

Given the horrific economic situation, it is not surprising that a major political realignment was in store. The Republicans nominated Vietnam War hero and Arizona Senator **John McCain**, after a bitter set of primaries. The GOP also revealed a deep fissure within the party. Social and religious conservatives—activists who vote and participate intensely—now constituted the "base" of the Republican electorate. These individuals highly disapproved of the government spending and deficits necessitated by the recession. McCain had voted for the bailout, and he had a reputation as a maverick within the party. In a move that surprised almost everyone, he picked **Sarah Palin**, the governor of Alaska, as his running mate. Palin was highly popular with conservatives, but she had little experience in national politics. It was a year of surprises for the Democrats, too.

As the primary season began, virtually all commentators assumed that Senator Hillary Clinton of New York would be the Democratic nominee. She was experienced, articulate, and possessed a loyal following of voters and contributors. This was not, however, just another election year. Soon, Senator **Barack Obama** of Illinois began to attract a great deal of attention, based on his soaring rhetoric, personal charisma, and desire for dramatic change. Democrats detected a winner, in spite of Obama's relative inexperience in politics. Once he entered the race, the game changed. As an African American, he was able to energize racial minorities—an important bloc of votes for Democrats. His calm demeanor (reporters referred to "No Drama Obama") seemed just right during a crisis. As an early opponent of the Iraq war, he was also better equipped to criticize the Bush policies than Clinton, who had voted to grant Bush permission to invade Iraq. Obama proved to be an able candidate, with a disciplined campaign that eventually overtook Clinton, who had enjoyed an early lead.

On January 20, 2009, the first African American President in history was inaugurated. Obama defeated McCain by winning the traditional battleground states, including Virginia and Florida. Analyses of the votes indicated a surge of support for Obama among younger voters. Promising change, Obama and running mate, Senator **Joe Biden** of Delaware, basked in a glow of wonder along with the nation, as it crossed a dramatic milestone. Americans said repeatedly that they never dreamed such an event would occur in their lifetime. As the financial crisis worsened, a new atmosphere of confidence could be detected, not just in the United States but all over the world. It would not last long, however, as the traditional honeymoon period quickly faded and partisan "politics as usual" resumed.

Successful presidents tend to achieve their major priorities early—a fact the Obama team knew quite well. Spurred by the financial meltdown, the administration obtained Congressional approval for an economic **stimulus package** totaling $787 billion, as projected deficits climbed into the trillions. The money went largely to the states, which were devastated by a huge decline in tax revenue, and to help rebuild the infrastructure of roads, bridges, and electrical grids. It was the largest public works measure ever and the most significant since the New Deal. Much of the revenue was also directed toward "green" projects designed to steer the nation toward energy independence and a healthier environment. Obama had also pledged to begin work in earnest to mitigate the effects of **global climate change**, which scientists said was largely the result of "greenhouse gases" released into the atmosphere by various forms of industrial and automobile emissions.

President Obama achieved a measure of bipartisan support in Congress as he focused on the war in Afghanistan, sending in an additional 30,000 troops to that fractured nation, where the Taliban was reportedly providing support for organizations responsible for numerous terrorist attacks. The president had supported this war from the beginning, in contrast to his opposition to the war in Iraq.

Perhaps the most striking of the various "bailout" policies of the Obama Administration involved direct financial aid to the automotive industry, in particular to Chrysler and General Motors—troubled firms that sputtered into bankruptcy in the wake of the financial crisis. Politicians found it unacceptable to allow these companies to fail, for it would have resulted in thousands of layoffs. In addition to the nearly $7 billion in direct loans to GM, the U. S. Treasury extended $43 billion in other funds, for a total of $50 billion. The non-debt portion was converted to stock shares, representing a 60 percent stake in the company owned by the U.S. taxpayers. The newly reorganized GM managed to pay back the cash fairly quickly, but the federal government was still the majority stockholder of the company. Chrysler also received federal help. Nonetheless, President Obama stated repeatedly that he wanted the government to "get out of the car business" as quickly as possible.

The most ambitious and controversial proposal of the Obama administration was in the field of health care reform, which had been on the U. S. political agenda for over a century. Virtually all developed nations had found a way to provide adequate and affordable health care to their citizens, while the United States still had more than 30 million people without health insurance, in a system consuming one-sixth of the gross domestic product and little evidence of better health to show for it. Finally, after more than a year of extremely acrimonious debate, Congress enacted an overhaul of the health care system, the **Patient Protection and Affordable Care Act**. It was the most ambitious domestic legislative accomplishment since the Great Society programs of the 1960s. Unlike previous historic reforms, however, the bill was passed on a purely partisan basis, with Republicans united in opposition.

In 2010 many commentators could not recall a time when the country was so deeply divided. But a reading of history clearly demonstrates that sharp disagreements over policy are nothing new. Around 1800, many will recall, it was not uncommon for political disagreements to be settled by duels. Certainly the labor disputes, the Civil Rights era, and the debate over the war in Vietnam during the twentieth century produced plenty of acrimony—and no shortage of violence. As noted earlier, it is not difficult to detect a pendulum effect to social change in the United States, with reforms followed by reaction and retrenchment, which, in turn, stimulates more reform. Finally, more than one observer has noted an optimistic quality to the American character. Simply put, Americans always have been and remain an optimistic people, always willing to believe that problems can be solved and things will get better. If the past is any indication, the United States will continue to reinvent itself in dramatic ways as its people try to fulfill the original promise.

✤ Chapter Review

Identify

George H. W. Bush	*Bush* v. *Gore*
election of 1988	No Child Left Behind
end of the Cold War	Osama bin Laden
Saddam Hussein	al-Qaeda
Operation Desert Storm	Patriot Act
Persian Gulf War	Taliban
election of 1992	WMDs
Bill Clinton	unilateralism
Ross Perot	Iraqi insurgency
Hillary Clinton	John Kerry
Clinton health care plan	red states and blue states
NAFTA	Nancy Pelosi
congressional elections of 1994	Great Recession
Newt Gingrich	Ben Bernanke
election of 1996	TARP
Kenneth Starr	"bail out"
Whitewater investigation	"too big to fail"
Monica Lewinsky	John McCain
Balkans War	Sarah Palin
ethnic cleansing	Barack Obama
Kosovo	Joe Biden
Slobodan Milosovic	stimulus package
election of 2000	global climate change
George W. Bush	Patient Protection and
Al Gore	Affordable Care Act
Joseph Lieberman	

Short Paragraph

1. What were the causes of the end of the Cold War?

2. What were the major controversies of the 1990s?

3. What were the results of September 11, 2001?

4. Why did Barack Obama win the election of 2008?

Declaration of Independence

(On June 7, 1776, Richard Henry Lee submitted a resolution to The Continental Congress declaring the independence of the United States. The resolution was referred to a committee consisting of Jefferson, Adams, Franklin, Roger Sherman, and Robert Livingstone, who were directed to draft a Declaration embodying this resolution. The committee reported its draft on June 28; the Declaration was adopted on July 2 and signed on July 4.)*

THE UNANIMOUS DECLARATION OF THE
THIRTEEN UNITED STATES OF AMERICA

When, in the course of human events, it becomes necessary for one people to dissolve the political bands which have connected them with another, and to assume among the powers of the earth, the separate and equal station to which the laws of nature and of nature's God entitle them, a decent respect to the opinions of mankind requires that they should declare the causes which impel them to the separation.

---

*This note is *not* part of the document; it is an annotation from *The Constitution of the United States and Related Documents,* edited by Martin Shapiro. Copyright © 1973 by Harlan Davidson, Inc.

We hold these truths to be self-evident, that all men are created equal, that they are endowed by their Creator with certain unalienable rights, that among these are life, liberty and the pursuit of happiness. That to secure these rights, governments are instituted among men, deriving their just powers from the consent of the governed, that whenever any form of government becomes destructive of these ends, it is the right of the people to alter or to abolish it, and to institute new government, laying its foundation on such principles and organizing its powers in such form, as to them shall seem most likely to effect their safety and happiness. Prudence, indeed, will dictate that governments long established should not be changed for light and transient causes; and accordingly all experience hath shown that mankind are more disposed to suffer, while evils are sufferable, than to right themselves by abolishing the forms to which they are accustomed. But when a long train of abuses and usurpations, pursuing invariably the same object evinces a design to reduce them under absolute despotism, it is their right, it is their duty, to throw off such government, and to provide new guards for their future security.—Such has been the patient sufferance of these colonies; and such is now the necessity which constrains them to alter their former systems of government. The history of the present King of Great Britain is a history of repeated injuries and usurpations, all having in direct object the establishment of an absolute tyranny over these states. To prove this, let facts be submitted to a candid world.

He has refused his assent to laws, the most wholesome and necessary for the public good.

He has forbidden his governors to pass laws of immediate and pressing importance, unless suspended in their operation till his assent should be obtained; and when so suspended, he has utterly neglected to attend to them.

He has refused to pass other laws for the accommodation of large districts of people, unless those people would relinquish the right of representation in the legislature, a right inestimable to them and formidable to tyrants only.

He has called together legislative bodies at places unusual, uncomfortable, and distant from the depository of their public records, for the sole purpose of fatiguing them into compliance with his measures.

He has dissolved representative houses repeatedly for opposing with manly firmness his invasions on the rights of the people.

He has refused for a long time, after such dissolutions, to cause others to be elected; whereby the legislative powers, incapable of annihilation, have returned to the people at large for their exercise; the state remaining in the meantime exposed to all the dangers of invasion from without, and convulsions within.

He has endeavored to prevent the population of these states; for that purpose obstructing the laws for naturalization of foreigners; refusing to pass others to encourage their migration hither, and raising the conditions of new appropriations of lands.

He has obstructed the administration of justice, by refusing his assent to laws for establishing judiciary powers.

He has made judges dependent on his will alone, for the tenure of their offices, and the amount and payment of their salaries.

He has erected a multitude of new offices, and sent hither swarms of officers to harass our people, and eat out their substance.

He has kept among us, in times of peace, standing armies without the consent of our legislature.

He has affected to render the military independent of and superior to the civil power.

He has combined with others to subject us to a jurisdiction foreign to our constitution, and unacknowledged by our laws; giving his assent to their acts of pretended legislation:

For quartering large bodies of armed troops among us:

For protecting them, by a mock trial, from punishment for any murders which they should commit on the inhabitants of these states:

For cutting off our trade with all parts of the world:

For imposing taxes on us without our consent:

For depriving us in many cases, of the benefits of trial by jury:

For transporting us beyond seas to be tried for pretended offenses:

For abolishing the free system of English laws in a neighboring province, establishing therein an arbitrary government, and enlarging its boundaries so as to render it at once an example and fit instrument for introducing the same absolute rule into these colonies:

For taking away our charters, abolishing our most valuable laws, and altering fundamentally the forms of our governments:

For suspending our own legislatures, and declaring themselves invested with power to legislate for us in all cases whatsoever.

He has abdicated government here, by declaring us out of his protection and waging war against us.

He has plundered our seas, ravaged our coasts, burned our towns, and destroyed the lives of our people.

He is at this time transporting large armies of foreign mercenaries to complete the works of death, desolation and tyranny, already begun with circumstances of cruelty and perfidy scarcely paralleled in the most barbarous ages, and totally unworthy the head of a civilized nation.

He has constrained our fellow citizens taken captive on the high seas to bear arms against their country, to become the executioners of their friends and brethren, or to fall themselves by their hands.

He has excited domestic insurrections amongst us and has endeavored to bring on the inhabitants of our frontiers, the merciless Indian savages, whose known rule of warfare, is an undistinguished destruction of all ages, sexes and conditions.

In every stage of these oppressions we have petitioned for redress in the most humble terms: our repeated petitions have been answered only by repeated injury. A prince, whose character is thus marked by every act which may define a tyrant, is unfit to be the ruler of a free people.

Nor have we been wanting in attention to our British brethren. We have warned them from time to time of attempts by their legislature to extend an unwarrantable jurisdiction over us. We have reminded them of the circumstances of our emigration and settlement here. We have appealed to their native justice and magnanimity, and we have conjured them by the ties of our common kindred to disavow these usurpations, which, would inevitably interrupt our connections and correspondence. They too have been deaf to the voice of justice and of consanguinity. We must, therefore, acquiesce in the necessity, which denounces our separation, and hold them, as we hold the rest of mankind, enemies in war, in peace friends.

We, therefore, the representatives of the United States of America, in General Congress, assembled, appealing to the Supreme Judge of the world for the rectitude of our intentions, do, in the name, and by the authority of the good people of these colonies, solemnly publish and declare, that these united colonies are and of right ought to be free and independent states; that they are absolved from all allegiance to the British Crown, and that all political connection between them and the state of Great Britain, is and ought to be totally dissolved; and that as free and independent states, they have full power to levy war, conclude peace, contract alliances, establish commerce, and to do all other acts and things which independent states may of right do. And for the support of this declaration, with a firm reliance on the protection of Divine Providence, we mutually pledge to each other our lives, our fortunes and our sacred honor.

John Hancock

NEW HAMPSHIRE
Josiah Bartlett
Wm. Whipple
Matthew Thornton

MASSACHUSETTS BAY
Saml. Adams
John Adams
Robt. Treat Paine
Elbridge Gerry

RHODE ISLAND
Step. Hopkins
William Ellery

CONNECTICUT
Roger Sherman
Sam'el Huntington
Wm. Williams
Oliver Wolcott

NEW YORK
Wm. Floyd
Phil. Livingston
Frans. Lewis
Lewis Morris

NEW JERSEY
Richd. Stockton
Jno. Witherspoon
Fras. Hopkinson
John Hart
Abra. Clark

PENNSYLVANIA
Robt. Morris
Benjamin Rush
Benja. Franklin
John Morton
Geo. Clymer
Jas. Smith
Geo. Taylor
James Wilson
Geo. Ross

DELAWARE
Caesar Rodney
Geo. Read
Tho. M'Kean

MARYLAND
Samuel Chase
Wm. Paca
Thos. Stone
Charles Carroll of Carrollton

VIRGINIA
George Wythe
Richard Henry Lee
Th Jefferson
Benja. Harrison
Thos. Nelson, Jr.
Francis Lightfoot Lee
Carter Braxton

NORTH CAROLINA
Wm. Hooper
Joseph Hewes
John Penn

SOUTH CAROLINA
Edward Rutledge
Thos. Heyward, Junr.
Thomas Lynch, Junr.
Arthur Middleton

GEORGIA
Button Gwinnett
Lyman Hall
Geo. Walton

APPENDIX
B

The Constitution of the United States

PREAMBLE

We the People of the United States, in order to form a more perfect Union, establish Justice, insure domestic Tranquility, provide for the common defence, promote the general Welfare, and secure the Blessing of Liberty to ourselves and our Posterity, do ordain and establish this CONSTITUTION for the United States of America.

ARTICLE 1
[THE CONGRESS]*

SECTION 1. [GENERAL GRANT OF POWER]

All legislative Powers herein granted shall be vested in a Congress of the United States, which shall consist of a Senate and House of Representatives.

SECTION 2. [HOUSE OF REPRESENTATIVES: ELECTION, QUALIFICATIONS, APPORTIONMENT AMONG THE STATES, VACANCIES, POWER OVER INTERNAL ORGANIZATION, IMPEACHMENT]

The House of Representatives shall be composed of Members chosen every second Year by the People of the several States, and the Electors in each State shall have the Qualifications requisite for Electors of the most numerous Branch of the State Legislature.

---

*The notes in brackets and the footnotes are not part of the document; they are annotations from *The Constitution of the United States and Related Documents*, edited by Martin Shapiro. Copyright © 1973 by Harlan Davidson, Inc.

No Person shall be a Representative who shall not have attained to the Age of twenty-five Years, and been seven Years a Citizen of the United States, and who shall not, when elected, be an Inhabitant of that State in which he shall be chosen.

[Representatives and direct Taxes shall be apportioned among the several States which may be included within this Union, according to their respective Numbers, which shall be determined by adding to the whole Number of free Persons, including those bound to Service for a Term of Years, and excluding Indians not taxed, three fifths of all other persons.][1] The actual Enumeration shall be made within three Years after the first Meeting of the Congress of the United States, and within every subsequent Term of ten Years, in such Manner as they shall by Law direct. The Number of Representatives shall not exceed one for every thirty thousand, but each State shall have at Least one Representative; and until such enumeration shall be made, the State of New Hampshire shall be entitled to chuse three, Massachusetts eight, Rhode Island and Providence Plantations one, Connecticut five, New York six, New Jersey four, Pennsylvania eight, Delaware one, Maryland six, Virginia ten, North Carolina five, South Carolina five, and Georgia three.

When vacancies happen in the Representation from any State, the Executive Authority thereof shall issue Writs of Election to fill such Vacancies.

The House of Representatives shall chuse their Speaker and other Officers; and shall have the sole Power of Impeachment.

SECTION 3. [THE SENATE: NUMBER, STAGGERED TERMS, QUALIFICATIONS OF SENATORS, OFFICERS, IMPEACHMENT]

The Senate of the United States shall be composed of two Senators from each State, chosen by the Legislature thereof,[2] for six Years; and each Senator shall have one Vote.

Immediately after they shall be assembled in Consequence of the first Election, they shall be divided as equally as may be into three Classes. The Seats of the Senators of the first Class shall be vacated at the Expiration of the second Year, of the Second Class at the Expiration of the fourth Year, and of the third Class at the Expiration of the sixth Year, so that one-third may be chosen every second Year; and if Vacancies happen by Resignation, or otherwise, during the

---

[1] Altered by Amendment XVI. The three-fifths rule was eliminated by Amendments XIII and XIV.

[2] See Amendment XVII

Recess of the Legislature of any State, the Executive thereof may make temporary Appointments until the next Meeting of the Legislature, which shall then fill such Vacancies.

No Person shall be a Senator who shall not have attained to the Age of thirty Years, and been nine Years a Citizen of the United States, and who shall not, when elected, be an Inhabitant of that State for which he shall be chosen.

The Vice-President of the United States shall be President of the Senate, but shall have no Vote, unless they be equally divided.

The Senate shall chuse their other Officers, and also a President pro tempore, in the absence of the Vice-President, or when he shall exercise the Office of President of the United States.

The Senate shall have the sole Power to try all Impeachments. When sitting for that Purpose, they shall be on Oath or Affirmation. When the President of the United States is tried, the Chief Justice shall preside; And no Person shall be convicted without the Concurrence of two thirds of the Members present.

Judgment in Cases of Impeachment shall not extend further than to removal from Office, and disqualification to hold and enjoy any Office of honor, Trust or Profit under the United States: but the Party convicted shall nevertheless be liable and subject to Indictment, Trial, Judgement and Punishment, according to the Law.

SECTION 4. [ELECTIONS AND TIME OF MEETING]

The Times, Places and Manner of holding Elections for Senators and Representatives, shall be prescribed in each State by the Legislature thereof; but the Congress may at any time by Law make or alter such Regulations, except as to the Places of Chusing Senators.

The Congress shall assemble at least once in every Year, and such Meeting shall be on the first Monday in December, unless they shall by Law appoint a different Day.[3]

SECTION 5. [POWER OF CONGRESS TO REGULATE ITS INTERNAL BUSINESS]

Each House shall be the Judge of the Elections, Returns and Qualifications of its own Members, and a Majority of each shall constitute a Quorum to do Business; but a smaller Number may adjourn from day to day, and may be authorized to compel the Attendance of absent Members, in such Manner, and under such Penalties as each House may provide.

---

[3] See Amendment XX

Each House may determine the Rules of its Proceedings, punish its Members for disorderly Behavior, and, with the Concurrence of two thirds, expel a Member.

Each House shall keep a Journal of its Proceedings and from time to time publish the same, excepting such Parts as may in their Judgment require Secrecy; and the Yeas and Nays of the Members of either House on any question shall, at the Desire of one fifth of those Present, be entered on the Journal.

Neither House, during the Session of Congress, shall without the Consent of the other, adjourn for more than three days, nor to any other Place than that in which the two Houses shall be sitting.

SECTION 6. [COMPENSATION, PRIVELEGES, AND DISABILITIES OF MEMBERS]

The Senators and Representatives shall receive a Compensation for their Services, to be ascertained by Law, and paid out of the Treasury of the United States. They shall in all Cases, except Treason, Felony, and Breach of the peace, be privileged from Arrest during their Attendance at the Session of their respective Houses, and in going to and returning from the same; and for any Speech or Debate in either House, they shall not be questioned in any other Place.

No Senator or Representative shall, during the Time for which he was elected, be appointed to any civil Office under the Authority of the United States, which shall have been created, or the Emoluments whereof shall have been encreased during such time; and no Person holding any Office under the United States, shall be a Member of either House during his Continuance in Office.

SECTION 7. [MODE OF PASSING LAWS, REVENUE LAWS, OVERRIDING PRESIDENTIAL VETOES]

All Bills for raising Revenue shall originate in the House of Representatives; but the Senate may propose or concur with Amendments as on other Bills.

Every Bill which shall have passed the House of Representatives and the Senate, shall, before it become a Law, be presented to the President of the United States; If he approve he shall sign it, but if not he shall return it, with his Objections to that House in which it shall have originated, who shall enter the Objections at large on their Journal, and proceed to reconsider it. If after such Reconsideration two thirds of that House shall agree to pass the Bill it shall be sent, together with the Objections, to the other House, by which it shall likewise be reconsidered, and if approved by two thirds of that House, it shall become a Law. But in all such Cases the Votes of both Houses shall be determined by Yeas and Nays, and the Names of the Persons voting for and against the Bill shall be entered on the Journal of each House respectively. If any Bill shall not be returned by the President within ten Days (Sundays excepted) after it shall have been presented to him, the Same shall be a Law, in like Manner as if he had signed it, unless the Congress by their Adjournment prevent its Return, in which Case it shall not be a Law.

Every Order, Resolution, or Vote to which the Concurrence of the Senate and House of Representatives may be necessary (except on a question of Adjournment) shall be presented to the President of the United States: and before the Same shall take Effect, shall be approved by him, or being disapproved by him, shall be repassed by two thirds of the Senate and House of Representatives, according to the Rules and Limitations prescribed in the Case of a Bill.

SECTION 8. [THE POWERS OF CONGRESS: TAXATION, LOANS, COMMERCE, NATURALIZATION, BANKRUPTCIES, COINAGE, POST, PATENTS AND COPYRIGHTS, COURTS, ADMIRALTY LAW, WAR, MILITIA, FEDERAL DISTRICTS, THE NECESSARY AND PROPER CLAUSE]

The Congress shall have Power To lay and collect Taxes, Duties, Imposts and Excises, to pay the Debts and provide for the common Defence and general Welfare of the United States; but all Duties, Imposts and Excises shall be uniform throughout the United States;

To borrow money on the Credit of the United States;

To regulate Commerce with foreign Nations, and among the several States, and with the Indian Tribes;

To establish an uniform Rule of Naturalization, and uniform Laws on the subject of Bankruptcies throughout the United States;

To coin Money, regulate the Value thereof, and of foreign Coin, and fix the Standard of Weights and Measures;

To provide for the Punishment of counterfeiting the Securities and current Coin of the United States;

To establish Post Officers and post Roads;

To promote the Progress of Science and useful arts by securing for limited Times to Authors and Inventors the exclusive Right to their respective Writings and Discoveries;

To constitute Tribunals inferior to the supreme Court;

To define and punish Piracies and Felonies committed on the high Seas, and Offenses against the Law of Nations;

To declare War, grant Letters of Marque and Reprisal, and make Rules concerning Captures on Land and Water;

To raise and support Armies, but no Appropriation of Money to that Use shall be for a longer Term than two Years;

To provide and maintain a Navy;

To make Rules for the Government and Regulation of the land and naval Forces;

To provide for calling forth the Militia to execute the Laws of the Union, suppress Insurrections and repel Invasions;

To provide for organizing, arming, and disciplining the Militia, and for governing such Part of them as may be employed in the Service of the United States, reserving to the States respectively, the Appointment of the Officers, and the Authority of training the Militia according to the discipline prescribed by Congress;

To exercise exclusive Legislation in all Cases whatsoever, over such District (not exceeding ten Miles square) as may, by Cession of particular States, and the acceptance of Congress, become the Seat of the Government of the United States, and to exercise like Authority over all Places purchased by the Consent of the Legislature of the State in which the Same shall be, for the Erection of Forts, Magazines, Arsenals, dock-Yards, and other needful Buildings;—And

To make all Laws which shall be necessary and proper for carrying into Execution the foregoing Powers, and all other Powers vested by this Constitution in the Government of the United States, or in any Department or Officer thereof.

SECTION 9. [LIMITATIONS ON THE NATIONAL GOVERNMENT: SLAVE TRADE, HABEAS CORPUS, EX POST FACTO LAW, DIRECT TAXES, EXPORT DUTIES, DISCRIMINATION BETWEEN STATES, PUBLIC FUNDS, TITLES OF NOBILITY]

The Migration or Importation of such Persons as any of the States now existing shall think proper to admit, shall not be prohibited by the Congress prior to the Year one thousand eight hundred and eight, but a tax or duty may be imposed on such Importation, not exceeding ten dollars for each Person.

The privilege of the Writ of Habeas Corpus shall not be suspended, unless when in Cases of Rebellion or Invasion the public Safety may require it.

No Bill of Attainder or ex post facto Law shall be passed.

No capitation, or other direct Tax shall be laid, unless in Proportion to the Census or Enumeration herein before directed to be taken.[4]

No Tax or Duty shall be laid on Articles exported from any State.

No Preference shall be given by any Regulation of Commerce or Revenue to the Ports of one State over those of another: nor shall Vessels bound to, or from one State, be obliged to enter, clear, or pay Duties in another.

---

[4] See Amendment XVI

No Money shall be drawn from the Treasury, but in Consequence of Appropriations made by Law; and a regular Statement and Account of the Receipts and Expenditures of all public Money shall be published from time to time.

No Title of Nobility shall be granted by the United States: And no Person holding any Office of Profit or Trust under them, shall, without the Consent of the Congress, accept of any present, Emolument, Office, or Title, of any kind whatever, from any King, Prince, or foreign State.

SECTION 10. [LIMITATIONS ON THE STATES]

No State shall enter into any Treaty, Alliance, or Confederation; grant Letters of Marque and Reprisal; coin Money; emit Bills of Credit; make any Thing but gold and silver Coin a Tender in Payment of Debts; pass any Bill of Attainder, ex post facto Law, or Law impairing the Obligation of Contracts, or grant any Title of Nobility.

No State shall, without the Consent of the Congress, lay any Imposts or Duties on Imports or Exports, except what may be absolutely necessary for executing its inspection Laws: and the net Produce of all Duties and Imposts, laid by any State on Imports or Exports, shall be for the Use of the Treasury of the United States and all such Laws shall be subject to the Revision and Controul of the Congress. No State shall, without the Consent of Congress, lay any duty of Tonnage, keep Troops, or Ships of War in time of Peace, enter into any Agreement or Compact with another State, or with a foreign Power, or engage in War, unless actually invaded, or in such imminent Danger as will not admit of delay.

ARTICLE 2
[THE PRESIDENT AND THE EXECUTIVE DEPARTMENTS]

SECTION 1. [GENERAL GRANT OF POWER: MODE OF ELECTION, QUALIFICATION OF PRESIDENT, PRESIDENTIAL SUCCESSION, SALARY, OATH OF OFFICE]

The executive Power shall be vested in a President of the United States of America. He shall hold his Office during the Term of four Years, and, together with the Vice-President, chosen for the same Term, be elected, as follows

Each State shall appoint, in such Manner as the Legislature thereof may direct, a Number of Electors, equal to the whole number of Senators and Representatives to which the State may be entitled in the Congress; but no Senator or Representative, or Person holding an Office of Trust or Profit under the United States, shall be appointed an Elector.

[The Electors shall meet in their respective States, and vote by Ballot for two persons, of whom one at least shall not be an Inhabitant of the same State with themselves. And they shall make a List of all the Persons voted for, and of the Number of Votes for each; which List they shall sign and certify, and transmit sealed to the Seat of the Government of the United States, directed to the President of the Senate. The President of the Senate shall, in the Presence of the Senate and House of Representatives, open all the Certificates, and the Votes shall then be counted. The Person having the greatest Number of Votes shall be the President, if such Number be a Majority of the whole Number of Electors appointed; and if there be more than one who have such Majority, and have an Equal Number of Votes, then the House of Representatives shall immediately chuse by Ballot one of them for President; and if no Person have a Majority then from the five highest on the List the said House shall in like Manner chuse the President, but in chusing the President, the Votes shall be taken by States, the Representation from each State having one Vote; A quorum for this Purpose shall consist of a Member or Members from two-thirds of the States, and a Majority of all the States shall be necessary to a Choice. In every Case, after the Choice of the President, the Person having the greatest Number of Votes of the Electors shall be the Vice-President. But if there should remain two or more who have equal Votes, the Senate shall chuse from them by Ballot the Vice-President.][5]

The Congress may determine the Time of chusing the Electors, and the Day on which they shall give their Vote; which Day shall be the same throughout the United States.

No person except a natural born Citizen, or a Citizen of the United States, at the time of the Adoption of this Constitution, shall be eligible to the Office of President, neither shall any Person be eligible to that Office who shall not have attained to the Age of thirty-five Years, and been fourteen Years a Resident within the United States.

In Case of the Removal of the President from Office, or of his Death, Resignation, or Inability to discharge the Powers and Duties of the said office, the same shall devolve on the Vice-President, and the Congress may by Law provide for the Case of Removal, Death, Resignation or Inability, both of the President and Vice-President, declaring what Officer shall then act as President, and such Officer shall act accordingly, until the Disability be removed, or a President shall be elected.

The President shall, at stated Times, receive for his Services, a Compensation, which shall neither be increased nor diminished during the Period for which he shall have been elected, and he shall not receive within that Period any other Emolument from the United States, or any of them.

---

[5] Superceded by Amendment XII

Before he enter on the Execution of his Office, he shall take the following Oath or Affirmation—"I do solemnly swear (or affirm) that I will faithfully execute the Office of President of the United States, and will to the best of my Ability, preserve, protect and defend the Constitution of the United States."

SECTION 2. [POWERS OF THE PRESIDENT, THE EXECUTIVE DEPARTMENTS, TREATIES AND APPOINTMENTS]

The President shall be Commander in Chief of the Army and Navy of the United States, and of the Militia of the several States, when called into the actual Service of the United States; he may require the Opinion in writing, of the principal Officer in each of the executive Departments, upon any subject relating to the Duties of their respective Offices, and he shall have Power to Grant Reprieves and Pardons for Offenses against the United States, except in Cases of Impeachment.

He shall have Power, by and with the Advice and Consent of the Senate, to make Treaties, provided two-thirds of the Senators present concur; and he shall nominate, and by and with the Advice and Consent of the Senate, shall appoint Ambassadors, other public Ministers and Consuls, Judges of the supreme Court, and all other Officers of the United States, whose Appointments are not herein otherwise provided for, and which shall be established by Law: but the Congress may by Law vest the Appointment of such inferior Officers, as they think proper, in the President alone, in the Courts of Law, or in the Heads of Departments.

The President shall have Power to fill up all Vacancies that may happen during the Recess of the Senate by granting Commissions which shall expire at the End of their next Session.

SECTION 3. [PRESIDENTIAL MESSAGES, ADJOURNMENT AND CALL OF CONGRESS, RECEIVING AMBASSADORS, GENERAL EXECUTIVE POWER]

He shall from time to time give to the Congress Information of the State of the Union, and recommend to their Consideration such Measures as he shall judge necessary and expedient; he may, on extraordinary Occasions, convene both Houses, or either of them, and in Cases of Disagreement between them, with Respect to the Time of Adjournment, he may adjourn them to such Time as he shall think proper; he shall receive Ambassadors and other public Ministers; he shall take Care that the Laws be faithfully executed, and shall Commission all the Officers of the United States.

SECTION 4. [IMPEACHMENT]

The President, Vice-President and all civil Officers of the United States, shall be removed from Office on Impeachment for, and Conviction of, Treason, Bribery, or other high Crimes and Misdemeanors.

ARTICLE 3
[THE FEDERAL COURTS]

SECTION 1. [GENERAL GRANT OF POWER, TERMS OF OFFICE, AND SALARY OF JUDGES]

The judicial Power of the United States shall be vested in one supreme Court, and in such inferior Courts as the Congress may from time to time ordain and establish. The Judges, both of the supreme and inferior Courts, shall hold their offices during good Behaviour, and shall, at stated Times, receive for their Services a Compensation which shall not be diminished during their Continuance in Office.

SECTION 2. [JURISDICTION OF UNITED STATES COURTS, TRIAL BY JURY]

The judicial Power shall extend to all Cases, in Law and Equity, arising under this Constitution, the Laws of the United States and Treaties made, or which shall be made, under their Authority;—to all Cases affecting Ambassadors, other public Ministers and Consuls; —to all Cases of admiralty and maritime Jurisdiction; —to Controversies to which the United States shall be a Party;—to Controversies between two or more States;—between a State and Citizens of another state;[6]—Between Citizens of different States;—between Citizens of the same State claiming Lands under Grants of different States, and between a State, or the Citizens thereof, and foreign States, Citizens or Subjects.

In all Cases affecting Ambassadors, other public Ministers and Consuls, and those in which a State shall be Party, the supreme Court shall have original Jurisdiction. In all the other Cases before mentioned, the supreme Court shall have appellate Jurisdiction, both as to Law and Fact, with such Exceptions, and under such Regulations as the Congress shall make.

The trial of all Crimes, except in Cases of Impeachment, shall be by Jury, and such Trial shall be held in the State where the said Crimes shall have been committed; but when not committed within any State, the Trial shall be at such Place or Places as the Congress may by Law have directed.

---

[6] See Amendment XI

SECTION 3. [TREASON]

Treason against the United States, shall consist only in levying War against them, or in adhering to their Enemies, giving them Aid and Comfort. No Person shall be convicted of Treason unless on the Testimony of two Witnesses to the same overt Act, or on Confession in open Court.

The Congress shall have power to declare the Punishment of Treason, but no Attainder of Treason shall work Corruption of Blood, or Forfeiture except during the Life of the Person attainted.

ARTICLE 4
[THE STATES]

SECTION 1. [FULL FAITH AND CREDIT]

Full Faith and Credit shall be given in each State to the public acts, Records, and judicial Proceedings of every other State. And the Congress may by general Laws prescribe the Manner in which such Acts, Records and Proccedings shall be proved, and the Effect thereof.

SECTION 2. [PRIVELEGES AND IMMUNITIES, EXTRADITION, FUGITIVE SLAVES]

The Citizens of each State shall be entitled to all Privileges and Immunities of Citizens in the several States.

A Person charged in any State witll Treason, Felony, or other Crime, who shall flee from Justice, and be found in another State, shall on demand of the executive Authority of the State from which he fled, be delivered up, to be removed to the State having Jurisdiction of the Crime.

No Person held to Service or Labour in one State, under the Laws thereof, escaping into another, shall in Consequence of any Law or Regulation therein be discharged from such Service or Labour, but shall be delivered up on Claim of the Party to whom such Service or Labour may be due. [7]

SECTION 3. [NEW STATES, REGULATION OF THE TERRITORIES]

New States may be admitted by the Congress into this Union; but no new States shall be formed or erected within the Jurisdiction of any other State, nor any State be formed by the Junction of two or more States, or parts of States, with-

---

[7] Superceded by Amendment XIII

out the Consent of the Legislatures of the States concerned as well as of the Congress.

The Congress shall have Power to dispose of and make all needful Rules and Regulations respecting the Territory or other Property belonging to the United States; and nothing in this Constitution shall be so constructed as to Prejudice any Claims of the United States, or of any particular State.

SECTION 4. [GUARANTEE OF A REPUBLICAN FORM OF GOVERNMENT, PROTECTION AGAINST INVASION AND DOMESTIC VIOLENCE]

The United States shall guarantee to every State in this Union a Republican Form of Government, and shall protect each of them against Invasion; and on Application of the Legislature, or of the Executive (when the Legislature cannot be convened) against domestic Violence.

ARTICLE 5
[AMENDMENTS]

The Congress whenever two-thirds of both Houses shall deem it necessary, shall propose Amendments to this Constitution, or, on the Application of the Legislatures of two-thirds of the several States, shall call a Convention for proposing Amendments, which, in either Case, shall be valid to all Intents and Purposes, as part of this Constitution, when ratified by the Legislatures of three-fourths of the several States, or by Conventions in three-fourths thereof, as the one or the other Mode of Ratification may be proposed by the Congress; Provided that no Amendment which may be made prior to the Year One thousand eight hundred and eight shall in any Manner affect the first and fourth Clauses in the Ninth Section of the first Article; and that no State, without its Consent, shall be deprived of its equal Suffrage in the Senate.

ARTICLE 6
[PUBLIC DEBT, THE SUPREMACY CLAUSE, OATHS, RELIGIOUS TESTS]

All Debts contracted and Engagements entered into, before the Adoption of this Constitution, shall be as valid against the United States under this Constitution, as under the Confederation.

This Constitution, and the Laws of the United States which shall be made in Pursuance thereof; and all Treaties made, or which shall be made, under the Authority of the United States, shall be the supreme Law of the Land; and the Judges in every State shall be bound thereby, any Thing in the Constitution or Laws of any State to the Contrary notwithstanding.

The Senators and Representatives before mentioned, and the Members of the several State Legislatures, and all executive and judicial Officers, both of the United States and of the several States, shall be bound by Oath or Affirmation, to support this Constitution; but no religious Test shall ever be required as a Qualification to any Office or public Trust under the United States.

ARTICLE 7
[RATIFICATION]

The Ratification of the Conventions of nine States shall be sufficient for the Establishment of this Constitution between the States so ratifying the Same.

Done in Convention by the Unanimous Consent of the States present the Seventeenth Day of September in the Year of our Lord one thousand seven hundred and Eighty seven and of the Independence of the United States of America the Twelfth. In Witness whereof We have hereunto subscribed our Names.

Go. *Washington*
Presid't and deputy from Virginia

DELAWARE
Geo: Read
John Dickinson
Jaco: Broom
Gunning Bedford jun
Richard Bassett

SOUTH CAROLINA
J. Rutledge
Charles Pinckney
Charles Cotesworth Pinckney
Pierce Butler

NORTH CAROLINA
Wm Blount
Hu Williamson
Richd Dobbs Spaight

MARYLAND
James McHenry
Danl Carroll
Dan: of St. Thos Jenifer

GEORGIA
William Few
Abr Baldwin

PENNSYLVANIA
B. Franklin
Robt. Morris
Thos. Fitzsimons
James Wilson
Thomas Mifflin
Geo. Clymer
Jared Ingersoll
Gouv Morris

NEW HAMPSHIRE
John Langdon
Nicholas Gilman

NEW YORK
Alexander Hamilton

NEW JERSEY
Wil: Livingston
David Brearly
Wm. Paterson
Jona: Dayton

MASSACHUSETTS
Nathaniel Gorham
Rufus King

VIRGINIA	CONNECTICUT	Attest:
John Blair	*Wm Saml Johnson*	*William Jackson,*
James Madison, Jr.	*Roger Sherman*	Secretary.

AMENDMENT I [8]
[THE ESTABLISHMENT OF RELIGION; FREEDOM OF RELIGION, SPEECH, PRESS, ASSEMBLY, PETITION]

Congress shall make no law respecting an establishment of religion, or prohibiting the free exercise thereof; or abridging the freedom of speech, or of the press; or the right of the people peaceably to assemble, and to petition the Government for a redress of grievances.

AMENDMENT II
[RIGHT TO BEAR ARMS]

A well regulated Militia, being necessary to the security of a free State, the right of the people to keep and bear Arms, shall not be infringed.

AMENDMENT III
[QUARTERING OF SOLDIERS]

No Soldier shall, in time of peace be quartered in any house, without the consent of the Owner, nor in time of war, but in a manner to be prescribed by law.

AMENDMENT IV
[SEIZURES, SEARCHES, AND WARRANTS]

The right of the people to be secure in their persons, houses, papers, and effects, against unreasonable searches and seizures, shall not be violated, and no Warrants shall Issue, but upon probable cause, supported by Oath or affirmation, and particularly describing the place to be searched, and the persons or things to be seized.

---

[8] The first ten Amendments were adopted in 1791

AMENDMENT V
[INDICTMENT BY GRAND JURY, DOUBLE JEOPARDY, SELF-INCRIMINATION, DUE PROCESS OF LAW, JUST COMPENSATION]

No person shall be held to answer for a capital, or otherwise infamous crime, unless on a presentment or indictment of a Grand Jury, except in cases arising in the land or naval forces, or in the Militia, when in actual service in time of War or public danger, nor shall any person be subject for the same offense to be twice put in jeopardy of life or limb, nor shall be compelled in any criminal case to be a witness against himself, nor be deprived of life, liberty, or property, without due process of law; nor shall private property be taken for public use, without just compensation.

AMENDMENT VI
[SPEEDY AND PUBLIC TRIAL BY JURY, RIGHT TO KNOW THE NATURE OF ACCUSATION, CONFRONTATION OF WITNESSES, RIGHT TO COUNSEL]

In all criminal prosecutions, the accused shall enjoy the right to a speedy and public trial, by an impartial jury of the State and district wherein the crime shall have been committed, which district shall have been previously ascertained by law, and to be informed of the nature and cause of the accusation; to be confronted with the witnesses against him; to have the compulsory process for obtaining witnesses in his favor, and to have the Assistance of Counsel for his defence.

AMENDMENT VII
[TRIAL BY JURY]

In suits at common law, where the value in controversy shall exceed twenty dollars, the right of trial by jury shall be preserved, and no fact tried by a jury, shall be otherwise reexamined in any Court of the United States, than according to the rules of the common law.

AMENDMENT VIII
[PROHIBITION OF EXCESSIVE BAIL AND CRUEL AND UNUSUAL PUNISHMENT]

Excessive bail shall not be required, nor excessive fines imposed, nor cruel and unusual punishments inflicted.

AMENDMENT IX
[RIGHTS RETAINED BY THE PEOPLE]

The enumeration in the Constitution, of certain rights shall not be construed to deny or disparage others retained by the people.

AMENDMENT X
[POWERS RETAINED BY THE STATES AND THE PEOPLE]

The powers not delegated to the United States by the Constitution, nor prohibited by it to the States, are reserved to the States respectively, or to the people.

AMENDMENT XI [9]
[SUITS AGAINST STATES]

The Judicial power of the United States shall not be construed to extend to any suit in law or equity, commenced or prosecuted against one of the United States by Citizens of another State, or by Citizens or Subjects of any Foreign States.

AMENDMENT XII [10]
[ELECTION OF PRESIDENT AND VICE-PRESIDENT]

The Electors shall meet in their respective states and vote by ballot for President and Vice-President, one of whom, at least, shall not be an inhabitant of the same state with themselves, they shall name in their ballots the person voted for as President and in distinct ballots the person voted for as Vice-President, and they shall make distinct lists of all persons voted for as President, and of all persons voted for as Vice-President, and of the number of votes for each, which lists they shall sign and certify, and transmit sealed to the seat of the government of the United States, directed to the President of the Senate;—The President of the Senate shall, in the presence of the Senate and House of Representatives, open all the certificates and the votes shall then be counted;—The person having the greatest number of votes for President, shall be the President, if such number be a majority of the whole number of Electors appointed; and if no person have such majority, then from the persons having the highest numbers not exceeding three on the list of those voted for as President, the House of Representatives shall choose immediately, by ballot, the President. But in choosing the President, the votes shall be taken by states, the representation

---

[9] Adopted 1798
[10] Adopted 1804

from each state having one vote; a quorum for this purpose shall consist of a member or members from two-thirds of the states, and a majority of all the states shall be necessary to a choice. And if the House of Representatives shall not choose a President whenever the right of choice shall devolve upon them, before the fourth day of March next following, then the VicePresident shall act as President, as in the case of the death or other constitutional disability of the President.—The person having the greatest number of votes as Vice-President, shall be the Vice-President, if such number be a majority of the whole number of Electors appointed, and if no person have a majority, then from the two highest numbers on the list, the Senate shall choose the Vice-President; a quorum for the purpose shall consist of two-thirds of the whole number of Senators, and a majority of the whole number shall be necessary to a choice. But no person constitutionally ineligible to the office of President shall be eligible to that of Vice-President of the United States.

AMENDMENT XIII [11]
[THE ABOLITION OF SLAVERY]

SECTION 1.

Neither slavery nor involuntary servitude, except as a punishment for crime whereof the party shall have been duly convicted, shall exist within the United States, or any place subject to their jurisdiction.

SECTION 2.

Congress shall have power to enforce this article by appropriate legislation.

AMENDMENT XIV [12]
[GUARANTEES OF DUE PROCESS AND EQUAL PROTECTION OF THE LAWS,
APPORTIONMENT OF HOUSE OF REPRESENTATIVES, DISQUALIFICATIONS FOR OFFICE]

SECTION 1.

All persons born or naturalized in the United States and subject to the jurisdiction thereof, are citizens of the United States and of the State wherein they reside. No State shall make or enforce any law which shall abridge the privileges or immunities of citizens of the United States; nor shall any State deprive any

---

[11] Adopted 1865
[12] Adopted 1868

person of life, liberty, or property, without due process of law; nor deny to any person within its jurisdiction the equal protection of the laws.

SECTION 2.

Representatives shall be apportioned among the several States according to their respective numbers, counting the whole number of persons in each State excluding Indians not taxed. But when the right to vote at any election for the choice of electors for President and Vice-President of the United States, Representatives in Congress, the Executive and Judicial Officers of a State, or the members of the Legislature thereof, is denied to any of the male inhabitants of such State, being twenty-one years of age, and citizens of the United States, or in any way abridged, except for participation in rebellion, or other crime, the basis of representation therein shall be reduced in the proportion which the number of such male citizens shall bear to the whole number of male citizens twenty-one years of age in such State.

SECTION 3.

No person shall be a Senator or Representative in Congress, or elector of President and Vice-President, or hold any office, civil or military, under the United States, or under any State, who, having previously taken an oath, as a member of Congress, or as an officer of the United States, or as a member of any State legislature, or as an executive or judicial officer of any State, to support the Constitution of the United States, shall have engaged in insurrection or rebellion against the same, or given aid or comfort to the enemies thereof. But Congress may by a vote of two-thirds of each House, remove such disability.

SECTION 4.

The validity of the public debt of the United States, authorized by law, including debts incurred for payment of pensions and bounties for services in suppressing insurrection or rebellion, shall not be questioned. But neither the United States nor any State shall assume or pay any debt or obligation incurred in aid of insurrection or rebellion against the United States, or any claim for the loss or emancipation of any slave; but all such debts, obligations and claims shall be held illegal and void.

SECTION 5.

The Congress shall have power to enforce, by appropriate legislation, the provisions of this article.

AMENDMENT XV [13]
[THE RIGHT OF ALL CITIZENS TO VOTE]

SECTION 1.

The right of citizens of the United States to vote shall not be denied or abridged by the United States or by any State on account of race, color, or previous condition of servitude.

SECTION 2.

The Congress shall have power to enforce this article by appropriate legislation.

AMENDMENT XVI [14]
[THE INCOME TAX]

The Congress shall have power to lay and collect taxes on incomes, from whatever source derived, without apportionment among the several States, and without regard to any census or enumeration.

AMENDMENT XVII [15]
[POPULAR ELECTION OF SENATORS]

The Senate of the United States shall be composed of two Senators from each State, elected by the people thereof, for six years, and each Senator shall have one vote. The electors in each State shall have the qualifications requisite for electors of the most numerous branch of the State legislatures.

When vacancies happen in the representation of any State in the Senate, the executive authority of such State shall issue writs of election to fill such vacancies: Provided, That the legislature of any State may empower the executive thereof to make temporary appointments until the people fill the vacancies by election as the legislature may direct.

This amendment shall not be so construed as to affect the election or term of any Senator chosen before it becomes valid as part of the Constitution.

---

[13] Adopted 1870
[14] Adopted 1913
[15] Adopted 1913

AMENDMENT XVIII [16]
[PROHIBITION]

SECTION 1.

After one year from the ratification of this article the manufacture, sale, or transportation of intoxicating liquors within, the importation thereof into, or the exportation thereof from the United States and all territory subject to the jurisdiction thereof for beverage purposes is hereby prohibited.

SECTION 2.

The Congress and the several States shall have concurrent power to enforce this article by appropriate legislation.

SECTION 3.

This article shall be inoperative unless it shall have been ratified as an amendment to the Constitution by the legislatures of the several States, as provided in the Constitution, within seven years from the date of the submission hereof to the States by the Congress.

AMENDMENT XIX [17]
[EQUAL SUFFRAGE FOR WOMEN]

The right of citizens of the United States to vote shall not be denied or abridged by the United States or by any State on account of sex.

Congress shall have power to enforce this article by appropriate legislation.

AMENDMENT XX [18]
[CONGRESSIONAL AND PRESIDENTIAL TERMS]

SECTION 1.

The terms of the President and Vice-President shall end at noon on the 20th day of January, and the terms of Senators and Representatives at noon on the 3d day of January, of the years in which such terms would have ended if this article had not been ratified; and the terms of their successors shall then begin.

---

[17] Adopted 1920
[18] Adopted 1933

SECTION 2.

The Congress shall assemble at least once in every year, and such meeting shall begin at noon on the 3d day of January, unless they shall by law appoint a different day.

SECTION 3.

If, at the time fixed for the beginning of the term of the President, the President elect shall have died, the Vice-President elect shall become President. If a President shall not have been chosen before the time fixed for the beginning of his term, or if the President elect shall have failed to qualify, then the Vice-President elect shall act as President until a President shall have qualified; and the Congress may by law provide for the case wherein neither a President elect nor a Vice-President elect shall have qualified, declaring who shall then act as President, or the manner in which one who is to act shall be selected, and such person shall act accordingly until a President or Vice-President shall have qualified.

SECTION 4.

The Congress may by law provide for the case of the death of any of the persons from whom the House of Representatives may choose a President whenever the right of choice shall have devolved upon them, and for the case of the death of any of the persons from whom the Senate may choose a Vice-President whenever the right of choice shall have devolved upon them.

SECTION 5.

Sections 1 and 2 shall take effect on the 15th day of October following the ratification of this article.

SECTION 6.

This article shall be inoperative unless it shall have been ratified as an amendment to the Constitution by the legislatures of three-fourths of the several States within seven years from the date of its submission.

AMENDMENT XXI [19]
[REPEAL OF PROHIBITION]

SECTION 1.

The eighteenth article of amendment to the Constitution of the United States is hereby repealed.

SECTION 2.

The transportation or importation into any State, Territory, or possession of the United States for delivery or use therein of intoxicating liquors, in violation of the laws thereof, is hereby prohibited.

SECTION 3.

This article shall be inoperative unless it shall have been ratified as an amendment to the Constitution by conventions in the several States, as provided in the Constitution, within seven years from the date of the submission hereof to the States by the Congress.

AMENDMENT XXII [20]
[LIMITATION OF PRESIDENT TO TWO TERMS]

SECTION 1.

No person shall be elected to the office of the President more than twice, and no person who has held the office of President, or acted as President, for more than two years of a term to which some other person was elected President shall be elected to the office of the President more than once. But this Article shall not apply to any person holding the office of President when this Article was proposed by the Congress, and shall not prevent any person who may be holding the office of President, or acting as President, during the term within which this Article becomes operative from holding the office of President, or acting as President during the remainder of such term.

SECTION 2.

This Article shall be inoperative unless it shall have been ratified as an amendment to the Constitution by the legislatures of three-fourths of the several

---

[19] Adopted 1933
[20] Adopted 1951

States within seven years from the date of its submission to the States by the Congress.

AMENDMENT XXIII [21]
[PARTICIPATION OF RESIDENTS OF THE DISTRICT
OF COLUMBIA IN PRESIDENTIAL ELECTIONS]

SECTON 1.

The District constituting the seat of Government of the United States shall appoint in such manner as the Congress may direct:

A number of electors of President and Vice President equal to the whole number of Senators and Representatives in Congress to which the District would be entitled if it were a State, but in no event more than the least populous State; they shall be in addition to those appointed by the States, but they shall be considered, for the purposes of the election of President and Vice President, to be electors appointed by a State; and they shall meet in the District and perform such duties as provided by the twelfth article of amendment.

SECTION 2.

The Congress shall have power to enforce this article by appropriate legislation.

AMENDMENT XXIV [22]
[THE POLL TAX IN NATIONAL ELECTIONS]

SECTION 1.

The right of citizens of the United States to vote in any primary or other election for President or Vice President, for electors for President or Vice President, or for Senator or Representative in Congress, shall not be denied or abridged by the United States or any state by reason of failure to pay any poll tax or other tax.

SECTION 2.

The Congress shall have power to enforce this article by appropriate legislation.

---

[21] Adopted 1961
[22] Adopted 1964

AMENDMENT XXV [23]
[PRESIDENTIAL SUCCESSION]

SECTION 1.

In case of the removal of the President from office or of his death or resignation, the Vice President shall become President.

SECTION 2.

Whenever there is a vacancy in the office of the Vice President, the President shall nominate a Vice President who shall take office upon confirmation by a majority vote of both Houses of Congress.

SECTION 3.

Whenever the President transmits to the President pro tempore of the Senate and the Speaker of the House of Representatives his written declaration that he is unable to discharge the powers and duties of his office, and until he transmits to them a written declaration to the contrary, such powers and duties shall be discharged by the Vice President as Acting President.

SECTION 4.

Whenever the Vice President and a majority of either the principal officers of the executive departments or of such other body as Congress may by law provide, transmit to the President pro tempore of the Senate and the Speaker of the House of Representatives their written declaration that the President is unable to discharge the powers and duties of his office, the Vice President shall immediately assume the powers and duties of the office as Acting President.

Thereafter, when the President transmits to the President pro tempore of the Senate and the Speaker of the House of Representatives his written declaration that no inability exists, he shall resume the powers and duties of his office unless the Vice President and a majority of either the principal officers of the executive department or of such other body as Congress may by law provide, transmit within four days to the President pro tempore of the Senate and the Speaker of the House of Representatives their written declaration that the President is unable to discharge the powers and duties of his office. Thereupon Congress shall decide the issue, assembling within forty-eight hours for that

---

[23] Adopted 1967

purpose if not in session. If the Congress, within twenty-one days after receipt of the latter written declaration, or, if Congress is not in session, within twenty-one days after Congress is required to assemble, determines by two-thirds vote of both Houses that the President is unable to discharge the powers and duties of his office, the Vice President shall continue to discharge the same as Acting President, otherwise, the President shall resume the powers and duties of his office.

AMENDMENT XXVI [24]
[EIGHTEEN YEAR OLD VOTING]

SECTION 1.

The right of citizens of the United States, who are eighteen years of age or older, to vote shall not be denied or abridged by the United States or by any State on account of age.

SECTION 2.

The Congress shall have power to enforce this article by appropriate legislation.

AMENDMENT XXVII

No law, varying the compensation for the services of the Senators and Representatives, shall take effect, until an election of Representatives shall have intervened.

---

[24] Adopted 1971

Presidents of the United States of America

TERM(S)	PRESIDENT	PARTY
1789–1793	George Washington	
1793–1797	George Washington	
1797–1801	John Adams	Federalist
1801–1805	Thomas Jefferson	Democratic-Republican
1805–1809	Thomas Jefferson	Democratic-Republican
1809–1813	James Madison	Democratic-Republican
1813–1817	James Madison	Democratic-Republican
1817–1821	James Monroe	Democratic-Republican
1821–1825	James Monroe	Democratic-Republican
1825–1829	John Quincy Adams	Democratic-Republican
1829–1833	Andrew Jackson	Democratic
1833–1837	Andrew Jackson	Democratic
1837–1841	Martin Van Buren	Democratic

1841	William H. Harrison	Whig
1841–1845	John Tyler	Whig
1845–1849	James K. Polk	Democratic
1849–1850	Zachary Taylor	Whig
1850–1853	Millard Fillmore	Whig
1853–1857	Franklin Pierce	Democratic
1857–1861	James Buchanan	Democratic
1861–1865	Abraham Lincoln	Republican
1865	Abraham Lincoln	Republican
1865–1869	Andrew Johnson	Union
1869–1873	Ulysses S. Grant	Republican
1873–1877	Ulysses S. Grant	Republican
1877–1881	Rutherford B. Hayes	Republican
1881	James A. Garfield	Republican
1881–1885	Chester A. Arthur	Republican
1885–1889	Grover Cleveland	Democratic
1889–1893	Benjamin Harrison	Republican
1893–1897	Grover Cleveland	Democratic
1897–1901	William McKinley	Republican
1901–1905	Theodore Roosevelt	Republican
1905–1909	Theodore Roosevelt	Republican
1909–1913	William H. Taft	Republican
1913–1917	Woodrow Wilson	Democratic
1917–1921	Woodrow Wilson	Democratic
1921–1923	Warren G. Harding	Republican
1923–1925	Calvin Coolidge	Republican
1925–1929	Calvin Coolidge	Republican
1929–1933	Herbert C. Hoover	Republican
1933–1937	Franklin D. Roosevelt	Democratic
1937–1941	Franklin D. Roosevelt	Democratic
1941–1945	Franklin D. Roosevelt	Democratic
1945	Franklin D. Roosevelt	Democratic
1945–1953	Harry S Truman	Democratic
1953–1957	Dwight D. Eisenhower	Republican
1957–1961	Dwight D. Eisenhower	Republican
1961–1963	John F. Kennedy	Democratic
1963–1969	Lyndon B. Johnson	Democratic

1969–1972	Richard M. Nixon	Republican
1972–1974	Richard M. Nixon	Republican
1974–1977	Gerald Ford	Republican
1977–1981	Jimmy Carter	Democratic
1981–1985	Ronald Reagan	Republican
1985–1989	Ronald Reagan	Republican
1989–1993	George H. W. Bush	Republican
1993–1997	Bill Clinton	Democratic
1997–2001	Bill Clinton	Democratic
2001–2005	George W. Bush	Republican
2005–2009	George W. Bush	Republican
2009–	Barak Obama	Democratic

Index

The United States: A Brief Narrative History, Third Edition
Developmental editor: Andrew J. Davidson
Production editor: Linda Gaio
Proofreader: Claudia Siler
Cartographer: Jason Casanova and Jane Domier
Page design & typsetting: Bruce Leckie
Printer: Versa Press, Inc.

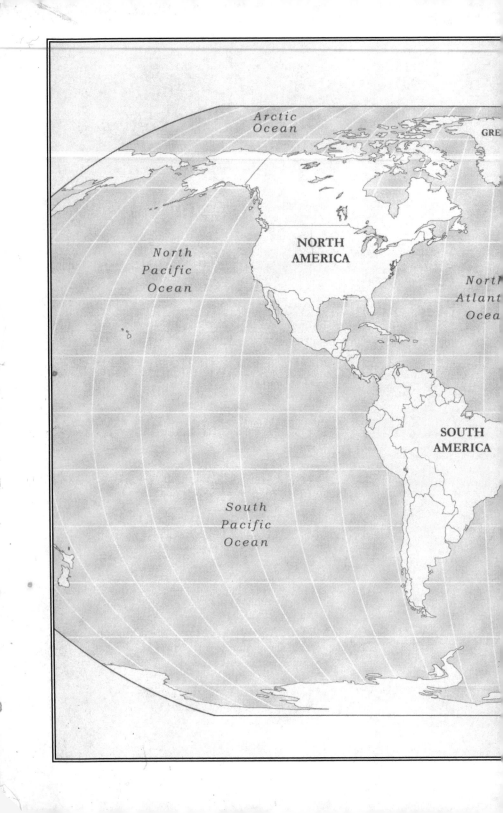